THE
BOOK
OF
VIPASSANA
SECRETS

BY NUMA

To my Dakinis
In Joy and in Sadness
In Equanimity and in Agitation

"After my death you will
be free to write anything."
— S.N. GOENKA

"'Venerable sir, which of
us has spoken well?'
'You have all spoken well,
each in his own way.'"
— THE BUDDHA
TO HIS DISCIPLES

CONTENTS

PREFACE*

"Dear Lord, grant me chastity — but not yet."
— ST AUGUSTINE

THOUSANDS OF YEARS BEFORE WOODY ALLEN AND DR REUBEN, THE questions people most wanted answered, even if they dared not ask, must already have been about sex. Every generation begins by believing that it has invented the ins and outs of the game and ends by realizing that there is nothing new under the sun — or under the bedroom lamp, whether it runs on bear grease, olive oil, or nuclear fission.

Questions about meditation are not likely, then, to displace our more urgent worldly pursuits, either in the West or anywhere else, at least for most of us most of the time. Buddhist metaphysics, which throws so sobering a light on our intimate inclinations, does not deny but emphasizes how powerful a force sexual energy is in propelling us from life to life: the entire realm we inhabit might be called the world of sex.[1] Were we not so entangled in our senses, we would not have been born here, or perhaps born at all, the Buddhists would say.[2]

---

* The quotations on the title page are taken from S.N. Goenka, *For the Benefit of Many*, p. 121, and from MN 32.17 (p. 312), respectively. St Augustine's famous prayer is one he recalls from his wayward youth in book 8 of the *Confessions*. All sources that I will be using repeatedly can be found in the final section on further readings. For the Pali Canon in general and my way of citing it in particular, see further down in the Preface. The cover image was taken at Datdawtaung Cave Temple in Burma by Lin Tun of Life Photography, Yangon, and I am reproducing it with his generous permission.

Buddhism has accumulated a great variety of resources over its 2500-year history, and it has rarely shrunk from engaging human life at the ground or the basement level. The Buddha[3] did not answer all outlandish questions that were put to him in his lifetime, but he never discouraged anyone from asking, except by pointing out the inutility of many intellectual preoccupations.[4] And so in the lands where his teaching travelled: Zen tells of ascetic seekers who finally attained enlightenment only when they penetrated a woman for the first time, and the favorite sage of the Bhutanese is said to have tumbled thousands of Himalayan maidens and subdued myriads of demons with the mighty thrust of his thunderbolt.[5] (Today's Bhutanese may insist that the towering specimen painted on so many of their houses have nothing to do with sex, but that only goes to show why they needed a saintly sex-instructor then, and why they still need him now.)

Where the plant of local tradition is still relatively green and tender, however, or among those merely interested in a general way, there can be a marked reluctance to expose the dirty linen that earlier generations might have been happy to drop off at the confession box, or that one would have no trouble leaving behind on a therapist's couch. It can be hard for us Western greenhorns not to feel like guests at the Buddha's banquet, and guests naturally feel obliged to be on their best behavior, or at least to keep up a measure of appearances with which they would gladly dispense at home.

I am writing this book, in other words, to make others feel a little more at home with the untidy aspects of their meditation, specifically with the practice I have learned from many a Vipassana retreat as taught by S.N. Goenka. (Goenkaji died in September 2013, but he remains alive to his students on the tapes and videos with which all his courses are taught.[6]) *I want to stress that this is not a book on how to meditate.* I will gladly leave the giving of instructions to Captain Goenka and his crew;[7] I would only be repeating what I have learned from them. They are expert teachers of a very far-reaching technique, indeed, and anyone serious about meditation will be well-served by taking a course with them. If I thought otherwise, I would have written a different book altogether. What I am offering, then, is not a challenge, but a supplement and a complementary perspective on the practical issues and the doubts and difficulties that surround a Ten-Day Vipassana marathon, as well as reflections on the myriad questions that I have asked and heard others ask over the years. In writing this book, I am thinking of anyone whose mind it has crossed to take the leap of faith into a course with Goenka, or who has already jumped but is still pondering what it all means. Whether the book might be useful to anyone else, I dare not say, though I will touch on many broader issues of meditation, Buddhism, and spiritual practice in general.

"Numa" might sound to some ears like Pali[8] for "rat," but I am thinking of the peacemaker who did not want to be made king over a city of warriors.[9] If the pseudonym will help to remind me that writing this kind of book (or perhaps any book) should not be about making publicity or a reputation for one's name, excellent. If it also reminds others of Nemo (Latin for nobody), even better: we are all nobodies in the end.

Let that be my secret. For the rest, there are no real secrets in the Dhamma: "Three things shine when exposed, not when concealed: the moon, the sun, and the Dhamma."[10] Or as Goenka puts it, "The Dhamma is an open book. No secrets."[11]

Although Buddhism in our parts tends to get shelved, for contingent historical reasons, in the New Age section, between the Mystics and the Gnostics, there is nothing esoteric about the Buddha's Teaching.[12] It is true that he often refused to answer questions as they were put, and there is a famous incident to illustrate that he did not share all that he knew: once he picked up some fallen leaves and asked his disciplines which were more, the leaves left in the forest or the ones gathered in his hand. Upon getting the obvious answer, the Awakened One declared that what he taught was to what he knew as the leaves in his hand were to those on the floor of the forest.[13] His point, however, was not to reserve special knowledge to the chosen few,[14] but rather to emphasize that many more things can be known than are necessary or helpful for solving the pressing problems at the heart of human life. Nor do all questions have answers in the terms in which they are put. When I say "secret," then, I merely mean such things as are not always expressed openly — be it out of fear, insecurity, or politeness.

Buddhism is not, in fact, the relativist playpen that it is sometimes taken to be by Westerners fed up with the rigidities of their own spiritual traditions, or what they see as such.[15] "Two bright qualities," the Buddha taught, "protect the world: moral shame and moral dread."[16] Thus the Teaching, while always sensitive to circumstances, makes decisive distinctions between the pure and the impure, the wholesome and the unwholesome, the karmically light and the karmically burdensome — between what is blamable and censured by the wise because it leads to harm and suffering, and what is unobjectionable and praiseworthy because it is conducive to a happy life, as the Buddha famously put it to the Kalamas of Kesaputta.[17] When I announce that I intend to wade into naughty territory, I do not mean to cross any serious moral lines; I am merely going to speak without inhibitions about matters that some may not be comfortable asking or discussing, and that others may not consider it proper to divulge.

To a point, I even sympathize with Goenka's conservative instincts — in the best sense of wishing to preserve something pure and unadulterated for the ages. He is operating, as all serious Buddhists probably should, under the impression of a troubling historical fact: after centuries of flourishing in its birthplace and spreading far and wide, especially under the Emperor Ashoka, the Buddha's Teaching was lost in India altogether. The legendary monastery whose land Anathapindika bought from Prince Jeta by covering the ground with gold coins[18] has long gone to ruins along with the ancient metropolis of Savatthi, "the city of wonder" no more;[19] the celebrated university at Nalanda, a mere memory; the very tree under which the Buddha attained enlightenment, cut down and burnt by a jealous queen, and later forgotten altogether before it was reclaimed by a Victorian enthusiast. Such is the sway of *Anicca*, the fact of impermanence that is at the very center of the Buddha's Teaching, to say nothing of the encrustations, distortions, and corruptions to which all traditions are heir.

Owing to my formation as a Goenka-student, my perspective on the Buddha's Teaching is dyed in the colors of the ancient scriptural tradition of the Pali Canon, whose claims cannot often be verified. Walking the Path requires faith — informed by reflection, study, and experience, but faith all the same — and mine inclines me to believe in the Pali narrative unless I have specific reasons to be skeptical. This predisposition may give my interpretations a hue that will not be to everyone's liking, but it is a case of dancing with the one that brought you, as well as of sincere conviction, and I could do no other.

Tradition holds that the first collection of the Buddha's teachings was compiled and authenticated by an assembly of 500 fully liberated monks who gathered a few months after the Buddha's death to recite what they could remember of the discourses they had witnessed over the years.[20] Back when Ananda had agreed to be the Buddha's attendant, he had stipulated that any talk he might miss should be repeated to him. It is therefore said that he heard every one of the Buddha's discourses for twenty-five years and that his prodigious memory allowed him to recall them verbatim.[21] The materials thus collected and codified were memorized and transmitted orally for some four hundred years before they were written down in Sri Lanka to safeguard them during a time of turmoil when at least one group of memorizers was reduced by famine and disease to a single survivor.

Over the following centuries, several Buddhist Councils were called to review and recertify the texts.[22] Eighteen early schools of Buddhism emerged, each with its own scriptures, but only one of them, the Theravadan school (or "Tradition of the Elders"), was able to transmit its canon more or less intact, or so it is believed.[23] The conventional belief that the Pali Canon mirrors the Awakened One's every word overstrains credulity, but there are still good reasons to think that much of what we are reading is not far from what contemporaries of the Buddha would have heard.[24] As with any set of texts passed down for as many as a hundred generations, it would be unwise not to recognize different layers of antiquity and authenticity, even if the borders between them are hard to discern.[25] Yet the coherence of the Canon remains astounding, as is its sheer volume: even if the pious certainties of the Theravadan faithful need to be tempered in light of scholarship and skeptical common sense, students of the Buddha's Teaching can check their understanding against thousands upon thousands of highly credible discourses that add up to a remarkably cogent and consistent overall picture.

In Pali, the Canon is called *Tipitaka* (or "three baskets") for its three main parts: first, the *Vinaya Pitaka* (Basket of the Discipline) that discuss the rules of monastic life together with the events that first gave rise to them; second, the *Sutta Pitaka* (or Discourses of the Buddha); and third, the *Abhidhamma*, or "Higher Dhamma."[26] I will draw most heavily on the second, the *Sutta Pitaka* — what Bhikkhu Bodhi has called "the living heart of the Buddha's Teaching"[27] — citing the most recent editions by Wisdom Publications for easy reference:

The *Digha Nikaya* (DN) or
Collection of *Long Discourses* [1995];

the *Majjhima Nikaya* (MN) or
Collection of *Middle-Length Discourses* [2005];

the *Samyutta Nikaya* (SN) or
Collection of *Connected Discourses* [2000];

the *Anguttara Nikaya* (AN) or
Collection of *Numerical Discourses* [2012].

Passages that appear in Bhikkhu Bodhi's anthology, *In the Buddha's Words* (BW) [2005], I will cross-reference by page number. Where I will use other translations, I will identify them in the footnotes.

The *Udana* and *Itivuttaka* are ancient texts from the *Khuddaka Nikaya*, the fifth, miscellaneous collection in the *Sutta Pitaka*, and I will be citing the translation by John Ireland unless noted otherwise.[28] For the *Dhammapada (Dhp.)* and *Sutta Nipata*, from the same fifth collection, I will use a variety of sources. *The Questions of King Milinda*, also in the *Khuddaka Nikaya*, I will be citing (as *Milinda*) in the edition by N.K.G. Mendis (BPS 2007).

The *Visuddhimagga* (*Vism.*) by Buddhaghosa is the principal non-canonical authority in the Theravadan tradition, a grand synthesis of all the commentaries still extant in Sri Lanka, then the center of the Buddhist world, about eight hundred years after the Buddha's death, but since lost.

On my brief forays into *Abhidhamma* territory, I will be guided by Bhikkhu Bodhi's expository edition of the *Abhidhammattha Sangaha* by Acariya Anuruddha, the classic primer used for such studies in the Theravadan world, published under the title *A Comprehensive Manual of Abhidhamma (Abh.)*.

Samuel Johnson wrote that "no man but a blockhead ever wrote except for money." I answer that no one but a blockhead could fail to see the problem with making money off the Dhamma. But contrary to myth and romance, Buddhist householders do not outgrow the need for food and clothes, for paying bills or rent, or even for buying cars and houses, perish the thought. Gratitude is as much a Buddhist virtue as renunciation, and I am offering my labor of love in hopes that we may all become more appreciative of the good things that come our way, and to treat them as the blessings they are, the gifts of grace and not just the fruits of our own meritorious efforts. *May all beings be happy.*

NOTES

1. Goenka, *For the Benefit of Many*, p. 31.

2. "Who can disentangle this tangle?" (SN 1.23 [p. 101]) is the great question towards which all Buddhist seeking is directed, and thus it stands at the very opening gates of the *Visuddhimagga* (I.1 [p. 5]).

3. "Buddha" is not a name, but an honorific meaning "the awakened one" that might be applied, loosely, to any "fully enlightened being who draws aside the veil in the world" (for this kind of usage see MN 92.8-10, p. 757). The given name of the best-known Buddha (who lived in Northern India in the 5th or 6th century BCE) was *Siddhartha*, of the *Gotama* clan and the *Sakyan* people. Hence he is sometimes called *Sakyamuni*, "Sage of the Sakyans," or *Sakyaputtiya*, "Son of the Sakyans."

Used more narrowly, as in "Gotama *the* Buddha," the term is commonly reserved for the pre-eminent enlightened being of his era, a discoverer and teacher of the Path liberated by his own efforts (technically a *sammasambuddha*). Hence the traditional formula for paying homage, also used by Goenka during courses: "*Namo tassa bhagavato, arahato, sammasambudhassa*," which invokes (with some variations in the translations) the exalted one, the conqueror of defilements, the fully self-enlightened Buddha. Since the teaching of the Buddhas is taken to be timeless, it is said that our Buddha *rediscovered* it as he might have an ancient, forgotten city in the jungle (SN 12.65 [p. 603 (BW 69)]). His role as the "arouser of the unarisen, declarer of the undeclared, the knower and finder of the Path" is stressed at MN 108.5 (pp. 880-881).

When the Buddha referred to himself, he used the term *Tathagata*, which has been interpreted in many elaborate and fanciful ways, most prominently by Buddhaghosa (*Sumangala-Vilasini*, tr. T.W. Rhys Davids, vol. 1, pp. 59-68). But the simplest etymology is also the most plausible: *tatha-gata*, "one who has thus gone," that is to say, who has arrived at the ultimate truth, the final goal of full liberation and enlightenment. "One who has thus come," *tatha-agata,* is another reasonable derivation that complements the first: one who returns to teach us about what he has discovered, as the Buddha did when he rejoined his five companions, which was also when he first claimed the title (MN 26:27 [p. 264]). (For more details and possibilities, see Robert Chalmers, "Tathagata," *The Journal of the Royal Asiatic Society* 1898/1, pp. 103-115, available online.)

4. Just before his death, the Buddha assembled his monks one last time and urged them to share any doubts or uncertainties remaining

in their minds — through a friend, if anyone were uneasy about asking the teacher directly! (See DN 16.6.5 [p. 270].) On speculative questions, see chapter 12.

5. For the best account of his adventures according to traditional texts in English translation by Keith Dowman, see *The Divine Madman: The Sublime Life and Songs of Drukpa Kunley* (London: Rider, 1980). Tradition credits the saintly sex-instructor with having taught 5000 girlfriends the finer points of intercourse (p. 69!), but as I shall have occasion to point out numerous times (in the context of 500-year epochs, for example), such numbers as 500 or 5000 are not to be taken as precise mathematical figures in most ancient texts, but as representations of considerable but uncounted quantities.

6. For some basic biographical information and the name Goenkaji, see the first question in chapter 8.

7. The worlds of medicine and corrections offer many apt metaphors for the tougher aspects of the Vipassana experience: a visit to the dentist, a surgical operation, physiotherapy, rehab, a mental hospital (hinted at by Goenka himself), a reform school, a camp for juvenile delinquents, a penitentiary for repeat offenders, etc. All these capture something about the discomfort, pain, anxiety, doubt, and sense of oppressive confinement that can grip students during a course. But perhaps the coloring needs to be lighter and a course might be better described as a ten-day flight around the globe with a respectable airline (economy class), a well-trained pilot, and a faultlessly attentive crew. (Even if it were business or first class, materially speaking, it would not help you much. Of course a pleasant environment can mitigate some of the stresses and strains, which is why Vipassana centers make such an effort to provide near-optimal external conditions. But in the end, a hospital bed is a hospital bed even if it were placed in a luxury hotel.)

8. The language of the oldest and most complete surviving Buddhist scriptures, the Pali Canon. Tradition holds that the Buddha spoke Pali, but scholarship has questioned that view, a point I will return to in chapter 2.

9. Plutarch, Life of Numa, 5.4-5: "The very points of my character that are most commended mark me as unfit to reign — love of retirement and of studies inconsistent with business, a passion that has become inveterate in me for peace, for unwarlike occupations, and for the society of men whose meetings are but those of worship and kindly intercourse. I should be a laughing-stock if I were to go about inculcating the worship of the gods and giving lessons in

the love of justice and the abhorrence of violence and war to a city whose needs are rather for a general than for a king." (Tr. Dryden-Clough with a few revisions)

10. AN 3.131 (p. 361).

11. Goenka, Day 11 Discourse. See also *The Art of Living*, p. 138: "There is no secrecy in Dhamma." The discourses I will be referring to are the standard English evening discourses recorded in California in 1991. So far as I know, no other English recordings are used on Ten-Day courses.

12. Paul Fleischman, specifically appointed by Goenka to represent Vipassana in university settings, distances himself emphatically from "New Age" thinking, claiming that "it leads people to construct lives of avoidance and denial" (*An Ancient Path*, p. 134). How such strident dismissals of a vast spectrum of opinion would be conducive to the "outreach" with which he is charged, I fail to see.

13. SN 56:31 (pp. 1857-58 [BW 360]). See chapter 12 for more details on the speculative questions that the Buddha deflected or refused to answer.

14. At DN 16.2.25 (p. 245) the Buddha rejects any suggestion that he might have held anything back "with the closed fist of a teacher" or favored anyone with special inside knowledge denied others. See also SN 47.9 (p. 1637).

15. The Buddha's Teaching culminates in an ultimate truth that is beyond all doubt and disagreement, indeed beyond mind and matter, space and time, and all dualism or distinction: *Nibbana*. At the intermediate level, there is the truth that only impersonal energy arises from moment to moment: all is a web of interdependent vibrations without any clear boundaries. But there is conventional truth, too, however crude it may be: we are not just imagining our interactions as selves, but we are construing them, unconsciously, in ways that are ultimately deluded. Thus we need to reckon with the conventional ways of perceiving the world, but if we remain content with what we see and hear ordinarily, we are like insects who circle the flame of a lamp until they fall into it (*Udana* 6.9 [Ireland, p. 92]).

16. AN 2.9 (p. 143). See also *Itivuttaka* 42 (Ireland, pp. 179-180).

17. An especially famous Sutta (AN 3:65 [pp. 279-283 (BW 88-91)]) to which I shall return several times.

18. *Cullavagga* 6.4.8-10 (*Life*, pp. 90-91). See also *Greatest Disciples*, p. 340.

19. The sensual pleasures once enjoyed to excess at Savatthi are alluded to in the *Udana* (7.3-4 [Ireland, p. 95-96]).

20. The main events of the First Council, held at Rajagaha during the rainy season following the Buddha's death, are recounted in chapter 11 of the *Cullavagga (Life,* pp. 333-340).

21. Hence the customary opening of the Suttas: *Evam me sutam* ("Thus have I heard"). Following a line in the *Theragata* (17.3, verse 1024), traditionalists say that Ananda received 84,000 teachings (82,000 from the Buddha, the rest from his disciples). Goenka takes this literally (*Satip. Discourses*, p. 14), but I disagree. The number is clearly a mythical one often attributed to divine beings: the longest-living gods, for instance, are supposed to endure for 84,000 great aeons (*Abh.*, p. 186, see also MN 83.6-11 [pp. 693-94]). A more realistic count for the *Sutta Nikaya*, on which Ananda was the expert at the First Council (*Cullavagga* 11.1.8), might exceed 10,000, but not by much. (Many Suttas are very short and there is a great deal of repetition and even outright duplication throughout the Canon.)

From what we know about feats of memorization in cultures relying on oral transmission (not to mention the *Guinness Book of World Records*), Ananda's alleged abilities may be a little more credible than it seems to us. Greek and Roman schoolchildren were able to recite the whole of Homer (28,000 lines) even after the introduction of writing, and memorizing the entire Koran (around 6000 verses) is still widely practiced in the Muslim world, as is memorizing the Vedas among Hindus.

22. The Second Buddhist Council was held in Vesali about a century after the Buddha's death (*Cullavagga*, chapter 12), the Third was convened by the Emperor Ashoka around 250 BCE. A Fourth Theravadan Council was called in the first century BCE in Sri Lanka, a Fifth and Sixth took place in Burma in 1871 and 1954, respectively.

23. Other Buddhist scriptural traditions do exist, especially in Chinese and Tibetan, but their materials are not as extensive and would have traveled much further in every sense, culturally as well as linguistically. In the end, the question which surviving tradition is the oldest and most authentic cannot be answered without recourse to faith, and all practitioners will have reasons favoring their own. What can be said with certainty is that the Buddha must have spoke a language closely related to Pali, and also that to translate Pali into another Indo-European language like English, with the sources still available for reference, is a very different proposition from

working with Chinese or Tibetan texts once produced from Sanskrit sources that are no longer extant, especially if the Chinese has to be translated again before being read in English.

24. I will return to this question, briefly, in chapter 2.

25. Also striking differences in *quality*. Many of the stories told about the gods in the Pali Canon are so silly, for example, that I am unable to take them seriously (see the question on the gods in chapter 12, especially my footnotes). Asked whether there are gods, the Buddha answered unequivocally (see MN 100.42 [p. 821]): the existence of higher realms inhabited by divine beings is a central feature the Buddhist cosmology. But the specifics of how these beings look and act are another matter, and many of the tales in the Canon sound to me as if they were echoes of folk-mythology that the Buddhists, like the Greeks, may have inherited from their common Proto-Indo-European ancestors, along with the shared features of their respective languages. (Likewise, the existence of hell-realms cannot be in doubt from a Buddhist perspective, but the delight in elaborating their topography is a human foible that has little to do with the Dhamma, though it does appear in the Canon, see MN 129.7-17 [pp. 1017-1019] and MN 130.10-27 [pp. 1032-1035].)

The many *Jataka*-tales about the Buddha's previous lives that bulk up the *Khuddaka Nikaya* enjoy high prestige in Buddhist lands, but they have never resonated with me. Like T.W. Rhys Davids, I doubt that they are specific to Buddhism, rather than adaptations from earlier Indian folklore (T.W. Rhys Davids, *Buddhist India* [Delhi 2005], pp. X.177 and XI.197). One of my discomforts with these stories, which appear in the other *Nikayas* as well (see MN 81 and 83, for example), is that they presuppose extremely ancient and evolved human civilizations (looking suspiciously similar to the India of the Buddha's times) in very remote ages that we have reason to believe were home only to cave men, or dinosaurs, or protozoa.

I grant that our science is hardly conclusive: while scientists are able to slice up our universe's first milliseconds into slivers so minute that it boggles the mind, they have come to acknowledge that 95 percent of what surrounds us is a mystery to them (24 percent dark matter, 71.5 percent dark energy). Given what room some of our most sophisticated scientific theories make for many more dimensions than we can experience, for vast galaxies in all directions, and perhaps even for parallel or multiple universes, we cannot rule out the existence of earlier Buddhas (each of whom could only have arisen, by the orthodox account, once the Dhamma had completely disappeared from a world-system). But making such possibilities credible would take more than a few rolling credits for extras in period costume. The gaudy puppet show at DN 14 [pp. 199-221] is not likely to convince any skeptic that the six ancient Buddhas identified by name are historical figures; if anything, it emphasizes the archetypal and legendary dimension to the whole Buddha-story.

Since the Buddha is also quoted as saying that "the sequence of a man's mothers and grandmothers," traced back in time, "would not come to an end" (SN 15.1 [p. 651 (BW 37)]), I am left wondering whether insight into the origin of species was among the Awakened One's revelations. Other stories in the Canon, like that of a world's beginning at DN 27.11-20 (pp. 410-413), are plainly mythical and have more in common with archaic Biblical stories than with any scientific understanding we have arrived at.

Such embarrassing rubbish as the "thirty-two marks of a Great Man" (ensheathed penis, giant tongue, head shaped like a turban etc.) is good only for reminding us that no scriptures are safe from corruption and absurdity (see MN 91-92).

26. The *Abhidhamma Pitaka* was produced by later generations of Buddhist scholars, but its adherents point to such passages as MN 32.8 (p. 309 and Note 362, p. 1226), MN 47.14 (p. 417), MN 69.17 (p. 575), and MN 103.4 (p. 848) for evidence that the conception of a "higher Dhamma *(Abhidhamma)*" already arose in the Buddha's lifetime.

27. Introduction to his *Numerical Discourses of the Buddha (Anthology)*, edited with Nyanaponika Thera (Vistaar 2000), p. 6.

28. John D. Ireland, *The Udana & the Itivuttaka* (Kandy: BPS, 1997).

CHAPTER ONE
FLIRTING

ACCORDING TO THE TEACHING OF THE BUDDHA, THE DHAMMA, WE get connected to the good things in life according to our past volitions, reaching far beyond this current existence back through beginningless time. The Dhamma does not teach fatalism,[1] but there are subtle causes behind all effects, and although we are free to choose, that choice is part of a complex fabric in which all things are interconnected and nothing happens without a reason. The decision to attend a Ten-Day course, seen in this light, is not just a mundane choice like any other, but a matter of one's deep karmic roots surfacing, a sign that we are ready to start walking the path of liberation for real.[2]

A possible approach to taking an introductory Ten-Day course would, accordingly, be to trust in the intuition that is drawing one forward and to take things as they come, without any expectations at all, with faith in and gratitude for the highly auspicious opportunity that is presenting oneself. To be human, according to the Teaching, is a great blessing, and never more than when one is introduced to Noble Eightfold Path and given a chance to experience its power.[3] However long the Path may be, after all, it must begin with the first step, and however small one's strides may seem, the end is already anticipated in the beginning. If you start to walk with determination, so the Buddhists believe, you will finish one day, even if that day seems a long way off.

Once the seed has been planted, it is bound to sprout sooner or later.[4]

On the other hand, the Buddha never asked anyone to be satisfied with mere hints or hunches. Thus, in a famous discourse to the Kalamas, who lived at the edge of a great forest and saw many spiritual teachers pass through their town professing clashing theories, the Buddha put the emphasis squarely on robust personal experience, at least at the outset of one's seeking.[5] Faith is a vital ingredient on the Path as well, but it should never be blind[6] and it may not be the best place to start when one is at a loss. It is fitting for you to be perplexed and in doubt, the Buddha reassured the Kalamas, because you are dealing with a truly confusing matter.[7] But if you look closely enough at the stock of your own experiences, you will be able to know for yourself what things are unwholesome and blamable, censured by the wise because they bring harm and suffering, and which are the opposite. Do not go only by what I tell you, he said, but by what you can confirm for yourselves. Then faith will come naturally and it will not be blind.

We all carry expectations whether we like it or not, and most of us like to have some sense of what we are getting into before we give up our car-keys and check ourselves into a facility that resembles a low-security prison, even if it is at Scandinavian levels of comfort.[8] An easy and direct way to get a feel for the dynamics of a Vipassana course is to watch one of the documentaries made about prison-programs near Delhi ("Doing Time, Doing Vipassana"), at a maximum-security facility in Alabama ("The Dhamma Brothers"), and at a women's jail in Seattle ("Changing from Inside"). The worldwide Vipassana website at Dhamma.org provides plenty of basic information about the tradition and the courses, including a popular talk and essay by Goenka on "The Art of Living." For more serious reading, the best book to start with on Goenka's approach specifically is *The Art of Living* by William Hart, the best general introduction to *The Noble Eightfold Path (NEP)* is Bhikkhu Bodhi's short but excellent book by that title.

There is no specific physical preparation for a course, but it would not hurt to have done a bit of yoga and to have experimented with different ways of sitting on the floor with a mat and a cushion. Arriving at a course as rested as possible would also be a plus.

NOTES

1. See the question on freedom in chapter 12.

2. Thus Goenka: "Nothing happens without a cause. None one comes to a course accidentally." (*Art of Living*, p. 145)

3. SN 56.47-48 (pp. 1871-72).

4. Goenka says very clearly in his courses that there is "every chance" that any practitioner of Vipassana might reach the "final goal." His exhortation to keep "starting again" and to practice as diligently and continuously as possible ("continuity is the secret of success") has everything to do with his conviction that if one keeps working at it, one is "bound to be successful, bound to be successful." (These characteristic turns of phrase are repeated throughout the Ten-Day course.

5. AN 3:65 (pp. 279-283 [BW 88-91]).

6. Faith is the first of the five spiritual faculties (*indriyas*), along with energy, mindfulness, concentration, and wisdom. The need to maintain balance between these five pillars of the practice is stressed in the *Visuddhimagga* (IV.45-49 [p. 128-29]). The Buddha discusses how faith gets "planted, rooted, and established" when it is "supported by reasons" (MN 47, esp. 47.16 [p. 418]). See also SN 55 (pp. 1788-1837) with many angles on "confirmed faith." The Buddha does call on the faith of followers who have good reasons to trust him (see for example SN 12.51 [p. 589]) and emphasizes the great benefits of such faith for heading towards enlightenment (MN 22.46-47 [p. 236]).

7. See also AN 8.12 (p. 1134), where the Buddha encourages a general to "make an investigation!"

8. The *Visuddhimagga* describes the kind of lodging most suitable for meditators of a greedy temperament: "It ought to be spattered with dirt, full of bats, dilapidated, too high or too low, in bleak

surroundings, threatened [by wild beasts], with muddy and uneven paths, where even the bed and chair are full of bugs." (*Vism.* III.97 [p. 107]) Persons struggling with ill-will, on the other hand, ought to be treated to "well-proportioned walls, posts and steps; with well-prepared frieze-work and lattice work; brightened with various kinds of painting; with an even, smooth, soft floor; adorned with festoons of flowers; ... the bed and chair covered with well-spread clean pretty covers; smelling sweetly of perfumes and scents set about for homely comfort." (*Vism.* III.98 [108]) I'm all for it! Or would that make me greedy? Oops...

CHAPTER TWO
THE LAY OF THE LAND

VIPASSANA IS A PALI WORD THAT MEANS "TO SEE THINGS AS THEY are" and so this type of meditation is often called "insight meditation" in English.[1] (Thus the Insight Meditation Society in Barre, Massachusetts, for instance, which was started by Goenka-students.) *Satipatthana* is Pali for the establishment of mindfulness, after the Buddha's most comprehensive discourses on meditative technique, and the term is sometimes used by other offshoots of the Vipassana tradition.[2]

The approach to meditation taught by S.N. Goenka is said to go back to the Buddha's day. In Burma, where Goenka grew up and got his Dhamma training, the story is told of how two monk-ambassadors sent out from India in Ashoka's time — Sona and Uttara — established the tradition in what was then called the Golden Land and how it is was supposedly transmitted ("in its pristine purity") from student to teacher for over two-thousand years.[3] So far the legend.

In modern times, the celebrated monk-scholar Ledi Sayadaw (1846-1923) has been called "the father of the insight meditation tradition in Burma."[4] Ledi is famous not only for his writings, but also for making a point of spreading both theoretical instruction and Vipassana meditation among the laity (some of his meditation centers still exist).[5] One of his lay students, U Thet (1873-1945), a

5

farmer later called by the honorific Saya Thetgyi, was identified by Ledi as his "great pupil" and charged with teaching the Dhamma to six thousand others, one of whom would turn out, in 1937, to be (Sayagyi) U Ba Kin (1899-1971). In 1952, U Ba Khin, by then Accountant General of newly independent Burma, founded his International Meditation Centre in Rangoon and it was there that S.N. Goenka (1924-2013) took his first ten-day course in 1955 (see the biographical sketch in chapter 8).[6] U Ba Khin and Goenka shared the vision of universalizing Vipassana[7] and when the latter set out to return the Dhamma to India in 1969, the former predicted that it would now spread around the world: "The clock of Vipassana has struck."[8] Today hundreds of Vipassana-centers around the world bear witness to their efforts.

Speaking loosely and from a Goenka-student's perspective, one might think of Ledi Sayadaw and Saya Thetgyi as the great-grandfathers of the modern Vipassana tradition, of U Ba Khin as the grandfather, and of Papa Goenka as the father. But in fact the family tree of Vipassana has many more branches. U Ba Khin's original center in Yangon still exists with its own lineage of teachers, and Mya Thwin (Mother Sayamagyi), another prominent U Ba Khin student, has established International Meditation Centres in several other countries. John Coleman, Ruth Denison, and Robert Hover (the aerospace engineer mentioned in Goenka's discourses[9]) were likewise authorized to teach by U Ba Khin himself. Sharon Salzberg and Joseph Goldstein, founders of the Barre center, also studied with Goenka, though not exclusively.

In his courses and talks, Goenka always made a strict distinction between *the Dhamma* — the Teaching of the Buddha — and *Buddhism*. He even went so far as to say that "whoever first used the word Buddhism or Buddhist, in any language, was the biggest enemy of Buddha's teaching, because the teaching had been universal, and now out of ignorance, he made it sectarian."[10] Goenka's principled stand against sectarianism is one of the attractions of his approach,[11] and anyone who has marveled at what strange blossoms the Buddhist tree has produced with the passage of time and the blending of cultures will have some sympathy for his attempt to recover the roots of the tradition. It is also true that the Buddha was not keen on making disciples: "Let him who is your teacher remain your teacher," he said to the wanderer Nigrodha and his friends.[12] The point is not to reverence any person, even that of a Buddha,[13] but to look to what he represents: "One who sees the Dhamma sees me; one who sees me sees the Dhamma."[14] (The custom of making Buddha-statues, incidentally, was not introduced for centuries after the Buddha's death and owed much to the influence of Greek sculpture.[15])

Whether the Dhamma can be distinguished as neatly as Goenka would like from historical Buddhism is another matter. It's one thing to say that the Buddha would have trouble recognizing himself perched on a pile of gold and gems in a Bangkok temple, or reduced to a business talisman in Singapore or Hong Kong, but quite another to pretend that a practitioner of the Dhamma like Bhikkhu Bodhi, perhaps the West's leading Theravadan scholar-monk, must be missing something because he is comfortable calling himself a Buddhist.[16] Most of the stories Goenka tells in his discourses come straight from the standard Theravadan repertoire, and however scientific and modern a bent he wishes to give to his claims, many of his positions are traditional Buddhist articles of faith recast for a contemporary global audience. The idea that the historic Buddha used the exact words of the Pali Canon, for instance, is one that few if any scholars accept.[17] There is little doubt that the Buddha would have spoken several Northern Indian dialects closely related to Pali, but the language of the Scriptures is most likely an amalgamation of different spoken idioms — partly Sanskritized for loftier style, and partly adapted to the structural needs of an oral tradition by which the texts were transmitted for about four-hundred years before they were first written down in Sri Lanka. To believe that Ananda's memory was such that he could recite thousands of sermons after having heard them only once is an act of faith, not of science or scholarship, as is the conviction that the Pali Scriptures could have escaped all corruption during four centuries of oral transmission and two millennia of copying manuscripts. Who is not susceptible to the siren-song of "the one and only way," the legend of a lone tradition that has miraculously survived the vagaries of time "in its pristine purity"?[18] Whether it is wise to give into such temptations we must all decide for ourselves.

But one should not get too hung up on minutiae. Prospective students will have to accept that Vipassana is a very practically-minded tradition that can sound almost dismissive of the intellect at times.[19] Opportunities for serious discussion and argument at Ten-Day courses are scant, at least before the exhilarating free-for-all of Day 10 (Metta Day), and first-timers especially will have to be prepared for some brooding if they are prone to intellectual misgivings. Students may raise any issue they wish during the noontime interviews, but they will rarely be given more than five minutes to do so (less during the short windows of opportunity to speak to the teacher after group sittings or during the question-period after 9 pm), and the often repetitive and predictable stock of Vipassana answers may leave something to be desired. The routine questioning (called "check-ins" in the lingo) that will take place at certain intervals during the course is not a setting conducive to pacifying restless intellects.[20]

The teachers are competent and experienced in their way, but they are not professors or philosophers, and their job is to guide students through the practice, not to engage them on the open field of intellectual battle.[21] If you are a stickler for no-holds-barred debate, you will spare yourself much anguish by accepting upfront that you have let yourself in for some brainwashing as part of your Vipassana experience. ("We must wash the dirty linen of our mind" is one of the lines in Goenka's Hindi chanting.[22]) Consider that putting your mental laundry through the hot-cycle may not be such a bad idea: unless you can accept that it needs a good scrubbing rather than merely another brainy workout, there's no point in putting yourself through the noble ordeal that is a Vipassana course.

NOTES

1. Walpola Rahula points out that *bhavana* carries much richer connotations of mental cultivation and development than "meditation" does in English (Rahula, p. 68).

2. See the box on *Satipatthana* at the outset of chapter 6.

3. See Goenka, *For the Benefit of Many*, p. 184.

4. Bhikkhu Pesala, editor of *A Manual of the Excellent Man* by Ledi Sayadaw (BPS 2000), p. v.

5. Who Ledi's teacher was is not known: he only mentioned that he had received the technique from a monk in Mandalay whose name has not been recorded.

6. Short biographies and other materials about these figures compiled by the Vipassana Research Institute can be found online or in a printed collection of commemorative materials entitled *Sayagyi U Ba Khin Journal* (VRI 1998), specifically pp. 75-84. See also part I of *The Clock of Vipassana Has Struck*.

7. Thus Goenka: "U Ba Khin's technique wasn't a special technique of meditation, but a way of explaining things, ... a way of expressing Dhamma that non-Buddhist English-speaking people could understand." (*For the Benefit of Many*, p. 66) See also *Clock of Vipassana*, p. 90: "It's an old technique that he taught in a modern way."

8. Goenka, *For the Benefit of Many*, p. 176.

9. Day 8 Discourse. The other scientist mentioned (the "bundle of misery" at UC Berkeley) was Donald A. Glaser, whose invention of the "bubble chamber" won him the 1960 Nobel Prize in Physics (Day 3 Discourse, *Art of Living*, pp. 32-33).

10. Goenka, *For the Benefit of Many*, p. 152. See also p. 110 and p. 126: "No, I am not a Buddhist."

11. The story of the blind men and the elephant, which Goenka tells in his discourses to illustrate the folly of sectarian quarreling, is an old Indian tale that precedes Buddhism; in the Buddhist Canon, it can be found in the *Udana* (6.4 [Ireland, pp. 86-88, BW 214-15]).

12. DN 25.23 (p. 393). At MN 56.17 (p. 484) the Buddha encourages a new follower whose family had long supported the Niganthas (or Jains) to keep giving to them, even though his disagreements with the founder of Jainism, Nigantha Nataputta (Mahavira to his

followers), were stark: "The Nigantha Nataputta had just died ... and his lay disciples were disgusted, dismayed, and disappointed with his pupils, as they were with his badly proclaimed and badly expounded Dhamma and Discipline, which was unemancipating, unconducive to peace, expounded by one not fully enlightened, and was now with its shrine broken, left without a refuge." (MN 104.2 [p. 853]) The Buddha was not coy about establishing his precedence: "The glow worm shines only as long as the sun has not risen. Even so the wanderers [other seekers] shine only as long as Fully Awakened Ones do not appear in the world." (*Udana* 6.10 [Ireland, p. 93])

13. Thus AN 6.42 (p. 906): "Let me never come upon fame, and may fame never catch up with me." Unlike Agamemnon in Aeschylus, the Buddha could not be tempted to step on any precious fabrics laid out before his feet (MN 85.5-7 [p. 704-705]).

14. SN 22.87 (p. 939). See also *Itivuttaka* 92 (Ireland, p. 217) and AN 10.172 [p. 1513]): "[The Blessed One] has become knowledge, he has become the Dhamma."

15. It is said that the first Buddha-statue was made on orders of Menander I, the King Milinda who presents his Questions to the monk Nagasena, in the second century BCE.

16. U Ba Khin too was quite "proud and satisfied" to call himself a Buddhist, as Goenka acknowledges (*Clock of Vipassana*, p. 41).

17. Thus Bodhi: "The entire [Pali Canon] has been preserved in a Middle Indo-Aryan language, one closely related to the language (or, more likely, the various regional dialects) that the Buddha himself spoke. We call this language Pali, but the name for the language actually arose through a misunderstanding. The world *pali* properly means 'text,' that is, the canonical text as distinct from the commentaries... At some point, the term was misunderstood to mean 'the Pali language,' and once the misconception arose, it took root and has been with us ever since. Scholars regard this language as a hybrid showing features of several Prakrit dialects used around the third century B.C.E. subjected to a partial process of Sanskritization. While the language is not identical with any the Buddha himself would have spoken, it belongs to the same broad linguistic family as those he might have used and originates from the same conceptual matrix." (BW 9-10)

18. On "the one and only way," see the box on *Satipatthana* in chapter 6.

19. Not that the Buddha's Teaching can be said to slight the intellect. "Without knowledge," it says in the *Dhammapada*, "there is no meditation," and vice versa: the two cannot be separated (see *Dhp.* XXV.13/372, AN 6.47 [p. 919]). Along with exceptional energy, steadfastness of purpose, and great loving-kindness, a keen intellect is considered one of the four marks of maturity expected of an advanced practitioner, or bodhisatta (*Manual of the Excellent Man*, p. 19). "We shall be of great learning here" is presented as a Buddhist resolution at MN 8.40 (p. 127). Thus also MN 115.2 (p. 925): "We shall be wise men, we shall be inquirers." In sum, the qualities of the heart and the qualities of the mind need to go together if one is truly to develop on the Path (Rahula, p. 46).

20. Think of these aptly-named and highly standardized encounters on analogy with checking in at an airport. You will be asked a set of routine questions and you might as well stick to the expected unless you have good reasons not to. When you are asked whether you did your own packing, you answer "yes" even though your butler or mother may have done it for you. When you are asked whether you have left your luggage unattended, you answer "no" even though you have not been carrying your bags around chained to your wrist as if they were the U.S. President's nuclear football. You should never lie or pretend, of course, but keep it simple. You will not be barred from a Goenka-flight for departing from the script, but neither are you likely to get more than a few stock responses out of your teacher on these occasions. Just try to start a discussion and see for yourself...

21. At some point in his discourses, Goenka has the nerve to call his courses "Dhamma seminars." Do not be fooled. What you have signed up for is a lecture course at best, in which the main teacher is above being questioned and his teaching assistants are neither disposed nor trained to entertain serious challenges.

22. Goenka, *Gem Set in Gold*, p. 73.

CHAPTER THREE
FOREPLAY

VIPASSANA CENTERS HAVE SPRUNG UP ALL AROUND THE WORLD AT a remarkable pace, especially over the past fifteen to twenty years, and since the basic structure of courses is everywhere the same (with Goenka's instructions always played in English and teachers usually able to speak at least some), students may in principle apply anywhere in the world. Doing a first course at home is probably advisable, but it is not a strict requirement, and the appeal of sitting in India, Burma, or Thailand is obvious. Some centers (in Thailand for example) have in the past set quotas for foreigners, supposedly because of language concerns, but from what I've heard, Goenka did not approve.

It would be inappropriate, in the context of living off the charity of others, to assign ratings based on the amenities and the level of comfort on offer at a center, but you should be aware of how crowded Indian courses can be, for example, and how rugged the living arrangements. There are also cultural differences around body-functions that can affect your experience considerably, and it may be worth making some discreet inquiries if you are bothered by such things. Of course it would be ideal to treat annoyances as simply part of one's equanimity training,[1] but you will be challenged enough no matter what. (The full implications of volunteering as a server in a place like India should be considered with care lest there be a rude awakening.)

Regardless of where you apply, you will be asked to provide personal information that you would not want published in the newspaper or shared with the goons that guard the US border. Unlike your credit card company or the IRS, the Vipassana folk who will process your application understand that you have entrusted them with something they are obliged to protect, and I have never heard of a security breach.

When you are asked to divulge intimate details about your physical and mental health, or about your history of using or abusing drugs, it is not done in order to weed you out; the purpose of the Vipassana courses is to help those who need it most, not to put barriers in their way. The information is required, instead, to ensure that your teachers will be aware of your situation and that they will be able to give you the help and attention necessary. On courses with as many as a hundred students or more, it is not always possible to accommodate individuals facing particular difficulties, but you can be sure that the centers are doing what they can and that no one is going to read your application looking for reasons to reject it. You would not be doing yourself any favors by hiding anything.

The Buddhist precept against intoxicants (as well as the one against sexual misconduct) tends to be read with unfashionable strictness by Goenka and his helpers. During courses, you must abstain completely from all drugs. There have been cases of students smoking up in the woods, but that is considered utterly unacceptable in a Vipassana setting. Ordinary smoking, although it is not considered a violation of the precepts, is also strictly forbidden. I have been amazed by the depth and range of personal drug-related expertise brought to Vipassana courses by some of the students. Not only had they tried everything, they had listed it freely on their applications and still been accepted. So long as there is some readiness to look beyond a life of drugs, experienced users may even make particularly good meditators, inasmuch as they are on closer terms with suffering and perhaps more open-minded in some ways. Let it be said that they may have a particularly hard time with a course; but then one never can tell.

There are certain legitimate practices, types of energy-work especially, that may raise red flags — Reiki for example. From what I understand, Vipassana meditation is not incompatible with the practice of Reiki as such, but the organization takes the line that mixing the two at a high level of intensity is potentially dangerous.[2]

Advanced practitioners in other traditions, especially spiritual teachers committed to other approaches, may not be accepted because Goenka does not look favorably upon combining techniques — partly because there are potential dangers, partly out of a principled concern about the inutility of eclecticism. Goenka's approach would have you identify the most suitable and congenial spot where to dig your spiritual well, and then to commit yourself to working for depth until you hit water, rather than starting over and over again, digging here, there, and everywhere.[3] Cases are handled individually and fairly flexibly, except when they are not.

Most centers have a rule that you may only be registered for one course at a time, but they will allow you to be waitlisted for several. Course availability varies drastically by center and season. Sometimes it is possible to get a seat at a few days' notice, other times there are no open spots for months.

OTHER COURSES

In addition to the standard Ten-Day courses with which every student must begin her training,[4] there are three other types of courses for returning students (called "Old students" in the lingo): single-day and three-day courses, open to all; Sati courses (eight-day courses for studying the *Mahasatipatthana Sutta*,[5] open to students who have sat at least three Ten-Day courses); and Long courses of twenty days and more with very stringent prerequisites (two years of sitting the full two hours every day, for starters, and much else besides). All courses follow the same daily schedule, with one third of the course devoted to Anapana meditation (mindfulness of breath), two thirds to Vipassana.[6]

Very short Anapana courses for children and adolescents are also offered at many centers.

NOTES

1. See the box on equanimity at the outset of chapter 6. Nyanaponika Thera writes: "The method of transforming disturbances into objects of meditation, as simple as it is ingenious, may be regarded as the culmination of non-violent procedure. It is a device very characteristic of the spirit of Satipatthana to make use of all experiences as aids on the path. In that way, enemies are turned into friends; for all the disturbances and antagonistic forces become our teachers, and teachers, whoever they may be, should be regarded as friends." (*Vision,* p. 87) On turning hindrances into helpers for one's practice, see also Marcus Aurelius (*Meditations* VI.50, VIII.32, VIII.35, X.31).

2. From what I have heard, practitioners of Reiki are only admitted to Vipassana courses if they promise not practice their techniques during the ten days.

3. The image is used in Goenka's discourse on Day 10. Also Bodhi: "A spiritual tradition is not a shallow stream in which one can wet one's feet and then beat a quick retreat to the shore. It is a mighty, tumultuous river that would rush through the entire landscape of one's life, and if one truly wishes to travel on it, one must be courageous enough to launch one's boat and head out for the depths." (NEP I.3) Bodhi also likens the choice of a spiritual path to marriage: "One wants a partner for life, one whose companionship will prove as trustworthy and durable as the pole star in the night sky." (NEP I.4)

4. To provide more balance in my pronouns, and also because there are often more women on Vipassana courses than men, I will use the female pronoun for unnamed meditators unless there is a specific reason not to. Context should make it clear when I mean for pronouns of either sex to be understood inclusively.

5. See the box on *Satipatthana* in chapter 6.

6. See my brief discussion of the relationship between the two techniques in chapter 10.

CHAPTER FOUR
TEN DAYS IN THE HOT-TUB

IN THE UNIVERSE OF MEDITATION, THERE ARE MANY PLANETS OR traditions, and each planet is subdivided into many continents, countries, and regions. Thus Buddhism is only one tradition among many that have emphasized meditation; there are many kinds of Buddhism with very different techniques; and even the world of Vipassana has many distinct regions where different dialects are spoken and things are not understood the same way. So far as the Goenkan Republic of Vipassana is concerned, you must earn your passport by an introductory Ten-Day course. There are both longer and shorter courses that students may take eventually (see above), but the first course must always follow the basic Ten-Day format, which is the same everywhere it is offered. (Think of Goenka's organization as a kind of spiritual McDonald's with franchises around the world: there are minor allowances made for cultural context, but you should know what you are getting when you are ordering a Happy Meal anywhere in the world.)

A few centers start their Ten-Day courses on fixed days every month, but the more common format is for courses to run on a moving schedule from a Wednesday afternoon (Day 0) through a Sunday morning (Day 11). First-timers must commit to staying for the whole duration of a course in their applications, and they

16

are expected to reaffirm their commitment at registration time and again during the opening formalities on the evening of Day 0. Old students may apply to attend only part of the ten-day period, but this diminishes their chances of being admitted because full-time students are given priority. The management looks askance at departures on Saturday (Day 10), not for anyone's convenience but for energetic reasons. No one can detain you against your will, but if you leave without getting clearance, your course may not be considered full-time for the purposes of future applications. The course ends at 7 am on Day 11 and you should leave at least another hour or two for doing your part in the clean-up.

Centers may give students different instructions on when to arrive on Wednesday afternoon, but usually it is between 3 and 4 pm. There is no great harm done if you are a little early; just relax if you can, get used to the atmosphere, and keep your eyes open for opportunities to chat. You may find that the perspectives and experiences that other students bring to a course are as great a resource as your own preparations. Once the registration desk is open, you will need to fill out a form that mirrors your application with a bit of added space for talking about your background and motivations for coming. You will be asked to give up all items not permitted on a course (books, iPods, cigarettes, devotional items) as well as you car keys and cell phone. Although there is a number for friends or family members to call in dire emergencies, students agree to remove themselves from all contact with the outside world for the full duration of the course. Rooms are assigned (see "Beds and Bugs" below) and you will be left with some free time before a light supper is served (usually soup) and a short orientation talk specific to the center is played on tape. Talking is permitted until the night's opening formalities, but students have different ways of processing their jitters, and some like to keep to themselves or start the silence early.

Shortly before 8 pm, students will be summoned to the meditation hall by the first gong, which will be rung at all important occasions from now on. (Daily schedules are posted throughout the center and the rhythm of daily events, accompanied by the striking of the gong, will become intuitive to you within a day or two.) Students may still talk quietly, but they should keep their voices down around the hall; they will then be called into the meditation area one-by-one, starting with the most experienced meditator. For the purposes of Vipassana seniority, Long courses trump any number of Ten-Day courses and age is used to break ties. (Establishing a monastic hierarchy based on date of ordination was one of the strategies the Buddha used to break the hold of the incipient caste system at the time.[1] The story is told of a group of princes accompanied by their barber who made a point, when they were ordained, of letting their former servant go first so that he would become their superior.[2]) Everyone is assigned a specific seat: the more experienced towards the front, the new students towards the back.[3] Please do not change your seat without speaking to the course manager first, because the teachers and helpers will learn to identify you by your position in the hall. If you have not asked for a chair or a spot on the wall, you will still be able to get one, but only after the opening session, which runs for about an hour. Every seat comes with a mat and a cushion, and there are usually plenty of bolsters available in the antechamber of the hall, but it is always a good idea to bring your own.

NOBLE SILENCE

Noble silence commences as soon as you enter the meditation hall for the first time and it lasts until the special meditation on Metta (Loving-Kindness) that ends shortly before 10 am on Metta Day (Day 10). From now on you may only talk to the course manager (see below) or to the teachers. (If you need to alert someone to a serious problem or emergency, you should never hesitate to speak or even to shout, if necessary!)

You might say that the skies will hardly fall over a few quiet words, and you would be right; but even a few words can become a distraction, both to yourself and to the person you are addressing. (If you want to be strict, talking to yourself may be a minor violation of noble silence as well, but the most important thing is not to disturb anyone else.) Words multiply quickly and never fail to have a subtle agitating impact, especially when your mind is as sensitive as it will become on a Ten-Day course. Even communicating by glances or gestures (let alone reading or listening to music) can take one out of the deep introspection that makes the Vipassana technique so powerfully purifying. This may sound like mere dogma, but once you have experienced the magic of prolonged silence for yourself, you may come to appreciate why it is such a vital, well-guarded ingredient.

Purists are advised to keep their attention directed inward by always looking down when their eyes are open. A colorful story is told about a recluse by the name of Cittagutta, who lived in a cave that was famous for a beautiful wall-painting. One day a number of bhikkhus visited the recluse, wandered about his cave, and commented on the loveliness of the painting. "Painting? What painting?" asked the recluse. "For more than sixty years, friends, I have lived in this cave, and I have never seen any painting, because I have not looked up."[4] Goenka knows better than to tell this kind of story in the regular Ten-Day discourses, but be prepared for such edifying tales of the absurd to come up during Long courses.[5] You can always wash them down by drinking more of the Kool-Aid. Or console yourself with the thought that they are not actually in the Canon.

HOW TO SIT

In marked contrast to other schools of meditation, especially Zen, neither Goenka nor any of his helpers will tell you much about how to sit — save for one reference each, in the initial instructions given for Anapana and Vipassana, to the helpfulness in the long-run of keeping one's back and neck straight. (Judging by the culture of drooping that prevails in many courses, the message tends to get lost among so many others.) The logic for not providing any guidance is not made explicit; presumably the idea is to get students to figure things out for themselves, as they all seem to do sooner or later, partly by experimenting and partly by watching what others are doing (even if you are supposed to keep your focus inward).

The first and most common way to sit is cross-legged, either in a half-lotus position with one tucked leg or in the so-called "easy position" with one leg in front of the other. The full-lotus position is more of an aesthetic than a meditative ideal, and it should only be used if it is truly comfortable because otherwise it can result in a lot of strain.

The second common way is to sit in the Japanese kneeling position, either with a pillow or with a meditation bench to keep the pressure off your heels.

The third is to sit in a chair or with your back against the wall.

The positioning of your hands is not considered important at Vipassana centers. So long as you don't put them down the front of your pants, you may do with them whatever feels most comfortable.

Props and cushions can be used in too many ways for me to discuss here, but you will get plenty of ideas from the "game of thrones" that you will see your fellow meditators playing with ever greater refinement as the days progress. It can be amusing, if a little melancholy, to see what ingenuity goes into the doomed effort to keep pain at bay by tweaking one's seat. The great insight that only personal experience will make believable is that our most effective weapon in the fight with pain is to stop feeding our aversion by ceasing to react as much as possible. The Old students sitting so still in the front row aren't doing it because they are showing off their toughness; they are doing it because it turns out to be easier once one has acquired the knack for it.

As I gradually migrated, over several courses, from the wall to the kneeling position to sitting in the easy cross-legged position, I was surprised to discover that what had seemed most forbidding (sitting cross-legged) was in the end the most tolerable, and what might seem easiest (sitting in the chair) in fact the hardest if one has to spend many hours in a single position. But that is only my experience, and the key is to find out what works for you, always understanding that no matter how you sit, the pain will find you before long, because it is ultimately coming from the mind.[6] The weak spots on the body that seem to be getting so sore are like the cracks through which steam is escaping from a pressure cooker. So long as you are building up the pressure, the steam will keep discharging in unpleasant ways, if not in one place, then in another. To realize as much, not in theory but in your own practical experience, is one of the great liberating discoveries that Vipassana has to offer.

INJURY, HEMORRHOIDS, AND OTHER WORRIES

New students often worry about injuring themselves by so much sitting on the floor, but the only case I know of is the ironic one of a very experienced student who was bent on staying in the full lotus position throughout a course, and who ignored all messages his body was sending him. Pain is an inevitable part of the process, but there is a difference between sensations that appear during a sitting but go away within a few minutes after one has gotten up, and those that persist. Except during sittings of strong determination (see below), you may take breaks or change your position whenever you see fit, and there is only a single session longer than an hour, the ninety-minute introduction to Vipassana on Day 4. A judicious exploration of pain and its meaning is an important part of meditation, but simply disregarding the body or deliberately torturing yourself is not.[7]

Many students fear that they might be cutting off circulation in their legs during meditation. I am told that such fears are groundless[8] — the sensations are caused by irritated nerves, not lack of blood — but that doesn't make the worries any less real or intense. If you are concerned in advance, why not do some research now; during a course, you may always speak to a teacher when doubts and anxieties are threatening to overwhelm you. It is remarkable what force even the most trifling and far-fetched thoughts acquire when they've swirled around your meditation-addled head for a few hours. Try not to feed them unduly, but keep your attention on the breath and the sensations whenever you can.

There is a folk-myth, especially around Japanese Zen monasteries, that frequent meditation causes hemorrhoids (supposedly the Chinese character for the ailment may be read to suggest "temple-illness"). Some of the most experienced Vipassana teachers are doctors, and one of them assured me, during a course when I got worried, that hemorrhoids are caused not by sitting meditation, but by straining on the pot. If Zen monasteries are hotbeds of the complaint, it would be because of the habit of rushing bodily functions, not because of the protracted sittings. Nor are you putting yourself at any serious risk of blood clots unless you were planning to sit all day without moving, which you wouldn't be allowed to do anyway.

THE OPENING FORMALITIES

The opening session on the night of Day 0 follows a traditional Buddhist format with a few variations specific to Goenka.

Goenka will begin his chanting by paying homage to the Buddha with the traditional Pali formula: "*Namo tassa bhagavato, arahato, samma-sambudhassa.*" (Homage to him, the blessed one, the worthy conqueror, the fully self-enlightened Buddha, in Goenka's translation.[9])

While Goenka does explain most of the Pali he uses in the discourses, the chants are not translated or even identified. A translation of all Pali and Hindi used in a Ten-Day course is available under the title *The Gem Set in Gold*, but this is not made available to students until Metta Day (Day 10).

After the traditional homage, Goenka begins the first longish chant of the course, and it may be worth noting that it is not a traditional Pali text, but a Hindi chant of his own composition, as are many others during the course. His style of chanting is unusual: he claims to be broadcasting especially powerful vibrations,[10] but the effect is decidedly not music to everyone's ears.

Taking refuge in the Buddha, the Dhamma, and the Sangha (the Triple Gem) is another traditional Buddhist procedure, and Goenka explains how he understands the terms. (The Sangha to which one goes for refuge is not the present-day population of ordained monks and nuns, but the *Ariya-Sangha*: the community through time and space of all who have attained at least stream-entry, the first stage of Buddhist sainthood.[11])

Next come the Five Precepts, training rules by which students pledge to refrain from killing, stealing, sexual misconduct, lying, and the use of intoxicants. These shouldn't present great challenges during a closely supervised, silent Ten-Day course where the sexes are segregated, except for certain marginal points that I will touch on below.

Three additional precepts apply only to the Old students and don't have a great deal of relevance, to the point of being somewhat comical, except for the rule against eating in the afternoons. (Old students commit to abstaining from dancing, singing, music and worldly entertainments; wearing garlands, jewelry, or other adornments; using perfumes or cosmetics; and sleeping in high or luxurious beds![12])

The traditional formula for surrendering oneself to the Buddha (for proper guidance and protection) probably gives little occasion for squeamishness, and it is up to each student to interpret how much deference she is prepared to promise when she surrenders to her present teacher on similar terms. The online application process in North America clarifies that "students must declare themselves willing to comply fully and for the duration of the course with the teacher's guidance and instructions" but that "this acceptance should be one of discrimination and understanding, not blind submission."

Finally, students request to be taught Anapana meditation (mindfulness of the breath), and off they go on their adventure.[13] The traditional formula makes explicit the importance of Nibbana to all Buddhist striving: *"For the sake of witnessing Nibbana*, please teach me Anapana meditation."* Although the Dhamma brings many practical advantages for life in the world as well, "the holy life is grounded upon Nibbana, culminates in Nibbana, ends in Nibbana."[14]

I will refrain, as I promised, from discussing meditation instructions. Students should know, however, that Anapana is a challenge not just for them but for everyone, no matter how experienced: "Mindfulness of breathing is difficult, difficult to develop, a field in which only the minds of Buddhas and Buddha's sons [and daughters] are at home. It is no trivial matter, nor can it be cultivated by just anyone. In proportion as continued attention is given to it, it becomes more peaceful and more subtle. So strong mindfulness and understanding are necessary here."[15] For beginners and advanced meditators alike, trying to keep one's focus will often feel like struggling for balance on a beach-ball or sweeping a floor crawling with cockroaches.[16] The Dhamma is a regimen for poise and hygiene, mental as well as physical, not for resigning oneself to monkey-mind or parasite-infested living spaces; but just as even invading armies of insects should be chased out of our kitchens without undue resentment, so we should cultivate a friendly attitude towards our own agitated thoughts. They will calm down eventually, the way impurities in a glass of water will finally settle at the bottom. Just don't expect serenity to arrive quickly, or to last; you will fall off the beach ball before long and the cockroaches are not likely to yield to your broom for more than a moment. But that is quite all right, since the practice is not so much about succeeding as it is about trying again, and again, and again, perhaps in the spirit of Churchill's dictum than success is nothing other than going from failure to failure with undiminished enthusiasm (or if you prefer Zen: *shoshaku jushaku*, practice as a continuous succession of one mistake following another).[17]

SADHU, SADHU, SADHU

The opening session, like all group sittings, concludes with Goenka sharing his good will with all beings by chanting "*Bhavatu sabba mangalam*": *May all beings be happy*. Many Old students will then respond by saying "Sadhu, sadhu, sadhu" ("well said") and bowing three times.

The instructions posted on notice-boards (usually around the dining area) acknowledge that bowing to the floor at one's teachers' feet and glorifying their pearls of wisdom with chorales of acclaim are Eastern customs that students in the West may or may not find helpful, beneficial, or desirable. (Prostration has been a defining issue between the East and the West since at least the days of the ancient Greeks: Themistocles insisted that to crawl before the Persian "king of kings" in the expected Asian manner would be to betray his own culture, and he got his way.[18]) At Goenka-centers, at any rate, neither the response nor the bowing is required from anyone in whom the wish to join does not arise spontaneously. (It can be more obligatory elsewhere; when I sat at U Ba Khin's old center in Yangon, I was told that it was expected, and that was that.) In me, the desire to prostrate hardly ever arises, and since I tend to get seated in the front row, which may give others the mistaken idea that they should follow what I am doing, I usually make a point of not participating so that others feel free to do the same. At most, I will give a little bow, with hands folded before me, towards the teacher but really directed at the Buddha-nature in all of us that got expressed in the effort needed to make it through another hour on the mat.[19] Not only must we all fight our own battles, as Goenka is so fond of saying, but we must also choose which ones to wage with our egos since we can't be at war all the time. (The most original reason for bowing I heard from a Finnish boy who loved to bow because he considered it a pagan custom and wanted to rid himself of his Christian formation even while he was studying at a Seventh Day Adventist university in Thailand.)

The enthusiasm for bowing is nourished in part by the traditional Indian belief, upheld by Goenka himself, that good vibrations are absorbed with the top of the head,[20] while bad ones are given off by the soles of the feet. Thus the abandon with which you will see some Old students prostrating themselves, and thus the rule against pointing your feet at the teachers, even during the evening discourses. Whether you are prepared to believe that the best way to benefit from good vibrations is to mop the floor with your head, or that highly experienced teachers will really be contaminated by radiation from your feet, is up to you. (Dirty and smelly feet are another matter.[21] Goenka's many references to "*yatha-bhuta*," that is, learning to see and accept things "as they are, not as you would like them to be,"[22] should not be taken as encouragement to stop washing. Do by all means cultivate the Way of Mother Nature and tolerance towards all the strange smells emanating from others, but please do not force this practice on others, especially in the summer.)

You will sometimes see students from all kinds of backgrounds putting their palms together for a greeting in the Indian manner. It's a way to be friendly without breaking the center rule against physical contact, and it can be very nice or very annoying depending on one's frame of mind. I decided early on that I would rather break a rule than decline an outstretched hand, but that's another matter you will need to decide for yourself.

THE FIRST NIGHT

There is no need to anticipate any trouble, but do be aware that the opening session is the first occasion for the energies you have brought from the outside to clash with those of the center. That may sound like mumbo-jumbo to you, but I have come out of the first session unable to bear even moderate cold and shaking violently, or throwing up. Once the first dream I had during a course was that someone would come into my room and cut my throat! On Dhamma-land, at a meditation center! I must be a guy with issues, you say. Fair enough, but don't be surprised if your issues start surfacing with a violence you had not expected.

An image Goenka uses for illustration is that of an Indian housewife throwing water on hot charcoals so that they can be reused for cooking the next day. When the two elements meet for the first time, there can be an impressive clash. ("Choong!" says Papa Goenka.)

TEACHERS

In addition to the tapes and videos that provide the backbone of the course, there is always at least one on-site teacher available to answer questions and deal with complications. Teachers will be present in the meditation hall for Goenka's early morning chanting (around 5:45-6:30 am), for the group sittings and the brief instructions after the ten-minute recesses, and from 6 pm until the end of the night. Five-minute interviews at noontime can be scheduled by signing up on a list posted in or near the dining area.

Most courses are conducted jointly by a male and a female teacher, often but not always a couple. They are seated at the head of the hall on raised platforms not only as a mark of respect (questionable), because it is said to help them spread their positive vibrations (more questionable: why should a few inches matter?), but also for the more practical reason that it gives them a better view of meditators in the back rows (sensible enough). If there is a male and a female teacher, it will be the male handling the electronic controls and making announcements. (If you want to get indignant about such inequalities, save it for how the bhikkhunis get treated, see the next section.)

The process for appointing teachers is somewhat opaque, but it is not secret. Potential candidates are drawn from the ranks of students who make themselves known by sitting Long courses (which have very stringent prerequisites) and by doing a lot of Dhamma service. The rest is driven by intuitions about who would make a good teacher, with certain red flags. The gainfully employed and the married (or seriously committed) are probably at some advantage, because the organization is exceedingly wary of profit-seeking and hanky-panky.[23] The closest to a fixed principle in the selection process is that anyone who shows ambitions to be a teacher is eliminated from consideration. Or so Goenka has said.[24]

In addition to the teachers affiliated with centers, there are those with regional responsibilities or with specific outreach functions. There is also a global council of the most senior teachers (the cardinals, one might say) that take decisions for the organization as a whole. (After Goenka's death, no further popes are supposed to be appointed.)

For Old students to teach others without the organization's stamp of approval is frowned upon — hence the question on the application form. The strict line from Goenka is that only parents, teachers, and doctors are supposed to teach *Anapana* to their children, students, and patients,[25] but the main concern is that *Vipassana* not be taught casually.

MEN AND WOMEN

From the opening formalities through the morning of Day 10, a rigorous segregations of the sexes is maintained at all Goenka centers. That can be strange for many of us, who may never have been involved with any institution that did not let the sexes mingle freely; it was certainly strange for me, at first. The reason owes something to Asian traditionalism, no doubt, and to the fact that Goenka, before he became involved with Vipassana, was what he himself calls "a staunch, conservative Hindu"[26] rather than a hippie like most of the men and women who brought Vipassana to the West. (Thus also the rules on "modest clothing.") Close relatives of the Goenka school, such as the Insight Meditation Society at Barre, do not practice segregation.

Before letting the unfamiliar spoil your appetite for a course, however, you should know that one can become accustomed to the strange practice and even grow thankful for it. When your mind gets raw enough to reel with every passing mental stimulation and you think you can smell members of the opposite sex across a meditation hall the size of a basketball court, do you really want to sit next to a babe wearing lycra or a hunk in his muscle shirt? At any rate, the segregation policy is not up for debate, and you would only be wasting your time by challenging it. (The gender-criteria for where you will be expected to sit are not very nuanced. If your case cannot be easily accommodated, you may be exempted from the usual requirement to attend all group sittings in the hall, but you will not be allowed to choose which side to sit on.)

For a couple to sit a course together can be a very valuable and beautiful experience, but it can also bring its own challenges. It does not make introspection any easier to see your partner only a few feet away, yet not to be able to communicate in any way, especially if you are concerned that he or she may be having a hard time. You may also arrive at Metta Day on different wavelengths, which can be frustrating, but sitting together is still highly recommended.

BHIKKHUS AND BHIKKHUNIS

Although Vipassana is explicitly a lay tradition aimed at householders, and although Goenka disavows the Buddhist label, bhikkhus and bhikkhunis, Buddhist monks and nuns, will occasionally attend courses. When they do, the monks (but not the nuns) will usually be seated on elevated platforms like the teachers' and a point may be made of letting them be the first to leave the hall, among other small gestures of respect. These rituals of deference are mild by comparison to the shocking scenes you might witness in Burma or Thailand, for example, but you may still find them irritating and inappropriate to a Western setting. If you ask, you may be told that showing respect to the monks is not about deferring to any individual, but about honoring the bid for enlightenment in general; or that when the monks allow (or encourage) lay-folk to throw themselves at their feet, it has nothing to do with ego in robes, and everything with giving householders a chance to practice selflessness. Or perhaps you will be bought off with a reminder that you may earn extra points of merit by serving a monk rather than a lesser mortal, and so on. No doubt a strong case for such practices can be made from the Pali Canon, but one should be aware that when the Devil quotes Scripture for his purposes, he may be wearing the disguise of a Buddhist as easily as that of a born-again Christian. At any rate, the treatment of the monks at Goenka centers will not change any more than the separation of the sexes, so you might as well accept it, think of it what you may.

The situation of the bhikkhunis has been a complicated one from the outset. In the early days, when only men were allowed to join the Sangha, the Buddha was approached by Gotami (the aunt who had raised him because his own mother died shortly after giving birth) with the urgent plea to allow women to be ordained. After the Buddha had rejected her request three times, Ananda, his kindly assistant, saw Gotami crying in public, discovered the reason, and decided to take up her case.[27] He too was rebuffed until he changed his tack: instead of asking for anything, he merely inquired whether women were any less capable than men of the highest moral and spiritual discipline and attainment. The Buddha admitted that they were no less capable[28] — an unheard-of position at the time — and conceded the case, albeit with a string of special conditions for the bhikkhunis that border on the demeaning from a modern perspective. But Gotami gladly accepted the terms and women were henceforth admitted to the Sangha.

The Buddha realized how much resistance there would be to so radical a challenge to custom, even from within the Sangha. Women leaving their husbands and families to become nuns would present a serious challenge to male prestige and the social order, and many of the monks, after the Buddha had died, gave Ananda no end of trouble for his role in championing the bhikkhunis.[29] Monks and nuns living in close proximity would also be liable to distraction, temptation, and scandal, real or imagined. Hence the Buddha's gloomy prediction that with the admission of women to the Sangha, the expected lifespan of his Teaching in the world had been cut in half (complete with deplorable images of diseases befalling the crops in a field).[30] Before lamenting the Buddha's lack of vision, however, we might remember that he was speaking in an age when the great Pericles boasted in his Funeral Oration that the glory of an Athenian woman was to be seen and talked of as little as possible (rich as that was coming from the companion of Aspasia).[31] When the bhikkhuni lineage became extinct (or so Theravadan tradition holds) around the 12th century, owing in part to the burdensome rules for female ordination, the plot became yet more tangled, and the debate over the rightful place of women in the Sangha continues to this day.

NOTES

1. The Buddha and his disciples sought to discredit the caste system not by any frontal attacks, but by insisting on the meaninglessness of its distinctions (see MN 84, 90, 93, 96, 98). The great distinction is in the manner and direction of one's striving, not in one's blood (MN 90.11 [p. 737]). The five factors of striving identified by the Buddha are faith, health, sincerity, energy, and wisdom (MN 85.58 [p. 707]). On the connection between striving and seeing things with wisdom and equanimity, see MN 95.20,22 (p. 782-83) and especially MN 101.23 (p. 834).

2. *Cullavagga* 7.1.4.

3. Returning students ("Old students") will usually fill up the front row or two, but there is no quota set to achieve a fixed ratio between Old and new students, so it all depends on the course. Fewer than ten percent Old students would be unusual, as would more than a third, but both can happen.

4. *Vism.* I.104-105 (pp. 38-39).

5. Another favorite of the genre is about a monk (Maha-Tissa) who collapsed from hunger and fatigue in a field of mango trees. In

the *Visuddhimagga's* account, it is stressed that there were *ownerless* mangoes lying about that the monk wouldn't touch in the absence of someone to accept them from (because monks are supposed to beg their food, not help themselves to it). Mangoes, it appears, are not meant for saving starving humans from death, but for allowing them to prove their spiritual mettle by throwing away their lives on pseudo-moral points of pedantry. In the story, of course, Maha-Tissa gets rewarded for his righteousness by being saved (*Vism.* I.122 and Note [pp. 42, 754]).

6. The Buddha uses the image of two darts: the first one is the bodily sensation, the second one the mental suffering (SN 36.6 [p. 1264]). The same idea can be found in Marcus Aurelius: "You must not strive to resist the sensation, for it is natural: but let not [your judgment] add the opinion that it is either good or bad." (*Meditations* V.26. See also VII.16,33: let the body speak out if it suffers, but do not let your judgment add to the misery by losing its tranquility.)

7. The Buddha himself stressed that not all sensations should be explained as profound kammic patterns surfacing: some have such deep roots, others are just the consequences of bodily imbalances and disorders, of environmental factors, or of careless behavior (SN 36.21 [p. 1278-79]). Profound and shallow causes flow together in the stream of the sensations, and wisdom is needed in deciding how their signals are to be interpreted.

8. See also *Art of Living*, p. 99.

9. *Gem Set in Gold*, p. 1.

10. Thus his explanation, in the Ten-Day course, for why only he does the chanting; see also *Satip. Discourses*, p. 101.

11. See the question about Buddhist sainthood in chapter 12.

12. In the English opening formalities, Goenka smuggles in a ban on "cozy" beds, but that is his spontaneous invention and problematic. High beds were a status symbol in the ancient world and the precept is directed against pride, not reasonable comfort. Among the bhikkus' *Pacittiya*-rules (entailing confession), the eighty-eighth bans mattresses stuffed with "cotton down," which was the most luxurious material at the time; but pillows are permitted, so long as they are only for resting the head, not for showing off. "The purpose of all this is to keep bhikkhus from using furnishings that are extravagant and ostentatious," not to prevent them from making themselves comfortable at night. (Thanissaro Bhikkhu, *The Buddhist*

Monastic Code I: The Patimokkha Rules Translated and Explained [3rd Edition, 2013], pp. 418-19.)

13. Fleischman speaks of a "psychological safari" (*An Ancient Path*, p. 14).

14. MN 44.29 (p. 403). I will take up this topic again in the section on Doctrine.

15. *Vism.* VIII.211 (pp. 276-77).

16. I got the beach-ball image from Fleischman (*An Ancient Path*, p. 8), but I don't know whether it is original to him. The lovely metaphor of sweeping cockroaches is from Harris, p. 101.

17. *Zen Mind, Beginner's Mind*, p. 23.

18. Plutarch, Life of Themistocles, 27.2-4. Themistocles (527-459 BCE) was the great Athenian hero of the wars with Persia that meant to the ancient Greeks roughly what the War of Independence means to the Americans (myths included). He was also a great schemer, however, whose ultimate loyalty was always to his own overweening ambition, and he ended his days as a highly honored governor for the very Persians he had opposed so fiercely. From a Buddhist point of view, his life can only be read as a cautionary tale, but it is also among the most fascinating in the annals of ancient politics.

19. Talk of Buddha-nature is more at home in other Buddhist traditions, which take bowing to real extremes. See for example the section on Bowing in *Zen Mind, Beginner's Mind* (pp. 28-31), where it is said that every sitting should be concluded with *nine* bows to the floor, because by doing so one gives oneself up and lets go of one's dualistic ideas.

20. Goenka, *For the Benefit of Many*, p. 76, 159.

21. Many do not allow students to go barefoot because of the dirt it tends to track into the meditation hall.

22. See the box on *yatha-bhuta* in chapter 6.

23. Goenka, *For the Benefit of Many*, p. 150.

24. Goenka, *For the Benefit of Many*, p. 80.

25. Goenka, *For the Benefit of Many*, p. 169.

26. See the discourses and *Art of Living*, p. 143.

27. See AN 8.51 (pp. 1188-1192).

28. There is a sweet story told about the Buddha consoling a king (Pasendi) disappointed to hear that his wife (Mallika) had given birth to a girl: "A woman may turn out better than a man." (SN 3:16 [p. 178-179]) A tradition has nonetheless taken hold that a fully self-liberated Buddha (of which there can only be one until his dispensation has disappeared completely) must be male, though he may have been female in previous lives (MN 115.14-15 [p. 929]).

29. They made him formally acknowledge the "wrongdoing" of allowing the Buddha's remains to be first saluted by women and of exerting himself for the admission of women to the Sangha, among other charges (*Cullavagga* 11.1.10 [*Life*, pp. 339-40]). Such are the more arid suburbs of the Eternal City of Buddhism.

30. In *For the Benefit of Many* (pp. 156-57), Goenka is asked why the Buddha hesitated to ordain women and he answers that it was out of a concern for their safety ("nothing else") in dangerous times when rape was commonplace. Such considerations may have played their part, but to pretend that resistance to female ordination had only the women's own good in mind is at best naive, at worst disingenuous and ridiculous.

31. Thucydides, *History of the Peloponnesian War*, II.46 (Penguin, p. 151). Historians disagree about dating the Buddha's life, but the contending accounts would make him the contemporary of either Confucius (551-479 BCE) or Socrates (469-399 BCE). The life of Pericles falls in between (495-429 BCE).

CHAPTER FIVE
PILLOW TALK AND STAINED SHEETS

MOST OF THE THINGS YOU WILL NEED ARE JUST THE ONES YOU WOULD bring for an eleven-night stay anywhere else, but be aware that unless you are at a center that offers laundry service (mostly in Asia), you will not be given access to the machines and will have to make do with hand-washing.

If you have experimented with sitting on a mat and cushion at home and you find that a particular **cushion** works well for you, it would be a good idea to bring it. A **light shawl** to wrap yourself in during meditation will not only keep you warm, if necessary, it will also help to provide you with a measure of psychological comfort when you need it most. Think of it as your meditation blankie. Such things can matter more than you might imagine in the crucible of deep meditation.

There are many ways to get cold feet on a course, but why not protect yourself from the physical ones, at least, by bringing along some **comfy thick socks**?

Likewise with any item that will not get in your way, that does not run afoul of center rules, and that might help you feel more confident and at ease. Think of your stay as having to spend time at a hospital: bring whatever might help you feel better about the operation you are facing. You're supposed to leave your religious talismans at home, but I'm not aware of any rules against your **teddy-bear**. A friend in need is a friend indeed.

If a center asks you to bring your own **bed-sheets or a sleeping-bag**, please do so. Laundry is apparently a greater strain on center resources than one might imagine. Standard pillows are provided, but do bring your own cover.

(I bring my own comforter whenever I can — for reasons expressed so nicely by the English term for the thing.[1] One does not feel like a model renunciate lugging four or five duffle bags, granted, but I've never regretted being well-equipped on a course, only the reverse.)

An **alarm-clock** that is not too obnoxious and that will turn off after a minute or two may be a good alternative to what the centers can provide, which is often the brutalist plugged-in model that will scream all morning if it is not switched off.

Strict teachers will not let you wear **ear-plugs** in the hall, but at night they can be priceless, especially if you happen to have snoring neighbors.

Center mugs are not supposed to leave the dining area, so consider bringing your own. Also a **water bottle** or a thermos for hot drinks, which can be a nice source of good cheer during a winter course.

Deodorant is definitely a good idea, for your own comfort and the benefit of other meditators, but please avoid anything with an intense scent because intense meditation can make one very sensitive to such things. **Insect repellent** is permitted, including the noxious stuff that seems to be the only really reliable kind. (In Bihar they give you toxic coils to burn at night: they work. Once you have developed your equanimity enough, you will be able to handle the cancer.) The better-stocked centers (in Canada for example) may provide repellent when mosquitoes are rampant and **umbrellas** where it rains a lot, but don't count on it.

Most of the well-established center light their paths at night now so that a **flashlight** is not longer the indispensable necessity it once was, but bringing a small one might still be a good idea because you never know when it might come in handy. I always pack my **Swiss Army knife** just in case.

I bring my own rubber gloves for the clean-up at the end of the course, a good sponge or scouring pad, and some liquid scrub so that I can leave my sink shiny for the next student. Also a roll of paper towels, just in case. Centers will provide basic cleaning materials, but doing a fastidious job on your room is a good way to conclude the course in the proper spirit. Helping with cleaning the center at large is even better.

For the rest, be sure to read the instructions in your acceptance letter carefully because they may contain important information specific to your center.

THE COURSE MANAGERS

Noble silence or not, you are always allowed to speak to your course managers, but please only approach the one of your own sex unless you are facing an emergency. Course managers are your friends and allies with respect to all practical problems. They are not supposed to answer questions about meditative technique, but they are your lifelines to the teachers, whom they will contact on your behalf whenever necessary. Servers are giving ten days to look out for you, and chances are that you will come to love and admire them. Of course they are only human, they are working hard, and they are dealing with their own issues as they are looking after yours; so when something is making you unhappy, try to remember that the servers may be struggling at times as well and that what you are seeing may be getting clouded by all the inner dust you are stirring up with your meditation. Generally speaking, the poise and compassion of servers is one of the most impressive aspects of a course, and I remember how it was the volunteers, even more than Goenka himself, who drew me towards Vipassana when I first encountered it.

WHAT TO WEAR

Bring comfortable clothes and don't worry about making fashion statements, which would only be a distraction for others. You may get called on tight, revealing, or otherwise attention-drawing clothing (shorts and tank-tops, leggings and short skirts are not allowed[2]) but the volunteers are generally reluctant to say anything, so if you are sensible, you should be able to avoid problems. Religious pendants and other talismans worn around the neck, prayer bracelets, rosaries and crystals and the like are all against the rules, though this may or may not be enforced very strictly depending on how conspicuous such objects are. T-shirts with slogans made to be noticed are an invitation to complaint and trouble (you may be asked to turn them inside out). Remember that you are at the course to ratchet down your ego, not to advertise your personal style or your beliefs, and that you need to be sensitive to anything that might be a possible distraction to raw minds.

Goenka has said that black and red are not colors conducive to meditation, but with the qualification that it would be going to unhelpful extremes to make an issue of red or black clothing.[3] If you don't dress up as a fire hydrant for your course or show off your Goth wardrobe, you should be fine. (Then again you could try asking your on-site teacher whether Zen masters and Tibetan lamas are mere meditation rookies because they favor black and red robes, respectively.)

All things give off vibrations, but surely we should not get too preoccupied with possibly unwholesome emanations from inanimate objects.[4] I've heard teachers point out that a bracelet or amulet might carry unwelcome energies, but the much more decisive factor is always the purity of our minds. What could be more polluted, from a Dhammic perspective, than a battle-flag retrieved after the slaughter? Yet even it may be used to make monk's robes.[5] Robes presented by one king to another, though died in royal vainglory, are likewise acceptable.[6]

BEDS AND BUGS

Rooms are assigned according to course-seniority with some regard to age and special needs. This means that the more commodious single rooms (which may even come with small private bathrooms) tend to be given to the most experienced meditators. Younger students, especially, are very likely to have roommates on their first course, so bringing ear-plugs for the night is a good idea. (I have often thought that reversing the hierarchy would be more Dhammic, but not to the point of offering up my hard-earned privileges.)

Even without having to put up with a neighbor's snoring, many students have trouble sleeping during courses, especially on the first night. After a few days of adjustment, you may find that getting up at 4 am and going to sleep around 9:30 pm is easier than you expected, but the meditation will still stir up unconscious parts of your mind that can leave you highly agitated at night and that may well give you very strange and intense dreams. When you cannot sleep, try to follow Goenka's instructions and stay with your breath and your sensations to get some rest. The more you worry about your sleeplessness, the worse you will feel in the morning.

Sitting meditation at night is not allowed, and some centers lock the meditation hall overnight. The mundane reason is that you are supposed to save your energies for the daytime, but if you prefer a more exotic explanation, I've heard it said that at night certain benevolent spirits (devas and brahmas in Pali terminology) come to sit in the hall. (Don't let the news tempt you into trying to join their gatherings: unless you have a history of spontaneous visions, they are not likely to make themselves known to you.) Sitting in the earliest hours of the day can be a very powerful experience, but you may want to take it easy with such experiments, especially during your first course. If you end up coming back, you will have time enough to establish your reputation as a black sheep.

Problems with bed-bugs have arisen at certain centers, but you will be relieved to hear that living in harmony with such aggressive parasites is not part of the Vipassana training. On the contrary, the centers have developed rigorous protocols for addressing bug-related contingencies, and with this issue as with all, they really do have the interests of the students at heart, even if it may not always look that way to you in the heat of a tough course.

MEDITATING IN YOUR ROOM

During certain times of the day (from 4:30 to 6:30 am; usually for at least an hour before lunch; before 2:30 pm and after about 4 pm) students are free to meditate in their rooms or in their cells (see below). Some centers will make a point of telling students not to sit on their beds or use the blankets they sleep with for meditation. The idea behind devoting certain spaces and objects exclusively to meditation is that doing so will "grow vibrations," or if that doesn't sound convincing, at least create an association in the mind (perhaps even some kind of Pavlovian response) that might help give more focus to one's sittings.

But Vipassana is about discovering things for oneself, and if it turns out that you meditate well on your bed because it makes you feel safe, secure, and comfortable, I wouldn't let the general policy deter me.[7] If you find that sitting on your bed makes you sluggish, tired, and unfocused instead — which is not unlikely — better to sit in the chair provided or with a mat on the floor, or else to stay in the meditation hall, where you get to benefit from the group energy and where the atmosphere is generally the most conducive to serious meditation.

Goenka centers do not make many concessions to the devotional items that the human heart craves (prayer bracelets, amulets, or even Buddha statues are not allowed on a course), but meditation shawls are an exception. Bringing a nice one and using it for nothing but your sittings may help you a little during the course and will not only be a nice trophy afterwards, but also an inspiration to continue your practice at home.

BELLS AND WHISTLES

The first bell will be rung at 4 am and you can earn prodigious merit, if you are a returning student, by volunteering to get up five minutes earlier than every one else and making your loving rounds hitting a triangular Burmese gong with a wooden hammer at the right intervals and with the proper balance of gentleness and resolve. (Some students complain that the bell doesn't wake them up in the morning, but I cannot help wondering how keen they really are on hearing its clarion call.)

Bells will be used throughout the day to summon students to meditation or to announce mealtimes. To confirm that the food is ready, which can happen a few minutes behind schedule, the kitchen staff will ring a separate gong just outside the dining areas. Please wait for it before going in.

During interviews at noon, a small bell may tingle after about five minutes (or sometimes ten, if you are lucky and demand for interviews is at an ebb that day) to signal that it would be good if you could wrap up your discussion because others are waiting in line. Unfortunately the teachers do not operate the bell themselves and you therefore cannot seize it, as you might at a Zen temple, to force them to give you more attention.

Whistling is considered a violation of noble silence, especially when it is directed at members of the other sex.

BREAKFAST

Chances are that "the most important meal of the day" will not be your favorite part of meditation camp. (The designation "camp" is a holdover from the days when Vipassana courses were held under much more improvised conditions, but the hints of boot camp can still seem fitting at times.)

I imagine that breakfast in the early days was already what it is today, a stage for its leading characters, Mr Porridge and Ms Prunes, to strut their stuff. That Mr Porridge should have conquered Vipassana hearts with Anglo tendencies from

Herefordshire to Sydney does not surprise me. But how did Ms Prunes get into the picture? Were the two introduced by constipation-prone early Vipassana keeners (the model still gets made today), or are they meant as a "delicious breakfast choice for your little ones," as a top Google-hit informs me when I try to plumb the mystery?

At any rate, there it is: Porridge and Prunes, Prunes and Porridge, day after day. Cameos by Mademoiselle Slices d'Orange and the perfidious Dr Raisins have been reported, but don't count on them to make it to your show. (Until not so long ago, unpitted prunes were favored, presumably because they are cheaper. Some meditators miss the chance to test their early-morning mindfulness, but the costs of dental emergencies must at last have prevailed over the savings from cheaper ingredients.)

If you get tired of the prunes, I recommend a certified treat for the inner child:[8] try making the porridge with butter, brown sugar, cinnamon, and bits of orange or apple. Does that sound too self-indulgent for you? Have it your way, Dhamma warrior. Toughness has its place on the Path, and you will have plenty of opportunity to prove your mettle. When the Buddha sat down for the meditation that was going to bring his great breakthrough, he resolved not to get up until he had become fully enlightened, and let his bones be scattered in the attempt if necessary. So far so heroic. But let's remember, too, what was fueling his determination that legendary night: he had just resumed eating. And what had been his first meal? A bowl of sweet rice pudding (*khir*) from the hands of a pretty village girl. The Middle Way has its benefits.

Feel free to escape to toast and jam, or cereal with soy-milk, or even yogurt and fruit. Quitter.

Orange juice, a few types of tea (including black) and real coffee are usually provided.[9] I mean real in the limited sense of caffeinated. Perhaps they have espresso machines at the Swiss center (alas, no: I've since had a chance to check); in North America, expect the kind of no-name instant kernels that look, smell, and taste as if they might have been cat litter in a previous life. But despair not: with enough sugar, milk, and sensory deprivation, even the most plebeian cup of joe can be made pleasurable. You are in the Vipassana army now, so you'd better learn to drink your coffee like a soldier around the camp-fire who does not know whether he will survive long enough to have another cup.

(During my latest stint at a center, Nescafé had displaced the more noxious stuff. Part of Nestlé's drive for world-dominion, I reckon. Once all the Amazon's villages have been conquered by brand-name quality made in Brazil, what more natural campaign to wage than for the global archipelago of Vipassana centers?)

LUNCH AND FIVE O'CLOCK TEA

Lunch at 11 am tends to be so enjoyable, relatively speaking, that even non-vegetarians sometimes ask for the recipes at the end of the course. They are probably underestimating the power of the two secret ingredients — love on the part of the cooks,[10] hunger on the part of the eaters — but the results are still impressive when one considers how many of the volunteers haven't cooked with anything other than a microwave before (as one Canadian teacher likes to quip). Food is not rationed, and there are days when you may find yourself wolfing it down. Whenever that happens, be attentive and gentle with yourself; your mind and body are trying to compensate for what you are putting them through. (Best to keep an eye on leaving enough for others. Or else grab three helpings of dessert and experiment with meditator's guilt.)

Fasting is not allowed during the course, but Goenka does recommend that you should always keep about a quarter of your stomach empty for better meditation — a reasonable rule of thumb even if his body type does not suggest that he followed his own advice. (For an Indo-Burmese businessman of his background, chubbiness is as sure a mark of social status and attractiveness as trimness is for our own upwardly-mobile classes. When he quips about the "colossal evidence" that he is a householder and not a monk, meaning his wife, he may even be flirting with her, strange as it sounds. The body-beautiful crowd tends to be well-represented at courses, but a Vipassana center is not Bikram's Hall of Mirrors.)

Meat and eggs are not used in the Vipassana kitchens, but dairy may be.

Individual dietary arrangements can be made for pregnant women and students with special needs, but cooking for such large groups by all-volunteer teams is a sensitive point in the running of centers and you should try to make do as much as possible, within reason. If something has clearly been forgotten, on the other hand, you should not feel bad about asking for it.

No Earl Grey, cucumber sandwiches, or scones with Devonshire cream at 5 o'clock, alas. Only a bit of fruit if you are a new student, or a hot drink if you are not. Should you have specific health-related reasons for needing food in the afternoon as a returning student, you can get special permission, but don't expect to be heard on points of dietary philosophy.[11]

There is a group sitting right after the tea-period, so if you have drunk a lot, be sure to relieve yourself before heading into the meditation hall or you may make the hour even worse than it needs to be.

MEDITATION CELLS AND PAGODAS

Many centers have gone to considerable lengths and expense in order to provide individual meditation cells, often housed in Burmese-style pagodas. I personally find the Shwedagon Pagoda in rural Massachusetts as bizarre a sight as I would the Statue of Liberty on a street-corner in Yangon, but to each his own. Permission to sit in a cell will be given out, where available, by means of slips of paper on your cushion after a few days. More senior students are given priority, so you may or may not get a cell on your first course.

You can have mine: I prefer the ambience of a low-security prison to the charms of solitary confinement on death row. Tastes differ. I've only ever enjoyed one cell, when I was sitting at U Ba Khin's old center in Yangon. It was built into the side of a hill and had a steel door worthy of a military installation. Whether it had once been used as a bunker (Saya Thetgyi is said to have used a bomb shelter as his meditation cave) or whether such fortifications were necessary to withstand the tremors of U Ba Khin's shouting,[12] I don't know. All I was told, when I expressed my surprise at enjoying the cell, was that I had been put there because it was where Goenka used to sit. Dhamma works.

ARCHITECTURE AND AESTHETICS

All Goenka-centers in the world offer the same Ten-Day courses, and all subscribe to basic guidelines about how a Vipassana center should be run. Apart from the globalized menu they serve, however, they all operate independently through local charitable foundations with their own decision-making processes. All centers have their own charm: some sit on beautiful land; a few have big donors and special amenities; others are more architecturally sophisticated or try a little harder to make themselves attractive in other ways. Common to all is the sincere desire to offer students the best meditation environment possible given the local constraints, and the equally sincere absence of any expectation of getting anything in return. The centers do depend on donations to keep operating, but your happiness at the end of a course really is everyone's greatest reward. That may sound too good to be true, but go and see for yourself.

The fact that Vipassana centers are not selling a product, indeed not even advertising in any other way than word-of-mouth, also means that they can afford to look to substance rather than to appearances in a way that can be endearing and frustrating in about equal measures. At one North American center, on a plot once owned by the Boy Scouts no less, the dear Goenkanauts just spent almost two million bucks on the best meditation hall they could imagine while minding the bottom line. The state-of-the-art ventilation and heating system alone set them back half a million, and they put in recessed ceilings and indirect lighting for a touch of elegance, bless their hearts. Alas, when it came to calculating the height of the ceiling, utilitarian considerations predominated and they ended up with the coziest, most lovingly built garage in the world. Sigh.

So don't come to a Vipassana center expecting Zen gardens. Unless it's the one at the edge of Yosemite National Park, or the one in the Blue Mountains in Australia with its sunsets, or the one that has so spectacular a view of the Kathmandu Valley that boards have been put up to keep students from getting distracted. Or the center where peacocks roam the paths, or the one where the meditation cells have green marble floors and are big enough to sit a horse, or the one near the bridge on the River Kwai... Wait, I wasn't going to write any star-studded reviews for the discerning Vipassana traveler! The centers are all beautiful in their way because they are built with love. If that sounds too good to be true once more, go and find out for yourself.

KEEPING A DIARY AND OTHER WRITING

Taking notes during a Vipassana course is strictly forbidden because the mental noise created by writing is no less potent than what is generated by speech.

Is it conceivable that certain desperate writerly types might nonetheless filch every scrap of paper they can find — stooping so low as to go through the garbage and raid paper hand-towel dispensers — so that they might play at being Antonio Gramsci putting together his *Prison Notebooks*? Anything is possible with writers. But does that mean that you should consider following their example? I think not. Writers become writers because there is usually one thing they do well, and one thing only. They may be decent exponents of the art of living on paper, but as exhibits, they are hopeless cases. Better to do as they say, not as they do.

Of course using meditation time to write books in one's head (another common affliction among intellectual meditators) or even to memorize the list of ancient Roman emperors (only one case on record, but I can vouch for it![13]) is no better than to do some furtive scribbling. The point of a course is to keep your attention on your breath and on your sensations as continuously as possible; therein lies the magic. Other activities may have their merits, but they are not meditation.

NATURE-WORSHIP, SCULPTURES, AND PERFORMANCE ART

Students during courses have been known to become so enamored of nature's beauty that they have hugged and climbed trees or run into the woods in wild disregard of the course-boundaries. Whether any have stripped in the process, I don't know, but I wouldn't be surprised.[14] Please know that there will be little sympathy for such ecstatic displays of joy. Vipassana is a sober affair and you will be asked to desist from anything dramatic.

Irresistible surges of creative energy sometimes produce beautiful snow-men, inukshuks and balanced-rock sculptures, or happy messages laid out in pebbles across the center paths. All such productions, no matter how elaborate and lovely, are liable to be dismantled as soon as they are noticed, because they are taken to be distractions both for the artist and for the other students. If they are offered in the spirit of Tibetan sand paintings, made to last only for a moment past their completion, then so be it, but don't expect them to be left standing.

CLEAN-UP DURING THE COURSE

A number of small chores around the hallways and the shared bathrooms need to be performed from day to day. There are sign-up sheets posted where you may volunteer if you should feel like it. Strictly speaking, this is for Old students only, but if you feel the urge to sign up as a new student, no one will prevent you. There is no obligation at all, but you may find it surprisingly therapeutic.

NOTES

1. Nighttime is for resting and there are no extra points for being uncomfortable when you are sleeping (or trying to do so). As I have mentioned above, the insertion of a precept against "cozy beds" into the opening formalities is a spontaneous invention of Goenka's that appears nowhere in the printed materials. See also the question on sleeping in chapter 12.

2. As part of the applcation process, North American students are told that "dress should be simple, modest, and comfortable" and that "tight, transparent, revealing, or otherwise striking clothing (such as shorts, short skirts, tights and leggings, sleeveless or skimpy tops) should not be worn." I've seen a sign at a center add "baggy clothing is preferred." Haute couture it is not.

3. Goenka, *For the Benefit of Many*, p. 19.

4. Or the wholesome ones, for that matter, even if the making of relics — however implausible their provenance — seems to be an irrepressible human instinct everywhere. No sooner was the Buddha dead than his votaries in different parts of India started quarreling over who would get what share of his ashes (SN 16.6.24-25 [pp. 275-76]). Even Goenka's Global Pagoda (see chapter 11), for all the talk of rising above rites and rituals, has enshrined some donated relics on vibrational grounds (*For the Benefit of Many*, p. 133). To Goenka's credit, his courses do make it clear that one pays the highest respect to a Buddha not by reverencing a few mortal remains, authentic or not, but by walking resolutely on the path that he has pointed out: "*Imaya dhammanudhammapatipattiya, buddham pujemi.*" (*Gem Set in Gold*, p. 79). When the gods showered the Buddha with unprecedented honors before his death, he reminded Ananda that even in the face of such divine adoration, "the supreme homage" is paid by those who practice the Dhamma properly (DN 16.5.3 [p. 262]).

5. *Vism.*, II.17 (p. 62).

6. Ananda accepted such a robe from King Pasendi ("it was sent to me packed in a royal umbrella case by King Ajatasattu, sixteen hands long and eight hands wide") after the king had insisted three times on giving it to him (MN 88.18 [p. 726]). When another monarch, Udena, got angry because the ladies of the palace had donated 500 robes to the monks, it was Ananda who calmed him down by explaining how worn-out robes would get used as bed-

covers, then as pillow-cases, then as rugs, then as foot-towels, then as dust-cloths, then as shreds for brick-making (*Cullavagga* 11.1.14). Goenka tells this edifying story in one of the orientation-talks to Dhamma-servers, with the unintended consequence that even unredeemable junk has a way of collecting at centers.

7. Bed is best, I say, and I won't tolerate any slander — but that is a minority position. See the question on the benefits of sleeping in chapter 12.

8. The inner child holds a place of honor in Buddhism because of the pivotal part played in the story of the Buddha's enlightenment (and the inception of the Buddha's Middle Way) by his early memory of sitting under a rose-apple tree while his father was presiding over a ploughing ceremony in the surrounding fields (MN 36.31-32 [p. 340 ([BW 64])]). The psychological implications of the episode are brought out particularly well by Mark Epstein, *Going on Being* (Wisdom 2008), pp. 65-68. See also the question on the Middle Way in chapter 12.

9. Tea and coffee are not intoxicants in a sense that would run afoul of the precepts and U Ba Khin was fond of both (*U Ba Khin Journal*, p. 25 and *Clock of Vipassana*, p. 39).

10. "The food may be insipid or savory, it may be meager or abundant; but if it is given by a friendly hand, it becomes delicious." (*Jataka* 346)

11. See the question on the precept against eating after mid-day in chapter 8.

12. See the question on U Ba Khin in chapter 8.

13. Not because I was the culprit, but because he told me the story after a course: a puny, bespectacled twenty-year-old Turkish kid who dreamt of being Achilles or Alexander the Great. Needless to say he didn't think that Vipassana was quite right for him, though he lasted to the end of the course, perhaps because he wanted to get his emperors down pat before leaving.

14. It is reported that a monk once made the case for going naked, but the Buddha dismissed his proposal as foolish and improper (see *Mahavagga* 8.28.1).

CHAPTER SIX
BONDAGE DAY-IN-DAY-OUT

EQUANIMITY (*UPEKKHA*)

When faced with the vicissitudes of life
The minds of the wise remain unshaken —
Ever sorrowless, stainless, and secure.
The wise are everywhere invincible;
Wherever they go, they are safe.
Theirs are the greatest blessings.
— CONCLUSION TO THE MANGALA SUTTA[1]

EQUANIMITY REFERS TO A BALANCED, PATIENT, SERENE STATE OF MIND free of agitation. In a Vipassana context, it means observing the arising and passing of sensations without reaction or judgment, without distinguishing between the pleasant and the unpleasant, always understanding their innate quality of impermanence and impersonality. "Just as various winds blow in the sky ... so various sensations arise in the body."[2] Who would get attached to gusts of air?

As an ideal, equanimity forms a bridge between the Dhamma and Western traditions because it is also what the Stoics aspired to in Greek and Roman times. The English *equanimity* is derived from the Latin (the original Greek Stoics used the word *apatheia*) and it is said that "*aequanimitas*" was the last watchword given to the guard by the emperor Antoninus Pius on the night of his death at Lorium.[3] Antoninus's adoptive son, the emperor Marcus Aurelius, was one of history's most philosophical rulers[4] and his *Meditations*[5] read like reflections on the Dhamma with a Western flavor, especially in the translation by George Long.[6]

Goenka places equanimity at the very center of his instructions, emphasizing throughout his courses that "equanimity is purity," that "every moment of equanimity is a moment of your liberation," and that equanimity alone is the true yardstick of progress on the Path.[7] The doctrinal foundations for Goenka's approach are impeccable: *upekkha* is one of the four divine abodes or sublime states (*brahmavihara*);[8] it is one of the seven factors of enlightenment (*bojjhangas*) and one of the ten perfections (*paramis*); it is said to arise in conjunction with the highest *jhana*-states; and it is the immediate antidote, in the chain of dependent origination (*paticcasamuppada*), to reaction in general and craving and clinging in particular.[9]

A "storm" is a period of intense emotional or physical agitation that feels like the opposite of mental balance. In the Vipassana sense, however, equanimity can be maintained when such turmoil is observed with *detachment*.[10] Even when we cannot help reacting, we may still become aware of our reactiveness and thereby bring our minds into a kind of secondary equilibrium.[11] On the other hand, even mental balance can turn into an obstacle if it becomes an object of clinging.[12] Thus only equanimity, not any particular experience, however illuminating or sublime, is the yardstick of progress in Vipassana: what matters is not what passes through the mind, whether quietly or violently, pleasantly or unpleasantly, but only how *dispassionately* the arising and passing is observed.

Craving,[13] aversion, and ignorance generate and perpetuate the defilements that equanimity purifies. Some translations prefer to speak of "desire" instead, but that can be misleading because desires can be innocent and even wholesome, while cravings cannot. As Ajahn Sucitto points out, some form of desire (*chanda*) is needed to give direction to one's spiritual efforts:[14] "In fact, you could summarize Dhamma training as the transformation of craving (*tanha*) into wholesome desire (*chanda*)."[15]

So where does the line run between a craving and an innocent or wholesome desire? It's not always easy to tell, but there are a couple of questions you can ask to help you decide for yourself:

Why is it that you want something, and do you like the reason?

How does the desire feel when you look at it carefully, or are you perhaps eager not to look too closely?

How much of a rush are you in to get a green light?

How would you react if you didn't get what you want?

SANKHARA

Sankhara has almost as wide a range of meanings as *Dhamma*.[16] At its most sweeping, it refers to all "formations" or "conditioned things," thus to the whole of sentient existence — the *All* of the Five Aggregates (see chapter 7). Hence the phrase "*Anicca vata sankhara*" (Impermanent, alas, are all formations!)[17] that was used to announce the Buddha's death and that Goenka chants at the end of every Vipassana group sitting.[18] Hence also "*Sabbe sankhara anicca*" from the *Dhammapada*,[19] which expresses the same idea and is likewise included in the final chanting.[20]

In the context of a Ten-Day course, the term gets used more narrowly to identify the reactive mental patterns (volitional, emotional, or intellectual) that often manifest themselves as intense sensations on the body.[21] From what Goenka says during the course, one might get the impression that sankharas are always defilements, but meditation and other wholesome habit-patterns such as the ten perfections (or *paramis*, see chapter 7) are actually sankharas as well.[22] Nor are unwholesome sankharas always crude and unpleasant. Indeed sankharas of craving that surface in conjunction with subtle and pleasant sensations are said to be both more fundamental and even more difficult to uproot. That we would want to free ourselves, if only we could, from our reactions to unpleasant sensations is a given for most meditators; that freedom from attachment to the pleasant is even more important, because it is the twin (or even mother) of our other reactions,[23] may be harder to accept. Hence the Buddha's insistence that it is the destruction of *craving* that ends the flow of kamma and points the way to liberation.[24]

The logic of Vipassana as a technique of mental purification is that when the mind remains equanimous, even for a moment, it stops (or at least slows) the multiplication of sankharas. Just as the body draws on its reserves of fuel when it is not fed (or fed less), so old sankharas will rise to the surface of an equanimous mind-stream.[25] When these mental phenomena mirrored at the level of bodily sensations are observed with detachment, equanimously, the habit of blind reaction is broken, the sankharas' power is diminished or depleted, and some corner of the mind is cleaned up. It is a plausible story that fits well with the basic premise of modern psycho-therapy: namely that in order to undo the complexes that tie us up in mental knots, we need to face them without either shrinking from what is bothering us or reinforcing it with more reactive energy. Common sense is a good starting point, but the Buddha would have us ask for more and apply the test he proposed to the Kalamas: can we discover for ourselves, in our own experience, that the technique works as advertised, that it has wholesome, praiseworthy results, and that it leads to our welfare and happiness?[26]

SATIPATTHANA

Vipassana meditation as taught by S.N. Goenka™ presupposes a particular understanding of how mindfulness (*sati*) is to be established (*patthana*) in the most effective and profound way. Goenkanauts[27] tend to be fiercely committed to their interpretation of Satipatthana and keen on showing how it (and it alone) lines up with the Buddha's most explicit and comprehensive treatment of the matter, the *Mahasatipattana Sutta*.[28] In Goenkanauts' reading, the Sutta's opening lines point the way, *the one and only way*, towards "the purification of beings, for the overcoming of sorrow and lamentation, for the extinguishing of suffering and grief, for walking on the path of truth, for the realization of Nibbana."[29] As a translation for *ekayano maggo*, "the one and only way" is controversial at best,[30] but Goenka defends it resolutely, especially in his Long courses, which require students to subscribe to the formula in writing on their application forms.[31]

In fairness to Papa Goenka, the reason for striking so strident a tone is not so much triumphalism as his understanding of Vipassana in relation to *vedana*, that is, to bodily sensations. The Buddha's great discovery and the key to his liberation, goes the argument, was the role of *vedana* at the deepest level of the mind. Because everything that arises in the mind manifests itself at the same time as sensations in the body ("*Vedana-samosarana sabbe dhamma*"),[32] "observation of sensations offers a means — *indeed the only means* — to examine the totality of our being, physical as well as mental."[33] In contemplating *vedana* with awareness and equanimity, we are observing *the one nexus* "where the entire mind and body are tangibly revealed as impermanent phenomena," where all four aspects of establishing mindfulness in accordance with the Buddha's teaching run together.[34] Hence the priority given to mindfulness of sensations even over mindfulness of the breath.[35]

Goenka's approach is, on the whole, highly regarded across the traditions, both within and beyond the Buddhist world, but his tendency to sound as if he is presenting the one and only authentic way to practice and understand the Dhamma (whether that is really his intention or not) can raise eyebrows among some of the most thoughtful and respected practitioners in the field.[36]

YATHA-BHUTA

Yatha-bhuta (nana-dassana) refers in general to "the knowledge and vision of things as they really are"[37] and more specifically to understanding *the Four Noble Truths* (see next chapter) *as they really are (yathabhutam)*[38] — which is the distinctive teaching of the fully awakened ones in Buddhism.[39] Goenka uses the phrase to emphasize that we should observe phenomena as they occur naturally, without seeking to change or control them. Thus, during Anapana meditation, no effort should be made to make the breath either faster or slower, deeper or shallower, than it happens to be. Walking should be done at a natural pace, without slowing anything down deliberately, and all sensations, pleasant or unpleasant, should be seen and accepted "as they are, not as you would like them to be" — the formula Goenka keeps repeating and identifying with *yatha-bhuta*.[40]

Vipassana meditation takes you on a journey to the depths of your mind, to regions so unfathomable and so different from person to person that it may seem mere folly to make any generalizations at all. No two minds, no two moments, no two experiences are alike, and in the end, there is no telling where a Ten-Day course might lead you, or on what internal schedule. At the same time, if we were never prepared to simplify and generalize, we could not benefit from one another's experiences — in fact we could not think at all.

Take the early morning session from 4:30 to 6:30 am, the first full meditation period you are likely to experience (unless you can't get yourself out of bed and there is no Dhamma police making the rounds). The first thing you should know is that you are not expected to sit through two hours in one uninterrupted session. Taking breaks at your own discretion is certainly permitted, and how you use the two hours is up to you.[41] It will be your responsibility, for most of the course, to decide how hard you want to push yourself. You should also know that for the final 30-45 minutes of the session, Goenka always chants, with the teachers in the hall, which may turn out to be either a highlight for you or a low-point. (I'm not crazy about Goenka's chanting, but just today a good friend told me that it is always his favorite part.)

The late morning session runs from 8 to 11 am, and you will need to be in the hall for the full first hour from 8 to 9 am or the manager will come and get you. After a ten-minute recess, you will have to return for more instructions. Depending on the day, you will then be asked either to stay in the hall or you will be free to meditate in your room (or cell). For the periods that you may spend in your room, diligence will once again be your own responsibility. After a day or two, you will develop a good sense of whether the energy in the hall is congenial to you or not; but in most cases, you will find that it is better than in your room.

During the afternoon period from 1 to 5 pm, you may meditate on your own until 2:30 pm, when you need to spend another full hour in the hall for the second mandatory group sitting of the day. Afterwards, there will be a ten-minute recess again and instructions upon your return, much as in the morning.

If you will be listening to the evening discourses in English, you will be spending the whole evening in the hall. From 6 to 7 pm there is the third mandatory group sitting. After the ten-minute recess, there will be an evening discourse that usually runs a little over an hour, followed by another short recess. The day's program will conclude with a final mandatory group sitting of about half an hour depending on the day. At 9 pm you may either stay in the hall to ask or listen to questions, or else you may retire.

The times between meditation periods are for eating, resting, showering, and the like. If you are going to play hooky when you should be sitting, be sure to do it quietly in every sense. Showering or doing your laundry during meditation times is not only inconsiderate but also ill-advised because you will be drawing unwanted attention to yourself (assuming that you are not playing truant with an unconscious desire to get caught).

Your energies throughout the day are bound to wax and wane in mysterious patterns, with easy and difficult periods chasing each other like clouds across the sky. What I have noticed is that stronger and weaker periods do tend to cluster around certain times in one course, but around other times in another. Thus my preferred meditation period in one course has turned into my least favorite in another. In other words, be careful not to conclude that one period simply does or doesn't work for you. It may be so for the duration of a full course, but it may change completely in another.

If there is one thing you will learn in your course, it is that *Anicca* applies to meditational zeal as much as to anything else. You may reach a sitting in which you feel so lost, so forlorn and exhausted, that you cannot imagine doing another hour ever again; but after you've taken a short break and you've reluctantly sat down, you may find yourself sailing as you have never sailed before. Trust neither your despondency nor your exhilaration, and if possible, trust the latter even less than the former. A "bad" sitting (which is never in fact bad, however it may look to you[42]) always leaves room for hope; but there is nothing more treacherous than feeling that you have finally "gotten it" and now all will go smoothly at last. If you do not guard with the utmost vigilance against any attachment to such breakthroughs, you are setting yourself up for the harshest of falls. Everything passes, and more quickly than you think; cling to it, and you are already lost. Your lovely new toy will be torn from your hands no matter how much you clutch and scream; it never belonged to you, and never will. On the other hand, although you cannot hold on to any experience, insight, or revelation, no matter how sublime and overpowering, neither do you need to be afraid of forgetting it. Such things can neither be preserved at the surface of the mind, nor can they be lost at its depth. When the time has ripened for another peak, it will be built upon all the previous ones; and then you will be sent back down to the valley again, or to the subterranean bog.

Just as reliable predictions are impossible about the dynamics of your days, so there is nothing certain about the arc that your course is likely to take, if any. In my experience, the successive days have usually followed a rough pattern that may or may not be relevant to how things turn out for you.

Days 1 and 2 tend to be difficult days for everyone as tension slowly builds up against the background of a mind that has not quieted down much yet. All suffering is ultimately in the mind, but it will seem to you that your body is aching more and more, and you will be tempted to project that dynamic forward. The thought that things might keep going as they have been might get horrible enough, even in the first two days, to make you seriously consider quitting. If you brought sufficient determination (or desperation), you will probably tough it out, but know that everyone thinks about running away at some point in her first Ten-Day course. Goenka packed his bags on Day 2, and I spent the whole night of my first Day 4 sweating in my bed as I was contemplating a get-away. Students who go into a course most convinced that nothing could impel them to throw in the towel are usually the ones who suddenly disappear without a trace. (The rate of attrition on most courses no more than five to ten percent — in other words, 90 percent or more of the students make it through!)

Days 3 and 4 will drag you much deeper into the process, with a double effect. On the one hand, your mind may be getting clearer and more concentrated, possibly rewarding your efforts with the first "really good" sessions; but more and more stuff will be getting stirred up and your storms are likely to become more intense as well. It is about now that you might become aware of how violently you are yo-yoing between extremes of congratulating yourself on the best thing you have ever done, and cursing the day when you were crazy enough to sign yourself up for such a nightmare. A special complication is that in the afternoon on Day 4, you will have to face the toughest session of the course: the introduction to Vipassana meditation, which runs a full hour and a half and in which you will be urged, for the first time, to sit with a strong determination not to change your posture (*adhitthana*). There's nothing to be done when you arrive at this crucible but to bear the misery as best you can, keeping in mind what Bismarck said about life, but what might equally be applied to a Vipassana course, namely that it's like having one's teeth pulled by a clever dentist: one keeps thinking that the worst is yet to come until one discovers, with astonishment, that it's over already.[43]

From now on, all group sessions will be sittings of strong determination, but you will come to find them much more manageable than they may seem at first. The final few minutes will always be introduced by words you may come to love: *"Anicca vata sankhara, uppadavaya-dhammino."*[44] All things are impermanent (even sittings of strong determination); it is their nature to arise and pass away. In Buddhist countries, the formula is traditionally used in the context of funerals, but no one dies during group sittings, at least not when liberation is only a few minutes away.[45]

Days 5 and 6 tend to be days of alternating struggle and joy as the power of what you are doing becomes more and more evident while the storms keep lashing you, possibly with great violence. If you feel at the limit of your strength now, no wonder, but you have almost made it. After Day 6, though troubles may still come, you are sure to have gained the strength that will carry you through.

Days 7 to 9 are usually days of very serious, concentrated work, probably with a peak around Day 8 and a slight descent on Day 9 as you begin thinking about how close you are to the end and what may come after. By the evening of Day 9, you may feel like a runner who has spent her remaining energy in the final round. If so, it makes sense to take it easy in the morning of Day 10; but if you have the strength for a sprint on the final stretch, by all means give it your all until the finishing line.

The rest of Day 10 I shall discuss in chapter 10.

GOENKA'S EVENING DISCOURSES

For some students, Goenka's nightly discourses are the great delight of their Vipassana experience; for others, they are the pits. Love them or loathe them, all students must attend them over and over again, no matter how many courses they have taken. Lying down or making yourself truly comfortable is not allowed; you are not even supposed to point your feet forward when there are no teachers sitting upfront. But you should be able to get a spot on the wall or a chair if you need one. Many Old students close their eyes and meditate during the discourses, but if you are caught wearing ear-plugs, you will be asked to take them out.

Laughing at Captain Goenka's jokes is optional, and if you are listening to the discourses in translation, you may fail to see the humor in them. In the English version, however, which also allows you to watch Goenka's face as he is performing, you get the benefit of many more clues about when he is strictly serious, and when he is putting on a show. However much he may be getting on your nerves, at least he has a sense of humor. If you can believe it, a time is sure to come when his bedtime stories become so familiar that you would miss them, if you could not hear them again, as much as you miss Uncle Gulliver's endlessly repeated story, now that he is dead, about the time his boat got lost off Tasmania.

(The air of spontaneity that Goenka is able to preserve around his discourses is a remarkable feat of showmanship: by the time the standard English recordings were made, in 1991 in California, Goenka had taught over three hundred of his Ten-Day courses.[46] The reason he is so sure-footed, even speaking without notes, is simple: not only was he a gifted performer, he had also been testing and refining his lines for over twenty years. Perhaps the reason why only one set of recordings is used is that the similarity between different courses would give away Goenka's little secret.)

NOTES

1. That is, the Discourse on the 32 Greatest Blessings: *Sutta Nipata* 2.4 (Goenka, *Gem Set in Gold*, pp. 56-57), with my own revisions.

2. SN 36.12 (p. 1272).

3. *Augustan History*, Part I: "Life of Antoninus Pius" by Julius Capitolinus, par. 12 [Penguin, p. 106]. The reigns of Antoninus Pius (86-161 CE) and his adoptive son Marcus Aurelius (121-180 CE) have been traditionally considered the culmination of Rome's golden age as an empire. Thus the opening of Gibbon's *Decline and Fall of the Roman Empire*: "During a happy period (A.D. 98-180) of more than fourscore years, the public administration was conducted by the virtue and abilities of Nerva, Trajan, Hadrian, and the two Antonines. It is the design of this, and of the two succeeding chapters, to describe the prosperous condition of their empire; and afterwards, from the death of Marcus Antoninus, to deduce the most important circumstances of its decline and fall; a revolution which will ever be remembered, and is still felt by the nations of the earth." The melancholy postscript to Marcus's tenure as Rome's most philosophical emperor is that his efforts at showing more paternal affection than customary among Roman patricians (*Meditations* I.11-12) were crowned, as it were, by giving the empire one of its worst rulers, his son Commodus. (The movie "Gladiator" indulges in the pleasing fiction that Marcus sought at the last minute to prevent the ascension of his son, but there is nothing more than wishful thinking to support that story.)

4. Goenka tends to be rather dismissive of philosophy, as though it were no more than an intellectual game; but to the Stoics it retained its original meaning, which Thoreau captures so well in *Walden* ("Economy"): "To be a philosopher is not merely to have subtle thoughts, nor even to found a school, but so to love wisdom as to live according to its dictates, a life of simplicity, independence, magnanimity, and trust. It is to solve the problems of life, not only theoretically, but practically." [Vintage, p. 14]

5. The modern English title is fitting but more of an interpretation than a translation. The book was originally written as an inspirational private diary, entitled simply "To Himself". Far from a saint or a sage, Marcus was a practical man with philosophical inclinations who bore all the worldly responsibilities of ruling over an empire at the height of its power. His reflections were never intended to instruct anyone else, but to remind himself of lessons too easily

forgotten in the heat of battle, metaphorically as well as literally: he spent much of his life waging war under conditions well-depicted in the opening scenes of "Gladiator."

6. The insights of the Stoics may look a little crude beside the fully-elaborated Teaching of the Buddha, but they turn on the same essentials. Thus Marcus Aurelius emphasizes impermanence throughout: "all things are change" (*Meditations* VIII.6, see also IX.19,28,35); we are carried along by time as by a "furious torrent" (*Med.* VII.18, see also IV.43, V.23, IX.29). "In this flowing stream, on which there is no abiding, what is there of the things that hurry by on which a man would set a high price? It would be just as if a man were to fall in love with a sparrow flying by that has already passed out of sight." (*Med.* VI.15) The way to transform dissatisfaction and misery into wisdom is to "acquire the contemplative way of seeing how all things change into one another, and constantly to attend to it, and exercise oneself about this part. For nothing is so much adapted to produce magnanimity [or equanimity: see *Med.* X.8]" (*Med.* X.11). "[I]t is in the power of the mind [or soul: ψυχή] to maintain its own serenity and tranquility, and not to think that pain is an evil. For every judgment and movement and desire and aversion is within." (*Med.* VIII.28) True security can only be had if we see through the opinions we have formed based on the appearances of things, if we "penetrate" objects and "lay bare" what they really are, and if we also begin to understand that the self is not what it seems to be (*Med.* III.11, VI.13, VIII.40, XII.29). "Look within: within is the fountain of good, and it will ever bubble up, if you will ever dig." (*Med.* VII.59, see also II.8 and VI.3. And VIII.21: "Turn the body inside out and see what kind of a thing it is.") That we are meant to enjoy life (*Med.* VI.16, XII.29) is as much part of the Stoics' doctrine as the realization that this can only be done by keeping our attention focused resolutely on the present (*Med.* VII.29,54 and VIII.36). The idea that equanimity is not only about maintaining one's balance, but just as much about returning to it ("starting again"), can also be found in the *Meditations* (VI.11, X.8). Like Buddhists, Stoics are called to take refuge in their own minds (*Med.* VIII.48): "The mind that is free from passions is a citadel, for man has nothing more secure to which he can fly for refuge."

7. Such statements are made throughout the Ten-Day course; see especially Goenka's instructions on Days 6, 7, and 8. See also *The Art of Living*, p. 124-125: "Every moment in which we practice Vipassana properly, we can experience liberation... The highest quality of mind is equanimity based on full awareness of reality."

8. The other three divine abodes are dimensions of love: loving-kindness, compassion, and sympathetic (or altruistic) joy.

9. I will discuss these topics in chapter 7 on doctrine and in some of the questions in chapter 12 (*jhanas* and *bojjhangas*).

10. It is sometimes pointed out that *detachment* is too suggestive of drawing back and that *unattachment* would be the better term. See also the final question in chapter 12.

11. In chapter 7 on doctrine, I will offer a slightly broader interpretation of dependent origination than the one presented in the Ten-Day courses. Goenka emphasizes the importance of breaking the chain of becoming at the link between the arising of sensations (*vedana*) and the arising of craving and aversion (*tanha*); but by the logic of the construction, the chain can also be broken at the next link, when craving or aversion has already arisen. The window of opportunity, one might say, stays open just a little longer than Goenka allows.

12. Thus MN 106.10 (p. 872) about a bhikkhu who "obtains equanimity" but then "delights in that equanimity, welcomes it, and remains holding to it. As he does so, his consciousness becomes dependent on it and clings to it." The great instrument for liberation has turned into an obstacle: "A bhikkhu who clings," even if it is to equanimity, "does not attain Nibbana."

13. Where craving is contrasted with aversion, the Pali term is either *raga* or *lobha* with no clear distinction between the two (*U Ba Khin Journal*, pp. 276, 278). Where craving and aversion are identified with each other, like mirror images or like the two sides of the same coin, most importantly in the context of dependent origination (see chapter 7), the term used is *tanha* (lit. "thirst") (*U Ba Khin Journal*, p. 280).

14. The aspiration to Nibbana is a good example. As a matter of spiritual orientation, it is not only wholesome but expected, sooner or later, of all who are seriously committed to the Path. But if it turns into an object of craving, it becomes the antithesis of Buddhist practice.

15. Ajahn Sucitto, *Turning the Wheel of Truth* (Shambhala 2010), chapter 4, p. 50. MN 109.5 (p. 887) seems to identify *chanda* as the root of clinging, but this usage agrees so poorly with the rest of the Canon that Buddhaghosa, in his commentary on the *Majjhima Nikaya*, glosses it over (MN, Note 1038, p. 1319).

16. For a more thorough treatment, see Bodhi's "Anicca Vata Sankhara," BPS Newsletter Cover Essay No. 43 (3rd Mailing 1999), available online.

17. The pronouncement is made by Sakka, the ruler of the gods, at DN 16.6.10 (p. 271).

18. In his discourse on Day 5, Goenka interprets the phrase as applying to sankharas in the narrower volitional sense that he emphasizes throughout the course. Technically that's not correct, though the volitional sankharas are of course *Anicca* as well. (*The Art of Living* distinguishes more carefully between the narrower and the very wide meanings of *sankhara* on p. 97.)

19. The verse continues (*Dhp.* XX.5-7/277-79) "*Sabbe sankhara dukkha*" (all conditioned things are suffering), but "*Sabbe* dhamma anatta*" because even Nibbana, which *dhamma* comprehends but *sankhara* does not, is no-self.

20. See *Gem Set in Gold*, p. 68.

21. Sankharas in the volitional sense are what generates *kamma* or karma. In the chain of dependent origination, they constitute the crucial link following *vedana* or sensations where the cycle can be broken. See chapter 7 on Doctrine.

22. Goenka mentions wholesome sankharas in one sentence at the end of the discourse on Day 4, but he immediately sets them aside, presumably to avoid confusion. His omission becomes misleading on Day 7, when he says in the discourse that "a person is just the sum-total of his sankharas." That may be true, but it should not be taken to mean that we are just tangles of impurities and defilements: our personalities are complex mixtures of wholesome and unwholesome habits, just as common sense would tell us.

23. Thus Goenka: "Craving is the mother of aversion." (*Satip. Discourses*, p. 30)

24. SN 46.26 (p. 1586). The point that craving is the origin of suffering and the impetus behind renewed existence was already emphasized by the Buddha in his first sermon, on the "Turning of the Wheel" (SN 56:11 [p. 1844 (BW 76)]).

25. See *Art of Living*, p. 110: "Vipassana meditation is a kind of fasting of the spirit in order to eliminate past conditioning."

26. AN 3:65 (pp. 279-283 [BW 88-91]).

27. Those who have accepted Goenka as their Jason (or their Captain Kirk), their guide and leader on the sacred quest for the golden fleece of mental purity and liberation. Air Goenka does not advertise its connections as space travel, but their flights take travelers on an exploration of the inner universe on the premise that the depth within us is every bit as profound as the vastness that surrounds and that we can truly know the external world only by understanding the internal. Students do sometimes report traveling outward on a course (astral projections and such), but these are not authorized flight-routes at a Goenka center. Accidents can happen, of course, but it essential to Vipassana as understood by the Goenkanauts that every effort be made to keep one's attention strictly inward: *niccam kayagata-sati* (awareness always towards the body: see *Dhp.* XXI.4/293, *Gem Set in Gold*, p. 77).

28. That is, the "great" discourse on the establishment of mindfulness (DN 22 [pp. 335-350]), which differs from the "lesser" version at MN 10 (pp. 145-55) only in its lengthier treatment of the Four Noble Truths in section 5 (pp. 344-49 and p. 154, respectively). The discourses on mindfulness of breath and body presented side-by-side in the *Majjhima Nikaya* (*Anapanasati Sutta* [MN 118] and *Kayagatasati Sutta* [MN 119]) do not go beyond the Satipatthana Suttas.

29. DN 22.1 (p. 335 [BW 281]) in the translation by the Vipassana Research Institute (VRI 2006) that is used in Goenka's eight-day Sati courses for Old students.

30. The Goenkanauts may have Buddhist tradition on their side, but Bodhi points out, with reference to MN 12.37 (p. 170), that "the one-way path" would be more accurate (BW 281, 441, MN Note 135 [pp. 1188-89]). Nanamoli takes the same line in his translation for *The Life of the Buddha*, pp. 35, 349. Maurice Walshe, the editor of the *Digha Nikaya* for Wisdom Publications, side-steps the issue by translating "this one way" and points out that even the ancient commentators were not sure of the exact meaning of the phrase (DN 589). Bhikkhu Analayo in his rigorous *Satipatthana: The Direct Path to Realization* (Windhorse 2003) uses the word "indispensable," but favors "direct path" over alternatives that strike a more strident note (see pp. 27-29). The unnamed editors' introduction to the VRI edition of the *Mahasatipatthana Sutta*, p. vi, does also speak of Satipatthana as a "direct avenue," but only after having upheld "the one and only way."

31. Thus Goenka in his *Satipatthana Discourses* (p. 21): "*Ekayano maggo* (the one and only path) may appear to some to be narrow-minded.

Those who have not walked on the path, or have not walked on it very deeply, may feel uncomfortable. For those who have walked on it, it is clearly the one and only path. It is after all the universal law of nature." (See also *Ibid.*, pp. 96-97.) The disagreement, however, is not about the unity of the law of nature, but about whether there may be other equally valid ways to approach it. To say that anyone who insists on keeping such possibilities open must not have walked the Path very seriously does not help, but only aggravates the concern.

32. See *Satip. Discourses*, pp. 26, 51-52, 55, and "Vedana in the Practice of Satipatthana," the introduction to the VRI edition of the *Mahasatipatthana Sutta*, pp. vii-xv and Notes. As the basis for such an exclusive interpretation of Satipatthana, however, a few vague lines from two obscure Suttas (*Mula Sutta*: AN 10.58 [p. 1410] and *Samiddhi Sutta*: AN 9.14 [p. 1269]) are a rather feeble foundation. The VRI translates "Everything that arises in the mind flows together with sensations." (VRI, Vedana, p. viii) Bhikkhu Bodhi in the Wisdom edition of AN (p. 1410) has "all things converge upon feeling." The Pali Text Society version by F.L. Woodward reads "all things are conjoined in sensations." Thanissaro Bhikkhu offers "All phenomena have feeling as their meeting place."

33. VRI, Vedana, p. viii, italics added. A claim to exclusivity that seems to be flatly contradicted by SN 54.13 (pp. 1780-81): "Concentration by mindfulness of breathing is *the one thing* which, when developed and cultivated, fulfills the four establishments of mindfulness." (Italics added.)

34. VRI, Vedana, p. xiv.

35. See my discussion of Vipassana in relation to Anapana in chapter 8.

36. Thus Bhikkhu Bodhi in an e-mail correspondence (4 Dec. 2014, italics added): "I've done a few courses with Goenka and think the meditation system itself is fine, *provided it is not billed as the exclusive technique of insight practice handed down straight from the Buddha.*" Alas, that is exactly the billing it does often seem to receive.

As a results-oriented meditation teacher and a practical man, Goenka cannot be expected to take such nuanced and qualified positions as those of life-long scholars like Bodhi or Goldstein ("basically Talmudic scholars of Buddhism," Harris calls them with affection, p. 132). Still Goenka's taste for unambiguous, not to say strident interpretations (that are often highly incisive and convincing, it has to be said) can combine in unfortunate ways with the tendency of many of his students to defer to their teacher's pronouncements as if they were the final word and not just one man's contributions to an ancient discussion. The results can "border on a cult and a subtle kind of brainwashing," as Bodhi wrote to me in the same message.

For my own take on this vexatious subject, which many of the more independent-minded Vipassana students struggle with at some point or other, see the second question in chapter 8.

37. AN 8.81 (p. 1229); see also SN 56.22 (p. 1853).

38. In the *Mahasatipatthana Sutta* (DN 22:17 [p. 344], VRI edition, pp. 46-47), but also at SN 48:53 (p. 1696), SN 56:22-24 (p. 1853-1854 [BW 359]), etc. For Goenka's treatment of the concept, see *Art of Living*, pp. 105-106, and *Satip. Discourses*, pp. 81-83. Also Rahula, pp. 9, 17 ("to see things as they are, with right wisdom, objectively").

39. SN 56:24 (p. 1854 [BW 359]). At SN 28.2 (p. 278) the Four Noble Truths, called "the teaching special to the Buddhas" throughout the Canon, are said to comprise all that it is wholesome to know in the same way that an *elephant's footprint* can contain within its contours all the smaller footprints of other walking beings. (The Buddha often compared himself to a tusker — especially when he was ready for a break from the herd (AN 9.40 [pp. 1307-1308], *Udana* 4.5 [Ireland, p. 59]).

SN 56.45 (p. 1869-70) compares understanding the Four Noble Truths in all their profundity to a feat of archery beside which even Odysseus's pales (*Odyssey*, book 21). The common ordering of high meditative achievements in the Pali Canon is also telling: first the four *jhanas* (see below); then the knowledge of previous lives; then the full understanding of kamma (divine eye); then complete insight: "This is suffering." (See for example MN 51.20-26 [pp. 451-52].)

40. Of course one might object that controlled breathing or deliberately slow walking is surely no less *real* than any other kind of breathing or walking, but let's not nit-pick.

41. Some orthodox remedies for fighting off drowsiness and torpor (not all countenanced by Goenka) are discussed at AN 7.61 (p. 1060): reflecting on the Dhamma; reciting the Dhamma; pulling one's ears or rubbing one's limbs; splashing one's face with water; imagining a bright light; walking back and forth; lying down mindfully.

42. See the question on being a bad meditator in chapter 8.

43. The saying is widely quoted (even by Viktor Frankl in *Man's Search for Meaning*), but never with any indication of when or where Bismarck made the statement.

44. *Gem Set in Gold*, pp. 68, 78. In the Canon: DN 16.6.10 (p. 271).

45. See the question on dying at a Vipassana center in chapter 12.

46. The recording was made in August 1991 at Dhamma Mahavana, the California center at North Fork. This was Goenka's 358th Ten-Day course since the first one in July 1969 (held at Mumbai). (For a list of all courses taught by Goenka between 1969 and 1998, see *Sayagyi U Ba Khin Journal*, pp. 261-71).

CHAPTER SEVEN
TOYS, PROPS, AND BEDROOM FURNITURE (DOCTRINE)

FROM A VIPASSANA PERSPECTIVE, OUR MONKEY MINDS[1] INVARIABLY protest and theorize too much because that is how we divert and entertain ourselves; how we assert and affirm our *individual identities* (both words mere myths and misnomers, it is said, because there is nothing indivisible about a person and nothing that remains identical from one moment to the next); how we protect the illusion of being in control; and how we nourish and sustain an ego that is always threatened on all sides. That is one reason why Vipassana teachers can be so reluctant to enter into discussions — they also aren't trained for it and there isn't the time.

To some ears at least, "doctrine" may suggest overly abstract philosophizing, but in the context of the Buddha's Teaching, all doctrinal claims are supposed to be verifiable, sooner or later, by a meditator's direct personal experience. To reject the Vipassana technique on theoretical grounds would be to deprive oneself of an eminently practical tool that does not, at bottom, depend on any more than simple observation of what is happening in the body from moment to moment. "In this fathom-long body endowed with perception and mind" the Buddha found everything worth knowing without any need to travel to the ends of the world.[2]

Figure 1: The Twelve Links of Dependent Origination

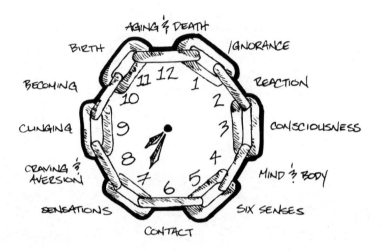

THE CHAIN OF BECOMING

Dismissing a theoretical formulation of the Dhamma is like denying a formula used to express the laws of gravity: one should feel free to reject whatever one has not been able to verify, but doing so will not protect one from the consequences of heavy objects falling on one's toes.

One doctrine, that of **Dependent Origination** (*Paticcasamuppada*), the Buddha considered nearly synonymous with his Teaching:[3] "One who sees dependent origination sees the Dhamma; one who sees the Dhamma sees dependent origination."[4] Arcane as it may seem, the Buddhist account of how life is reborn not only at death, but at every instant anew, is not a remote intellectual construct, not a creed or an article of faith, nor a philosophical tenet or thesis, but the central discovery (in the form of incontrovertible experience) said to have come to the Buddha under the Bodhi tree during the famous night of his final breakthrough. And not only the Buddha, but anyone who devotes himself to looking closely enough, can discover the same thing, namely how existence even in its most mundane manifestations is created in a twelve-step circular movement — the wheel of becoming with twelve spokes, or a closed chain with twelve links trapping us in ever-renewed life and suffering.

Given that we are dealing with a cycle of arising and passing away, one could begin with any step and trace the dynamic either in forward order (by origination) or in reverse order (by cessation).[5] Both directions are customary in Buddhism, with ignorance commonly taken as the first link. Since there are twelve links altogether, I find it evocative to superimpose them on a clock in forward order (see Figure 1: The Chain of Becoming),[6] so that the day begins with ignorance (the apt zero hour in digital format: 00:01-1:00) and ends with aging at the last hour (11:01-12:00) and death at midnight.[7] As a tool for making the phases of dependent origination more comprehensible and memorable, it has occurred to me to divide the cycle into four connected triads (not to be confused with the traditional expository model that distinguishes *three* segments and identifies them with successive lives):[8]

First Triad: (1) ignorance => (2) reaction (*sankhara*) => (3) consciousness =>
Second Triad : (4) mind and body => (5) six senses => (6) contact =>
Third Triad: (7) sensation (*vedana*) => (8) craving and aversion (*tanha*) => (9) clinging (*upadana*) =>
Fourth Triad: (10) becoming => (11) birth => (12) aging and death => back to ignorance

The *first triad* confronts us with the troubling but inescapable fact that in the Buddha's Teaching, the very flame of consciousness ("all is burning"[9]) is lit by the spark of ignorance and fueled by the habit of reaction (our old friend *sankhara*[10]). In the Buddhist understanding, then, the body with its brain and central nervous system does not give rise to consciousness (as one might imagine under the influence of materialist assumptions), but the mind-

Figure 2: The Clock of Vipassana

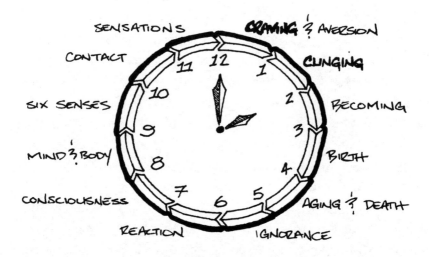

body phenomenon with its six senses arises *from* consciousness, though as soon as it has arisen, consciousness becomes enmeshed with mentality-materiality in a complex reciprocal and interdependent relationship.[11] Once the doors of the six senses have opened, contact with outside objects is inevitable. Thus the whole *second triad* merely traces the necessary physical consequences of consciousness having arisen.

The first link in the *third triad*, sensation (*vedana*) is the unavoidable consequence of contact, but the next two, craving-aversion (*tanha*) and clinging (*upadana*) are habitual responses that can be changed — the crucial point in the cycle from a meditator's point of view, as we shall see. Once craving and clinging have arisen, however, the *fourth triad* once more follows inescapably: becoming results in birth which leads to aging and death together with all the attendant sorrow and anguish, mental and physical, to which all life is heir. "Thus arises the entire mass of suffering."[12]

In order to throw the logic and power of the Vipassana technique into the sharpest relief, let us rotate the chain until the links of *sensation* and *craving* occupy the hours before and after 12, respectively, so that *the Clock of Vipassana*[13] (see Figure 2: The Clock of Vipassana) strikes midnight (or perhaps high noon) just after sensations have appeared, but before craving has arisen in response.[14] This moment is rightly stressed by Goenka as our moment of truth, because here ignorance can be overcome and reaction defeated by the cultivation of equanimity. That the Buddha's triumph[15] was specifically over his own craving or *tanha*, literally thirst,[16] is emphasized in the *Udana-gatha*, the "Verses of Joy" or "Song of Victory"[17] with which the Buddha rose from the meditation that had brought him full liberation and enlightenment: "The mind has been freed from conditioning; the end of craving has been reached. The glorious victory of the Buddha has come." Goenka emphasizes, plausibly, that craving is best nipped in the bud, before it blooms and multiplies, but the logic of dependent origination might also allow us to break the chain even when craving has already arisen, by observing its appearance with equanimity (what I call "secondary equilibrium" above).[18] If so, we might say that the window of opportunity stays open throughout the zero hour, until 1 am on our clock[19] — or even until 2 am if clinging (*upadana*) can be observed objectively as well.[20] From a Vipassana perspective the practical difference may not be great since craving and clinging will both be observed at the sensations level; but perhaps the beginnings of a doctrinal justification might be found here for practices that do not emphasize *vedana* to the extent that Goenka does.[21] (A point that could be stressed more in making the case for working with the sensations is how essential they are for constructing our sense of self. If we did not feel sensations, the Buddha emphasizes in the crucial *Mahanidana Sutta*, the idea that "I am" simply could not arise.[22] If that is how the illusion gets built up, surely the case for trying to undo it on the same terrain is nearly incontrovertible.)

But we should never be too sure of having understood the Buddha's Teaching by reasoning alone. When the Buddha emerged from the long meditation that had made him the

Awakened One, he mused how hard it was to grasp "this abstruse Dhamma that goes against the worldly stream," and he identified insight into the profundity of the Dhamma specifically with understanding dependent origination.[23] On one occasion when his trusted assistant Ananda spoke a little too confidently ("How profound this dependent origination is! And yet it appears to me as clear as clear!"), the Buddha admonished him: "Do not say that, Ananda, do not say that!"[24] However lucid a doctrine may appear to us, and however strong our faith, we must not presume that we have understood it until we have experienced it for ourselves in its full profundity.[25]

Theory and practice go together in the Dhamma.[26] Hence the Buddha's **Noble Eightfold Path** is both the practical strategy for moving towards enlightenment and liberation in this life and an "instrument of discovery"[27] that both begins and ends with *right view* (specifically of the Four Noble Truths). Right view in the truest sense is the fruit of the Path, reserved for the point of its completion: thus it is said that only the completely enlightened have "fully awakened to the Four Noble Truths as they really are."[28] On the other hand, without some preliminary recognition, there would be little reason to start on the journey or to keep moving.[29] Thus: "Just as the dawn is the forerunner and precursor of the sunrise, so right view is the forerunner and precursor of wholesome qualities."[30] So long as the Four Noble Truths appear dark or even depressing to us, however, we haven't understood them profoundly enough: "The breakthrough to the Four Noble Truths is accompanied only by happiness and joy."[31] The Noble Eightfold Path is meant to be "traveled joyfully" even if it may involve bumpy stretches.[32]

The eight aspects that make up the Noble Path are traditionally arranged in three groups:[33] *right speech*, *right action*, and *right livelihood* in the first (morality group: *sila*); *right effort*, *right concentration*, and *right mindfulness* in the second (concentration group: *samadhi*); and *right thought* and *right view* in the third (wisdom group: *pañña*).[34] Goenka offers his interpretation of these aspects in the evening discourses and they are most ably summarized and discussed by Bhikkhu Bodhi in *The Noble Eightfold Path*.

Right speech (samma-vaca) starts from the precept against lying and extends it to tale-bearing, backbiting and malicious gossip, flattery, harsh language, and useless chatter.[35] On the positive side, it enjoins not only truthful words, but mild, conciliatory, polite, timely, and wise speech.

Right listening did not make the list, but the Buddha illustrates beautifully how his disciples might learn to put up with speech that is disagreeable in five respects, namely untrue, untimely, harsh, ill-intentioned, and spoken with ill-will. "Herein you should train thus: 'Our minds will remain unaffected, and we shall utter no evil words; we shall abide with compassion for the speaker's welfare, with a mind of loving-kindness, without inner hate.'" Imagine yourself, the Buddha suggested, with a mind similar to the earth. Say someone comes along meaning to upset the earth by digging, scattering the soil, or spitting and urinating on the ground. Would the earth budge? Would it cease to be earth? Or imagine yourself with a mind similar to the river Ganges. Suppose someone came with a blazing torch and threatened to burn away the water? What would he gain?[36] Or imagine yourself with a mind similar to the softest kind of bag, well-loved and silky: could a man with a stick or a potsherd make it rustle and crackle?[37]

A related Buddhist favorite, told with slight variations in Goenka's discourses,[38] is the story of the brahmin Bharadvaja, who was enraged about the popularity the Buddha was gaining at the expense of the traditional priests. So he sought out the enemy and accosted him with abuse. When Bharadvaja had finished his tirade, the Buddha asked him whether he had ever entertained friends and guests at his house. Sure he had. "Did you offer them food and drink?" asked the Buddha. Naturally: so what? "But if

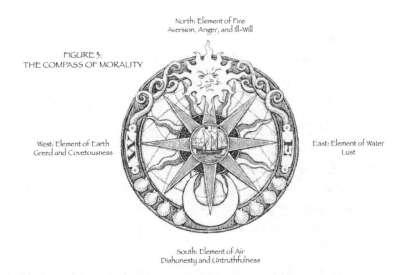

FIGURE 3:
THE COMPASS OF MORALITY

North: Element of Fire
Aversion, Anger, and Ill-Will

West: Element of Earth
Greed and Covetousness

East: Element of Water
Lust

South: Element of Air
Dishonesty and Untruthfulness

they did not wish to accept the food, to whom would it belong?" Bharadvaja was getting suspicious, but he answered that the food would still be his own, of course. "Just so do I refuse to accept the abuse and scolding that you have offered me. It still belongs to you, brahmin, it still belongs to you!" It is said that Bharadvaja was so impressed that he paid homage to the Buddha, asked to be received into the Sangha, and became one of the fully enlightened, the *arahants*.[39]

Right bodily action (samma-kammanta) comprises the precepts against killing, stealing, and sexual misconduct, with the precept against intoxication guarding all others (See Figure 3: The Compass of Morality).[40] It precludes all deliberate action to bring harm to any being, and it demands, on the positive side, considerate, helpful, and loving action.

Right livelihood (samma-ajiva) prohibits trading in arms, in living beings, in meat and other animal parts, in intoxicants and in poisons, as well as any mode of doing business that involves deception, false advertisement and misleading insinuations, slander, or scheming in any other way for gain in a greedy manner.[41]

The Buddha discussed workplace relations explicitly. Bosses are required to assign jobs according to the strengths of their workers, to pay them adequate wages and show concern for their health, to let them off at appropriate times and grant them vacations, and even to give bonuses and occasional gifts. Employees, in return, are expected to work conscientiously, not to waste time on the job, not to take anything that belongs to their employer, and to safeguard their employer's reputation.[42]

By *right effort (samma-vayama)* a meditator is called to put forth energy towards arousing and maintaining all things wholesome while avoiding and overcoming the contrary. It is here that the connection with meditation is perhaps most evident, since the effort required for a regular practice (as you are sure to discover) is considerable. The elements of *right concentration (samma-samadhi)* and *right mindfulness (samma-sati)* have a similarly evident relationship to the cultivation of awareness and equanimity by deliberate, regular practice, both formal on the mat and informal in every other situation. (In a Vipassana context, the phrase "*atapi sampajano satima,*" pivotal to the *Mahasatipatthana Sutta*, is stressed especially and understood to characterize contemplation "with ardent awareness and constant mindfulness of impermanence.")

If we look a little more closely, it becomes evident that meditation feeds and forms all eight dimensions of the Noble Eightfold Path. As we have seen, one might view the whole Path through the lens of purifying right view, and such progressive refinement is inconceivable without meditation. The eighth dimension of the Path, *right thought (samma-sankappa)* — the establishment of mental patterns free of craving and aversion, of ignorance, ill-will, or aggressiveness — is closely related to right view and requires the same meditative foundation.[43] For as the Buddha insisted, "Whatever someone frequently thinks and ponders upon, that will become the inclination of his mind."[44] Our views and thoughts sometimes seem to us as if they were growing above the ground of our mere habits and emotions, but in fact they have their roots deep in the soil beneath and it is meditative practice that waters, loosens, and fertilizes the earth.

One might also think of the Path as culminating in cleaning

up our thoughts, with morality as the foundation; concentration, mindfulness, and effort as the tools; insight and wisdom (right view) as the precondition. So if our struggle is finally for pure thoughts, one might ask, why not *begin* with the obvious and cultivate positive, non-judgmental thinking?[45] Why complicate things unnecessarily: isn't it all very simple? But no so fast. Certainly it is important, at all stages of one's journey on the Path, to make a conscious effort to stay away from unwholesome thoughts and to cultivate more wholesome ones. In one of his most striking discourses, the *Vitakkasanthana Sutta* on the removal of distracting thoughts, the Buddha offers some remarkably astute psychological advice on how to "knock out, remove, and extract a coarse peg by means of a fine one," among other techniques.[46] (In the *Itivuttaka*, there is the memorable image of stopping unwholesome trains of thought "as a rain-shower settles a cloud of dust."[47]) Only there can be much avoidance and denial lurking behind the peaceful facade of "positive thinking." The Path leads beyond suffering, but it does so by a direct confrontation with all that is unsatisfactory in life. These dark realities need to be faced or the purification of our minds will remain superficial, with the defilements receding beneath the surface of the mind (like "sleeping volcanoes"), where they can keep multiplying all the more safely because they are not fully acknowledged.[48]

(During the stormier moments of a course, trying to keep your thoughts together can feel like reading in a car does to a person prone to car-sickness. It will make you nauseous, and the best thing is not to think at all, if possible.[49])

The most succinct summary of the Path appears in the *Dhammapada*: "Abstain from all unwholesome actions, perform wholesome ones, and keep purifying your mind. This is the teaching of the Buddhas."[50] To keep turning our habits, mental or physical, in a more wholesome direction requires sustained training and a regular calibration of our emotional and moral compass such as only meditation can provide, at least by Buddhist accounts.

ॐ

The Noble Eightfold Path cannot be separated from the **Four Noble Truths** that were discovered and emphasized by the Buddha: first, the fact and scope of suffering (*idam dukkham:* this is suffering); second, how suffering arises; third, how it ceases; and fourth, the Path to be pursued for overcoming suffering. The Four Noble Truths themselves follow from the **Three Characteristics**[51] of all existence that become "gateways to deliverance" if they are properly observed: the *impermanence* of all things (*Anicca*), the basic *unsatisfactoriness* or liability to suffering of all sentient beings (*Dukkha*), and the *absence of self* (*Anatta*) wherever we imagine it.[52]

The technique of Vipassana directs our attention so resolutely towards **Anicca** that one might call it *a meditation on impermanence* first and foremost.[53] To become engrossed in the feeling of *Anicca* within,[54] Goenka's teacher U Ba Khin said in his best-known discourse, is to find a deep pool of quiet in the midst of all that is happening in the world: "*Anicca* is, for the householder, the gem of life that he will treasure to create a reservoir of calm and balanced energy for his own well-being and for the welfare of society."[55] The Pali Scriptures, too, attest to the great power of contemplating *Anicca*:[56] "More fruitful than the greatest alms-offering, than feeding a hundred *arahants* or a Buddha, than going for refuge or taking the five precepts, even than developing a mind of loving-kindness, would it be to develop the perception of impermanence just for the duration of a finger-snap."[57] It is because all things are so changeable, forever torn away from untrained minds seeking to hold them fast, that **Dukkha** becomes so prominent a feature of things: not only the raw suffering that we all recognize as such, but also the subtler forms of dissatisfaction that run like a subterranean current beneath all our sentient experiences.[58] "Have you ever experienced a single night or day, or half a night or day, that was entirely happy?"[59] the Buddha asked a skeptic. All that is dear and pleasant to us must suffer change, separation, and alteration,[60] yet to see the transience of things clearly is to begin coming out of the madness. Hence the urgency in the Buddha's last words: "All conditioned things arise and pass away: work out your deliverance with diligence!"[61]

The perception of *Anicca*, once sufficiently developed and cultivated, eliminates ignorance as the rising sun dispels the darkness and cold.[62] Its warming rays loosen our clinging and craving and melt the deluded belief in self, opening the way for understanding **Anatta**, the doctrine of no-self or impersonality or corelessness[63] — at once the most inaccessible and the most liberating of the three characteristics.[64] In the Buddha's day as in our own, it was common to acknowledge the dominion of *Anicca* over the body, but to keep attaching one's sense of self to a supposedly incorruptible mental element instead. The Buddha insisted, however, that consciousness, far from being less impermanent than the body, is even more fickle: "Just as a monkey roaming through a forest grabs hold of one branch, lets that go and grabs another, then lets that go and grabs another still, so too that which is called 'mind' and 'mentality' and 'consciousness' arises as one thing and ceases as another by day and by night."[65] Nothing changes so quickly as the mind:[66] consciousness, too, is no-self.[67]

The image of the monkey applies in another sense as well. Then as now, monkey-traps depended on their victims' unwillingness to give up something they are clutching, even if they could free themselves simply by letting go.[68] So it is said of us: we desperately cling to the very thing that causes our misery, the illusory self.[69] To use another of the Buddha's images, we keep running in circles like puppies on a leash, tied to a post, because we cannot let go of the belief that one phenomenon or another must define us as selves.[70] Yet, while we keep insisting that there must be some hard core to our identities as selves, and while the more determined among us commit such energies to seeking it out, we seem unable to find it no matter how hard we try and we keep getting tormented by ever the same questions, since time immemorial, about who or what we are, whether we truly exist or not, where we have come from, and where we are going.[71] All such "inward confusions," whether about the present, the past, or the future, can only be resolved one way according to the Buddha: by "clearly seeing, with correct wisdom, as it really is, this dependent origination and these dependently arisen phenomena."[72]

A memorable *Anatta*-story is told about the bark-cloth-wearing ascetic Bahiya, who came to realize that his liberation had not gone as far as he had imagined[73] and who set out walking across India to find the Buddha.[74] Before the gates of Savatthi, where the monks were gathering to collect alms in the city, Bahiya accosted the Awakened One, who asked him to have a little patience, because the time of the alms-round was not well-suited to giving a teaching. But the wanderer was not to be put off even for an hour: who knows what might happen to either of us even in a few minutes, he said, and demanded to be taught the Dhamma on the spot. When the Buddha relented after being importuned a second and a third time, the teaching he gave was deceptively simple: "In seeing there is only seeing, in hearing only hearing, in feeling only feeling, in knowing and understanding only knowing and understanding. There is no self to be found in it anywhere."[75] We are told that Bahiya understood right away and became fully liberated. (A close call, too, because before the Buddha even returned from his alms-round, Bahiya had been attacked and killed by a cow protecting her calf.)

The Questions of King Milinda were raised in a conversation between a Greek king established in Bactria by Alexander's conquests and the Buddhist monk Nagasena. The king, like most of us, is particularly puzzled by the idea that his sense of self is supposed to be a delusion. Nagasena answers him with the famous simile of the chariot. What part makes a chariot: is it the axle, or the wheels, or the body? All the parts make the vehicle, and none: "chariot" is only a designation, a label, a name for the sum of its parts.[76] And so with the self and personal identity: in the ultimate sense, there is no such thing, because there is nothing that remains "identical" behind the momentary phenomena that we are summarizing by a name. We understand that a river is merely a process of flow, that what we call its waters are never the same from one moment to the next. We know that the light of a candle is really a flicker, and that of a light-bulb the flow of electricity through a wire. If we spoke strictly, we would have to say that the person we saw (or were) a moment ago no longer exists; but to do justice to how we speak conventionally, and to our sense of close causal connection, the Buddha used the illustration of cream that gets churned into butter and then clarified into ghee.[77] The three are evidently not the same, but neither do they look completely distinct to us. Hence a classic Theravadan formula in the *Questions of King Milinda*: "*Na ca so na ca añño*," *neither the same nor another*.[78] (Perhaps instead of writing "I," we should get into the habit of writing "iiiiii" — but conventional simplifications have their legitimate uses so long as we understand their limitations.[79])

These attempts at explanation may sound feeble, even if no less a philosopher than David Hume came to similar conclusions about personal identity.[80] We should not be surprised if abstract reflection fails to convince us, nor disappointed or discouraged if even intellectual and devotional conviction cannot defeat our intuition that we are selves, even long after the delusion has been unmasked and confronted. Never is it truer that we can only really know what we see with the eye of experience than when it comes to *Anatta* and *Nibbana*.[81] Even stream-enterers who understand *Anatta* properly and who have had a first glimpse of *Nibbana* will not shed every vestige of "the conceit I am," which is the most tenacious and subtle of all mental impurities. According to the Teaching, the last traces of the self-illusion will be eliminated only at the very end of the Path, with the attainment of *arahanthood* itself. Until then, we may whittle away at its trunk,[82] but we will not be able to uproot it.[83] Thus the Suttas observe that the residual sense of self will linger like the smell of detergent on fresh laundry long after it has been thoroughly cleaned.[84]

The Buddha taught that not only *all persons* but *"all things* are empty of a self, and of anything belonging to a self," so that the whole world might be called "empty" in a specific sense.[85] Thus some of the most unforgettable lines in the *Visuddhimagga*: "Mere suffering exists, but none who suffers; doing exists, but there is no doer; Nibbana is, but no person enters it; the Path is, but no one travels on it... *Empty phenomena roll on*, that is the only right view."[86] As the Buddhist tradition developed in different directions, however, pronouncements about "this fleeting world: a star at dawn, a bubble in a stream, a flash of lightning in a summer cloud, a flickering lamp, a phantom, and a dream"[87] became more and more oracular, impressionistic, and perplexing. Such gems as "giving a Dharma talk in fact means that no talk is given"[88] or "not even the least trace of Dharma is to be found anywhere"[89] may have their own strange beauty, but I prefer to stick to the more plainspoken spiritual language of Goenka and the Theravadan heritage. "The light of human minds is perspicuous words."[90]

One of the great difficulties we face in trying to understand **Nibbana** is that while the Buddha's Path, if it is authentic, must necessarily lead towards it, even so innocent a word as "towards" is misleading in its implications. Nibbana does not exist in any particular direction either in space or in time; it is not a distinct realm and it cannot be either separated from nor identified with anything else. Our speech having evolved in tandem with our struggle for survival in a world perceived by our senses and interpreted by our shared conceptual habits, what lies beyond the self and the senses must exceed the reach of language as well. Thus, on the one hand, whatever words or concept we use to locate, characterize, or describe Nibbana will fail us;[91] on the other, Nibbana is so central a feature of the Buddha's Teaching that we cannot remain silent about it for long.[92]

The literal meaning of Nibbana is cessation or extinction, the snuffing out of our dissatisfaction, from the conflagrations of our agonies to the smallest sparks of agitation or unease. "All is burning," the Buddha taught in one of his most famous sermons, "burning with the fire of craving, the fire of aversion, and the fire of delusion; burning with birth, aging, and death; burning with sorrow, lamentation, pain, dejection, and despair."[93] Nibbana lies beyond the flames, beyond "the All"[94] of the **Five Aggregates**[95] — beyond the interaction of **matter** (*rupa*) with the four aspects of **mind**[96] (*nama/citta*: divided into consciousness, perception, sensation, and reaction[97]) — beyond space and time, and thus beyond anything for which our language, made to serve us in the world of our senses, could furnish us with adequate expressions. If we need to talk about the ultimately reality, we have to use such negative terms as *the unborn, unarisen, unmade, unconditioned* — but no words do it justice. Only one thing can be said with confidence, following the Buddha: "It is for the sake of final Nibbana without clinging that the holy life is lived."[98] If it were not for Nibbana, there could be no escape from suffering and the Four Truths would be bitter, not noble.[99] But escape *is* possible because "just as the water of a river plunges into the ocean and merges with the ocean, so the spiritual path, the Noble Eightfold Path, plunges into Nibbana and merges with Nibbana" (Bhikkhu Bodhi).[100]

I sometimes think of Nibbana on a crude analogy with dark matter or energy in Physics. For everyday purposes, limiting oneself to Newtonian perspectives is sufficient and appropriate, and so with one's Dhamma practice, which might flourish for years without the least thought given to Nibbana. Nonetheless, physicists tell us that Einstein's theories explain much more of the observable universe than do Newton's, and their most advanced accounts of the nature of things require the postulate of dark matter or energy even if we have no direct knowledge of it at all. Without it, none of our most powerful equations work out. Just so, the basic formulae of the Dhamma do not balance without Nibbana, even if it defies positive description. In fact, we are told that the shadow of dark matter or energy looms vastly larger than any of the stuff we know; and so it is with Nibbana, supposedly the truest thing (or *no-thing*) of all. Even the Four Noble Truths, the bedrock of the Teaching, are only finally understood when they are contrasted with the experience (or rather, the *non-experience*) of Nibbana.

Thus the Buddha's Teaching operates both at **the mundane** and at **the supra-mundane** level. The Noble Eightfold Path covers the entire landscape of human spiritual endeavor, from virtuous living in the fertile valley where householders make their homes (money, marriage, mumps and all) to the soaring peaks where recluses dwell in their caves and saintly beings survey the universe from the highest summits. The Buddha was happy to give practical encouragement to "laypeople who enjoy sensual pleasures, dwelling at home in a bed crowded with children, enjoying fine sandalwood, wearing garlands, scents, and unguents, and accepting gold and silver" no less than to a devoted couple hoping to be reunited in a future life.[101] But he also stressed that the time must come, if suffering is to have an end, when we recognize that the troubles of life are not rooted in this or that unsatisfactory aspect, but built into the very fabric of existence as imagined selves. (The *Mangala Sutta*, one of the most beloved Theravadan texts, captures in only a page or two the full sweep of the Buddha's vision, from the most practical and worldly to the most detached and sublime.[102])

At its most stark and fundamental, the Buddha's Teaching alerts us to the sobering fact that life is fueled by mental defilements — cravings, aversions, and ignorance — and that what comes into existence, examined closely enough, turns out to be only suffering arising.[103] Thus his insistence, so shocking to our ears, that "delight is the root of suffering"[104] and that "just as even a trifling amount of feces is foul-smelling, so too I do not praise even a trifling amount of existence."[105] To most of us, these are hardly glad tidings of great joy, and so long as the message sounds merely depressing to us, we'd better leave it aside. The

Figure 4: The Pyramid of the Paramis

purpose of the Dhamma is not to add to our woes, but to lighten our burdens. If the Teaching is true, the day must come when we will see that what looks so bleak to us now is really a message of hope and liberation, but it is up to us to decide when we feel ready to face its ultimate implications. It is in this context of readying oneself to the take the ultimate steps that the monastic option looms so large on the Buddhist horizon.[106]

The *Paramis* (or *Paramitas*) are the ten "cardinal" virtues in Theravadan Buddhism, the excellences or perfections that point the way towards liberation and buddhahood. Although each of the ten can be plausibly traced to the original teaching of the Buddha (so far as we can tell), they were not gathered together and turned into a conceptual tool until later. In the Vipassana context, *equanimity (upekkha)* is stressed especially,[107] but it is said that all ten qualities must eventually be perfected on the path of enlightenment — like jars (or Olympic swimming pools!) to be filled drop-by-drop with water.

For my own purposes, I have sometimes found it helpful to think of them as forming a pyramid (See Figure 4: The Pyramid of the Paramis) with *morality (sila)* at the foundation (a point untiringly stressed by Goenka).[108] In the next section, one's *commitment to truth (sacca)*,[109] *strong determination (adhittana)*, as well as *effort and energy (viriya)* express the will to enlightenment, which can be practiced, like morality, whether one is ready to begin doubting the self or not. *Wisdom (pañña), equanimity*, and *renunciation (nekkhamma)* in the next section appear like hinges to me that allow for self-making to be overcome, while *loving-kindness (metta), patience (khanti)*, and *selfless service and giving (dana)* mark the transcendence of self and put a shining top on the pyramid, as the Egyptians are said to have done when they first built their monuments to human vanity. But that is merely my ploy for remembering the ten and putting them in some conceptual order. For a more traditional and elaborate account, Ledi Sayadaw's *Manual of the Excellent Man* is a great resource so long as one is prepared to put up with a few Victorian rigors, including the title.

As a tool for taking stock, either to get encouragement or to identify weak spots, the Paramis make sense to me; but I am less fond of how they are more commonly used, namely as a kind of spiritual scorecard for tracking progress towards buddhahood over many lifetimes.[110] The Dhamma is about keeping our attention on the unique opportunity that a human birth affords all human beings, *in this lifetime*, right now.[111] Even if our different karmic pasts will affect how much use we are able to make of the opportunities presenting themselves, only Buddhas can see karmic trajectories clearly.[112] Instead of trying to tally our progress or quantifying our karmic obstacles, we should focus on the decisive fact that we are the masters of the present. Thus Goenka: "This is Vipassana: be masters of the present moment.[113]

ॐ

Of all the Buddha's doctrines, perhaps none has been as widely misunderstood as the teaching on **Kamma**, in part because no other has entered everyday speech to the same extent. When karma (the Sanskrit equivalent) is casually invoked, the intended meaning is usually that fate has caught up with someone. What can and will catch up with us, however, is not fate but the opposite, our own intentional actions — the volitional energy that shapes our actions and gives form to our states of mind.[114] "It is *volition* that I call kamma," the Buddha declared.[115] It is in this sense that beings are said to be "owners of their actions, heirs of their actions; they originate from their actions and are bound to their actions." But that is not all: they have "actions as their refuge" as well.[116] Our actions are like seeds we have scattered: they cannot be unsown, but they will sprout quickly or slowly, or not at all, depending on the soil and the water we give them with our present actions. It would be folly to imagine that we can simply evade the shadows of the past, but it would be equally mistaken to think that we must remain their prisoners. If the effect of past karma could not be modified by present action, liberation would be altogether impossible.[117] Thus the whole tendency of the Teaching is to stress how much power we hold as *masters of our present karma*, and if the lives of such Buddhist saints as Angulimala (a former serial killer who used to wear his victims' little fingers on a necklace around his neck[118]) or Kisagotami and Patacara (driven mad by loss and grief, as Goenka recounts in his discourses[119]) demonstrate anything, it is that even the most daunting karmic antecedents can be overcome.[120]

NOTES

1. SN 12:61 (p. 595), see below.

2. AN 4.45 (pp. 434-444); see also SN 2.26 (p. 158). "The taste of all the water in the ocean can be found in a single one of its drops." (*Vism.* XVI.60 [p. 513]) Thus also SN 35.116 (p. 1188): "I say that the end of the world cannot be known, seen, or reached by traveling. Yet I also say that without reaching the end of the world there is no making an end to suffering." On how the Buddha understood the origin and the end of the world, see immediately below and the question on Samsara in chapter 12.

3. See SN 12.65 (p. 602): "*Origination, origination* — thus in regard to things unheard before there arose in me vision, knowledge, wisdom, and light." Elsewhere, Bhikkhu Bodhi translates "*Arising, arising*" and the doctrine is also sometimes called *dependent or conditioned arising* in English, by Goenka for example (*Art of Living*, pp. 47-50). It is said throughout the Canon that the Four Noble Truths are the distinctive teaching of the Buddhas, but a direct connection between the two doctrines is made at AN 3:61 (p. 269).

4. MN 28.29 (p. 282); see also MN 26.19 (p. 260). At SN 12.41 (p. 579) attending closely and carefully to dependent origination is called "the noble method." When the Buddha summarizes the Dhamma for the wanderer Udayin (MN 79.7 [p. 655]), he uses the more general principle behind dependent origination: "When this exists, that comes to be; with the arising of this, that arises. When this does not exist, that does not come to be; with the cessation of this, that ceases." (See also MN 38.19,22 [pp. 355, 357].) The two formulations, general and specific, also appear side-by-side at the outset of the *Bodhi Sutta* (*Udana* 1.1-3 [Ireland, pp. 13-15]).

5. See *Gem Set in Gold*, pp. 43-44, *Art of Living*, pp. 49-50.

6. The ideas of the clock and of the triads (see below) are strictly my own illustrations; they have no traditional currency. The image of the clock would become very misleading if it were forgotten that its "hours" reflect only sequence, that the links in the chain are of very unequal durations in time, and that all occur so rapidly as to be nearly instantaneous (see footnote on the traditional expository method, below). Hence, when I use the image of a window opening for an hour or two below, I am not referring to any significant duration in time; I am only trying to explain an opportunity for practice with what may or may not be a helpful image.

7. Of course this requires *two* cycles on a twelve-hour clock, strictly speaking, so that aging and death occur between 23:01 and 0:00 on digital 24-hour time.

8. I find this traditional method of dissecting dependent origination unintuitive, unconvincing, and misleading, even for the purposes of exposition. My triads also identify phases, but these are more thematic than chronological: first comes the emergence of consciousness; second, physical manifestation; third, a brief opportunity for the cycle to be broken; last come the implications, renewed every moment (not just every lifetime), of keeping the wheel of suffering rotating. (That said, expository devices are a matter of taste: their value depends not so much on greater truth than on greater utility for helping us understand and remember.)

9. SN 35:28 (p. 1143 [BW 346]); see also *Dhp.* XI.1/146 and *Itivuttaka* 93 (Ireland, pp. 218-19). I will elaborate on the fire-imagery in the section on Nibbana, below.

10. In the narrower, volitional meaning, not in the sense that applies to all formation. See the box on the *sankharas* in chapter 6.

11. Thus the *Mahanidana Sutta* (DN 15), the longest and most detailed discourse on dependent origination, does not simply insist that consciousness is the condition for mentality-materiality (DN 15.3,21 [pp. 223, 226]), but immediately adds that mentality-materiality, once it has arisen, becomes the reciprocal condition for consciousness (DN 15.3,22 [pp. 223, 226]). Thus "the sphere of wisdom" opens up for us humans precisely in a state of being where consciousness and mentality-materiality always exist together (DN 15.22 [p. 226]). (See Bhikkhu Bodhi on the "reciprocal conditionality" or "essential interdependence" of the two ["the hidden vortex"] in the introduction to his translation of the *The Great Discourse on Causation: The Mahanidana Sutta and Its Commentaries* [Kandy: BPS 1995], pp. 18-22.)

12. For the chain of dependent origination (or conditioned arising) in forward order, see *Gem Set in Gold*, p. 43; in reverse order, p. 44. In the Canon, see SN 12.1-2 (pp. 533-536 [BW 353]).

13. One of U Ba Khin's favorite metaphors, but applied in my own way.

14. The point that craving is at the root of suffering and the impetus behind renewed existence was already emphasized by the Buddha in his first sermon, on the "Turning of the Wheel" (SN 56:11 [p. 1844 (BW 76)]). But clinging, too, is mentioned in the lines immediately preceding: an important consideration, as we shall see.

15. "The noblest victor is he who conquers himself." (*Dhp.* VIII.4-6/103-105, tr. Buddharakkhita) The idea is echoed in nearly identical terms by Jain: "Though a man should conquer thousands and thousands of valiant foes, greater will be his victory if he conquers nobody but himself." (*Uttaradhyayana Sutra* 9.34) Likewise Rumi: "The lion who breaks the enemy's ranks is a minor hero compared to the lion who overcomes himself." See also the Tao Te Ching, chapter 33, Proverbs 16:32, and Milton's *Paradise Regain'd*, book 2, lines 466-467: "He who reigns within himself and rules passions, desires, and fears, is more than a king."

16. *Tanha*, one might say with Walpola Rahula, is the great force that agitates the whole world (Rahula, p. 33). And not just our

world either: "Life in *any* world is incomplete, insatiate, the slave of craving." (MN 82.36 [p. 687], italics added)

Unlike *raga* and *lobha*, synonyms for craving and antonyms of aversion, the use of *tanha* implies the closest connection between the positive and negative aspects of craving: the negative, aversion, arises against unpleasant sensations only because pleasant ones are craved. Thus Goenka: "Craving is the mother of aversion." (*Satip. Discourses*, p. 30) The two reactions spring from the same source; they are merely two aspects of the same phenomenon.

17. The lines (*Dhp.* XI.8-9/153-154) appear under the first title in Goenka's *Gem Set in Gold*, pp. 45, 78, but they are sometimes translated under the other title as well (Acharya Buddharakkhita). The idea that they were the Buddha's first words after his enlightenment comes from the Commentaries.

18. See the box on equanimity at the outset of chapter 6. The observation of craving and aversion that has already arisen in the mind is not emphasized by Goenka, but some room is made for it in the practice of Satipatthana when it comes to *cittanupassana*, the observation of mind (*Satip. Discourses*, pp. 56-57, 61, 63).

19. Let me stress again that the clock is not about temporal duration, but only about illustrating a sequence. The contact-sensations-craving-clinging sequence occurs near-instantly, countless times in every moment, and to speak of hours would become terribly misleading if it were thought of in terms of keeping time.

20. Of course craving and clinging might be distinguished by saying that we crave when we reach for something new and that we cling when we try to hold on to it (see *Vism.* XVII.242 [p. 586], for example). But that distinction only captures the different external expressions of the same internal impulse of aggravated desire. The observation of either, to be objective and equanimous, would have to be of the energy behind the action, which seems practically indistinguishable to me in the two cases. (See also *Vism.* XVII.51 [p. 538], where clinging is defined in terms of craving.) If we look at the negative side, it seems even clearer that aversion is the opposite of craving as well as clinging. What remains is perhaps a distinction in the degrees of intensity. Hence it is fitting that "craving and clinging" so often appear in a joint phrase in the Suttas.

21. It's not my purpose to provide such justifications. The primacy of *vedana*-practice makes sense to me, both as a matter of theory and of personal experience in meditation. I merely think that the doctrine may leave room for other possibilities than the ones stressed by Goenka.

22. DN 15:30 (p. 227). Since the doctrine of dependent origination as a whole is presented at the Buddha's antidote to our inward confusions about the self (SN 12:20 [p. 552 (BW 355)]), the connection with other links to self-making might perhaps have been made by the Buddha as well. Yet in the *Mahanidana Sutta* the thought "I am" is identified exclusively with *vedana*.

23. MN 26.19 (p. 260).

24. DN 15.1 (p. 223), see also SN 12.60 (p. 594).

25. For another attempt at making sense of dependent origination intellectually, for what it's worth, see the question on Samsara in chapter 12.

26. *Pariyatti* (study) and *patipatti* (practice, meditation) are the commonly used terms, but they come from the Commentaries, not the Canon itself. (For Goenka's understanding of their relationship, see *Satip. Discourses*, pp. 2-3, 8-10.)

27. Bodhi, NEP, VIII.107.

28. SN 56:24 (p. 1854 [BW 359]). See the footnote on the Four Noble Truths in the box on yatha-bhuta.

29. Thus Bodhi: "The search for a spiritual path is born of suffering. It does not start with lights and ecstasy, but with the hard tacks of pain, disappointment, and confusion." (NEP I.1) Wisdom begins with perplexity, Socrates would agree: he is wisest, at least initially, who understands how little his wisdom is worth (Plato, *Apology*, 23). The perplexity of the Kalamas, too, is a most fitting starting point for exploring the Dhamma (AN 3.65 [p. 280 (BW 89)]).

30. AN 10.121 (p. 1503). See also SN 56.37 (p. 1861).

31. SN 56.35 (p. 1860).

32. MN 19.26 (p. 210 [BW 420]). At MN 45.6 (p. 407) we are told about someone who "by nature has strong lust" or struggles with a propensity to ill-will or ignorance. Such a meditator may be "[leading] the perfect and pure holy life" even while she is "in pain and grief, weeping with fearful face." Sometimes even the most wholesome spiritual practice can be like drinking "fermented urine mixed with various medicines" (MN 46.19 [p. 413]).

33. There is a strong logic, stressed by Goenka, to thinking of the Path as beginning with morality, progressing to concentration, and culminating in wisdom; but its components are best thought of not

as sequential steps, but as "intertwining strands of a single cable that requires the contribution of all the strands for maximum strength" (Bodhi, NEP, II.13).

34. On the possibility of starting the list not just with right view but with right thought as well, see my footnote on positive, non-judgmental thinking in the discussion of right thought below.

35. The range of what is considered "unprofitable talk" on a strict Buddhist understanding goes far beyond the precepts: "Talk of kings, robbers, ministers, armies, dangers, battles, food, drink, clothing, beds, garlands, perfumes, relatives, vehicles, villages, towns, cities, countries, women, heroes, streets, wells, the dead, trivialities, the origin of the world, the origin of the sea, whether things are so or are not so." (MN 122.12 [p. 974]. See also DN 1.1.17 [pp. 70-71] and SN 56.10 [p. 1843]) On the avoidance of disputatious talk, see SN 56.9 (p. 1842).

36. In the same spirit, the Buddha encouraged his son, Rahula, to "develop meditation that is like the earth ... like water ... like fire ... like air ... like space" (MN 62.13-17 [pp. 529-530]).

37. MN 21.10-19 (pp. 220-23). See also MN 28.8-9 (p. 279): "If others abuse, revile, scold, and harass a bhikkhu, he understands thus: 'This painful feeling born of ear-contact has arisen in me. That is dependent, not independent. Dependent on what? Dependent on contact.' Then he sees that contact is impermanent ... and his mind ... acquires confidence, steadiness, and resolution."

38. Discourse Day 8.

39. SN 7.2 (pp. 255-56).

40. A way to visualize the precepts that I have come up with, claiming no doctrinal orthodoxy (but see *Vism.* XIII.64 [p. 417]), is to think of them as arranged on a compass guarding the four directions from which moral danger might approach (See Figure 3: The Compass of Morality). (The missing precept against intoxication is more precisely a *training rule* enjoining abstinence from spirits and fermented drinks *that cause heedlessness and intemperate behavior.* In the conventional list of Ten Unprofitable Courses of Action, intoxicants do not appear; they are prohibited, in other words, not so much because of inebriation itself, but because of how they lower the threshold to transgression in the other moral directions. See also the questions on the precepts and on drugs in chapter 10.)

From the NORTH (Element of Fire) we are threatened by the impulse to kill and destroy, that is, by all forms of anger, aggression, and ill-will that lead to violence. (*Thanatos*, as Freud so aptly calls this force in *Civilization and Its Discontents*.)

From the WEST (Element of Earth) we are threatened by the impulse to steal and take what is not given, that is, by all forms of material greed and covetousness.

From the SOUTH (Element of Air) we are threatened by the impulse to lie, that is, by all forms of untruthfulness.

From the EAST (Element of Water), we are threatened by lustfulness, that is, by all forms of sensuous greed — Freud's *Eros* running wild.

And at CENTER of it all, the root of our trouble is ignorance or wrong view.

41. In an extended sense, the *Visuddhimagga* points out, fewness of wishes and contentment could also be included under right livelihood (*Vism*. XVI.86 [p. 519]). Acquisitiveness is considered a great root of suffering in Buddhism (MN 66.17 [p. 556]), and at least one young bhikkhu whom his father wished to lure back to family life with a pile of gold told his old man to "have this pile of gold coins and bullion loaded on carts and carried away to be dumped midstream in the river Ganges" (MN 82.22 [p. 683]).

42. DN 31.32 (p. 468 [BW 118]).

43. Ledi Sayadaw suggests that right view might be pictured as an arrow, right thought as the strength in the hand that pulls the bow (*The Noble Eightfold Path and Its Factors Explained* [BPS 1977, 1998] p. 67).

44. MN 19.6 (p. 208). Thus also Marcus Aurelius: "Such as are your habitual thoughts, such also will be the character of your mind; for the soul is dyed by the thoughts." (*Meditations* V.16)

45. The traditional pyramidal arrangement that crowns morality and concentration with right thought and right view at the top has its logic and merits: but one might with equal justification start with wisdom and begin the list with right view *and* right thought. Hence the *Mahacattarisaka Sutta* (The Great Forty) insists that "right view comes first" and is immediately followed by right thought (or right intention in some translations), with the other elements of the Path following suit (MN 117.3,4,34 [pp. 934, 938], see also *Art of Living*, pp. 134-135).

46. MN 20 (pp. 211-14).

47. *Itivuttaka* 87 (Ireland, p. 212).

48. A danger discussed, at least in passing, not only in Goenka's Ten-Day Discourses, but also in his talk on "The Art of Living" that is used as an introduction to Vipassana on the worldwide Dhamma. org website.

49. During Ayahuasca-ceremonies, where the mind unleashes comparable but even more violent tempests, thoughts can come to feel like chunks of glowing metal in a furnace, ready to burn you to the bone if you get too close to them.

50. *Dhp.* XIV.5/183 (*Gem Set in Gold*, p. 77).

51. Goenka introduces the Three Characteristics as the three aspects of wisdom in his first presentation on pañña in the Day 3 Discourse.

52. See *Dhp.* XX.5-7/277-279. I will be capitalizing the Pali for emphasis.

53. VRI, Vedana, p. xii: "The Buddha always stressed the importance of *anicca* because the realization of the other two [characteristics] will easily follow when we experience deeply the characteristic of impermanence." See below.

54. U Ba Khin also liked to speak of "*activating* anicca" (*U Ba Khin Journal*, p. 34, *Clock of Vipassana*, p. 98).

55. U Ba Khin, "The Essentials of Buddha-Dhamma in Meditative Practice," in *U Ba Khin Journal*, pp. 33-34 and *Clock of Vipassana*, pp. 117-118. Thus also Fleischman: "Anicca is what we run from; anicca is what we fear... Anicca is what drives the world mad. But the *experience* of anicca ... is a release, like a dip in a healing, cool, fresh river. Now I am washed away by the river; after so much fussing, I am carried along, alone in the current. But I can swim, or rather, float... The living ride on life like foam on the crest of a surge in the cosmic ocean." (*Karma and Chaos*, p. 91)

56. It should be clear that insight into *Anicca* is not just a Theravadan specialty, let alone the exclusive property of Vipassana practice as taught by Captain Goenka. Thus Suzuki: "The everything changes is the basic truth of existence. No one can deny this truth and all the teaching of Buddhism is condensed within it... When we realize the everlasting truth of 'everything changes' and find our composure in it, we find ourselves in Nibbana." (*Zen Mind, Beginner's Mind*, p. 91)

57. AN 9.20 (pp. 1276-77 [BW 178-79], condensed and edited).

58. Evident suffering is aptly called *dukkha-dukkha* in Pali, but

there are many more forms, crude or subtle, direct or indirect, exposed or concealed (see *Vism.* XVI.34 [p. 505]). Dukkha need not be experienced as acute dissatisfaction, but may take the more fundamental form of that chronic, if often latent, sense of unease and insecurity which Thomas Hobbes identified as the mark of our condition: "There is no such thing as perpetual tranquility, while we live here; because life itself is but motion, and can never be without desire, nor without fear, any more than without sense." (*Leviathan* VI.58) Thus Bodhi speaks of "that insecurity which is the deepest meaning of *dukkha*" (NEP, I.8). See also the "four summaries of the Dhamma" at MN 82.36 (p. 686-687): "Life in any world is unstable; it is swept away... Life has no shelter and no protection ... [Before long] one has to leave it all and pass on... Life in any world is incomplete, insatiate, the slave of craving." What Nibbana offers, by contrast, is precisely "supreme security" (MN 26.12 [p. 255]).

59. DN 9.34 (p. 166). Thus also Goenka: "We certainly do not wish to say that in life there is only *Dukkha* and not a vestige of any pleasure. But are the pleasures of the senses really something that can be called happiness? Does not that glitter of happiness contain within it the shadow of pain?" (*Clock of Vipassana*, pp. 164-165)

60. DN 16.3.48 (p. 252).

61. DN 16.6.7. In other words, "Meditate, do not be negligent, lest you regret it later. That is my instruction to you." (SN 43:1 [p. 1372 (BW 365)])

T.W. Rhys Davids's translation has been made famous by T.S. Elliott's *Waste Land*: "Work out your salvation with diligence." Sister Vajira and Francis Story translate "Strive with earnestness!" Bhikkhu Nanamoli has "Attain perfection through diligence," Maurice Walshe "Strive on untiringly."

The idea that everyone must make his own effort and that even Buddhas can only show the way could hardly be more central to the Teaching (*Dhp.* XX.4/276, *Gem Set in Gold*, p. 77). See also SN 45.139 (p. 1550): "Whatever wholesome states there are, they are all rooted in diligence." Goenka calls Vipassana "workism" in one of his discourses ("story is story: another boy goes to buy oil and falls down": see *Art of Living*, p. 131) and keeps exhorting students to "work, work, continue to work" throughout the course. Burmese Buddhism tends to be more relaxed ("May you reach Nibbana the quick and easy way" gets used as a salutation there), and I've heard it said that Goenka's tone is meant to counter that cultural tendency. It must also owe something to the example of U Ba Khin, who was said to be exceedingly strict and demanding even by the students who loved him most.

62. SN 22.102 (p. 961-962).

63. One of the Buddha's images for no-self was that of a banana tree whose layers are unrolled one by one without containing any core, any heartwood (see SN 22:95 [pp. 951-52 (BW 344)] and SN 35: 234 [p. 1233 (BW 348)]; also *Vism.* XX.16 [p. 631]).

If one pictures the eight aspects of the path to liberation as a wheel with eight spokes, one might discover *Anatta* in the hole at the center, the emptiness around which the wheel revolves. This fits well with an etymology for *Anicca* mentioned in one of Joseph Goldstein's talks: a "bad axle hole," that is, failure to understand *Anatta*, makes for a rough ride through life.

64. Nyanaponika Thera speaks of "the exhilaration of relief felt when the right, vice-like grip of 'I' and 'Mine' loosens; when the tension it produces in body and mind is relaxed; when we can lift, for a while, our heads above the fierce current and whirl in which the obsessions of 'I' and 'Mine' engulf us." (*Heart of Buddhist Meditation*, p. 52) Eventually the mind-body phenomenon will seem like a marionette or a doll that one looks after with zest and good will, but without clinging (*Heart*, p. 64, Dhp. *Vism.* XVIII.31 [p. 613-14]). The body ravaged by old age is compared to a once-charming "puppet" at SN 48.41 (p. 1687).

65. SN 12:61 (p. 595). Hence the common expression "monkey-mind." A related image is that of our thoughts thrashing "like a fish taken from his watery home and thrown on the dry ground" (*Dhp.* III.2/34, tr. Babbitt). See also SN 35.127 (pp. 1197): "The mind is wanton."

66. AN 1.48 (p. 97). It is the lightning speed of our mental processes that sustains the illusion of self: like a "whirling firebrand" that appears as a circle in the dark (*Vism.* XX.104 [p. 656]) or like a reel of film that gives the impression of continuous movement because it is played too quickly for our eyes to discern the several frames.

67. SN 35:234 (pp. 1232-33 [BW 348]). At MN 38.1-7 (pp. 349-351) a bhikkhu is reprimanded for the "pernicious view" that consciousness persists. It does not, but rather arises anew in dependence on conditions from moment to moment. To be precise, it is not one, but six parallel consciousnesses that give the illusion of unity: five connected to the senses, one to the mind (MN 38.8 [p. 351]). On the six distinct consciousnesses, see also *Satip. Discourses*, p. 88.

68. The trap described at SN 47.7 (p. 1633-34) is less clever than the African version, but the story is more or less the same. The African

trap places some desirable object in an opening just wide enough for a monkey's hand; so long as she is clutching the object, the monkey cannot free herself, but she will not usually give it up even when she sees the hunters coming for her.

69. Are we born with this clinging, one might ask, or do we acquire it by learning? The Suttas answer that infants do not have any notion of identity yet, but that the underlying tendency to develop one is strong within them (MN 64.3 [p. 537], see also MN 78.8 [p. 649]). Presumably no child could survive for long without it, nor can birth occur, according to the Buddhist conception of Samsara, without a strong disposition to craving and clinging. (See also the question on having children in chapter 12.)

70. SN 22.99 (p. 957).

71. SN 12:20 (p. 552 [BW 354-55]). See also MN 2.7 (p. 92) and MN 38.23 (p. 357).

72. SN 12:20 (p. 552 [BW 355]).

73. A very common, very old problem: see the story of Dhammadinna and the elephant, *Vism.* XX.111-113 (pp. 657-58).

74. *Udana* 1.10 (Ireland, pp. 19-22). He walked some 700 miles: from Suparapattam, near present-day Mumbai, all the way to Savatthi in northern India (see Ireland, pp. 119-20, *Satip. Discourses*, p. 33).

75. I am giving a very free rendition here. See *Udana* 1.10 (Ireland, p. 21); *Art of Living*, pp. 116-117; *Satip. Discourses*, p. 34. Also Rahula, pp. 26, 42: "Thought itself is the thinker... In the same way it is wisdom that realizes. There is no other self behind the realization."

76. *Milinda* I.1 (pp. 28-31). See *Vism.* XVIII.25-28 (pp. 612-13). Also *Satip. Discourses*, p. 67. The ancient Athenians preserved the ship that had once brought home Theseus from Crete by replacing its decayed planks one by one until none of the original wood remained. Whether the vessel was still the same or not was a question that divided the ancient philosophers even then (Plutarch, Life of Theseus, 23.1).

77. DN 9.52-53 (p. 169).

78. *Milinda* II.1 (p. 40). See the *Visuddhimagga*: "With a stream of continuity there is neither identity nor otherness. For if there were absolute identity in a stream of continuity, there would be no forming of curd from milk. And yet if there were absolute otherness, the curd would not be derived from the milk... And if [we could not speak

of identity at all] there would be an end to all worldly usage, which is hardly desirable." (*Vism.* XVII.167 [p. 568]; see also MN 139.12 [p. 1084] on respecting normal usage.) Thus also Nyanaponika Thera: "[T]hough there is no identity between successive states of consciousness, there is also no complete diversity since some factors and groups always overlap... [C]hange always involves two complementary aspects, dissolution and connection, which are like two faces turned in opposite directions." (*Abhidhamma Studies*, pp. 44-45) A famous fragment from Heraclitus (ca. 535–475 BCE) reads: "We both step and do not step into the same river. We are and are not." (Diels-Kranz 91) No fragments have been found with the idea that "all is in flux (*panta rhei*)," for which Heraclitus is most famous, but Diogenes Laertius quotes him saying that "everything flows like a river" (*Lives and Opinions of Eminent Philosophers*, book IX, section 6 of the entry on Heraclitus).

79. Thus DN 9.53 (p. 169): "These are merely names, expressions, turns of speech, designations in common use in the world, which the Tathagata uses without misapprehending them."

80. *Treatise of Human Nature* (I.iv.6).

81. The two are finally found to go together: the moment *Anatta* is revealed in its full profundity, it is said, one has arrived at stream-entry, the point from which the reality that lies beyond all sentient existence, *Nibbana*, becomes visible and progress irreversible. (Even to use the word "beyond" is problematic: Nibbana is not a state or a realm or the result of anything; it simply *is* in an ultimate way that defies our language and our concepts. See Rahula, pp. 40-41.)

82. Nyanaponika Thera speaks of "fluency exercises" by which we refine our concepts and mental habits in a gradual change of outlook from the viewpoint of "self" to that of "no-self" (*Abhidhamma Studies*, pp. 9-10). Thus also *Vision*, p. 27: "Just as, according to similes given by the Buddha, the handle of a hatchet is wasted away by constant use; just as the strongest ship-ropes will become brittle by constant exposure to wind, sun, and rain and finally fall asunder — so will constant acts of giving up, of letting go, wear thin and fragile the once so stout and unbreakable fetters of craving and ignorance, until one day they drop off completely." (For the similes, see SN 22.101 [p. 961].)

83. It is nonetheless a common experience in Anapana meditation for the sense of self to dissolve temporarily when one becomes sufficiently absorbed in observing the breath. Sustained meditation on the sensations, as taught during a Ten-Day course, will

demonstrate sooner or later how much the construction of our selves depends on identifying with our sensations and claiming them as our own, as well as how high a price we pay for that habitual turn of mind. That the idea of self could not arise without such sensations is emphasized at DN 16:30 (p. 227), as I pointed out above.

84. SN 22:89 (p. 945 [BW 405]). A slightly modernized version of the image. In the Buddha's day, the residual smell of "cleaning salt, lye, or cow dung" would have been more obviously displeasing.

85. SN 35:85 (pp. 1163-64 [BW 347]). At SN 55.53 (pp. 1833-34) we are told about "discourses by the Tathagata that are deep in meaning, supramundane, dealing with emptiness," but the term does not have the centrality it later acquired in the Mahayana traditions.

86. *Vism.* XVI.90 (p. 521) and XIX.20 (p. 622), combining Bh. Nanamoli's and Nyanatiloka Thera's translation in his *Buddha's Path*, pp. 168, 180 (italics added). When the Buddha was asked *who* is feeling and craving, *who* exists and ages and dies, and so on, he answered, "Not a valid question." (SN 12.12 [pp. 541-542], 12.35 [pp. 573-574]) The idea that the consequences of one's actions might be evaded if there is no self occurred to some students even in the Buddha's time and was firmly rejected as an attempt to "outstrip the Teacher's Dispensation" by spurious reasoning (MN 109.14 [p. 890]).

87. *Diamond Sutra*, Section 32, translated by A. F. Price and Wong Mou-Lam. The Pali Canon contains some similar images in the *Dhammapada* (XIII.3/170) and at SN 22.95 (pp. 951-953 [BW 343-345]). The world as a whole is not likened to a dream in the Theravadan tradition, but sensual pleasures certainly are (MN 54.19 [p. 471]).

88. *Diamond Sutra,* Section 21, translated by Thich Nhat Hanh (*The Diamond that Cuts through Illusion*, Parallax 2010, p. 24).

89. *Diamond Sutra,* Section 22, translated by Mu Soeng (*The Diamond Sutra*, Wisdom 2000, p. 129).

90. Thomas Hobbes, *Leviathan*, 5.20. "Words are wise men's counters," but how easy it is to get entangled in them Hobbes understood as well as the Buddha (*Leviathan* IV.12-13).

91. Although language can still offer approximations. Thus the *Abhidhamma* may be understood as an effort to develop a more strictly accurate vocabulary from the ultimate standpoint (*paramattha*) that does without conventional concepts such as the self (*Abhidhamma Studies*, pp. 3, 5, 15).

92. Zen Buddhists cherish a story that is not recognized as authentic by the Theravadans, recounted in the so-called Flower Sermon. Towards the end of his life, the Buddha assembled a small circle of followers, pulled up a lotus flower from a pond and presented it to his disciples, who did their best to expound upon the meaning of the plant dripping mud and water. Mahakassapa only smiled and began to laugh. The Buddha smiled, too: "What can be said I have said to you," he told his followers, "and what cannot be said, I have given to Mahakassapa." Thus also the final, seventh proposition in Wittgenstein's *Tractatus Logico-Philosophicus*, "Whereof one cannot speak, thereof one must be silent."

93. SN 35:28 (p. 1143 [BW 346]), *Dhp.* XI.1/146, *Itivuttaka* 93 (Ireland, pp. 218-219).

94. SN 35:26 (p. 1141 [BW 345]).

95. Fully to understand the Five Aggregates is to understand dependent origination, which governs their arising and passing away (SN 22:56 [p. 895 (BW 335)]). Likewise the Four Noble Truths cannot be separated from the other two doctrines, because what arises is only *Anicca arising* (SN 12:15 [p. 544 (BW 357)]). Thus Ledi Sayadaw: "Any wrong view can be dispelled by a knowledge of dependent origination. One is liable to fall into a false view only due to lack of this knowledge... One who has [also] gained insight into ... the Five Aggregates is a Buddhist of the higher attainment... One is a true Buddhist, however, only when one has realized the Four Noble Truths." (*Manual of the Excellent Man*, p. 98)

96. I will try to explain (for what it is worth) how this interaction shapes the different worlds and realms that Buddhism posits in the question on the gods in chapter 12.

97. In the Buddhist conception, the mind should not be identified only with the brain; the whole body contains the mind (*Art of Living*, pp. 29, 128).

The first aspect of mind, consciousness (*viññana*) simply registers the raw data of experience. All evaluation, judgment, and categorization on the basis of past experience is supplied by the second aspect, perception (*sañña*). Sensation (*vedana*) provides the emotional texture of mental life, and reaction (*sankhara*) is what perpetuates consciousness and existence, as we have seen in the discussion of dependent origination (*Art of Living*, pp. 26-27).

Our mental processes look problematic and unreliable by the Buddhist analysis because all new experiences are evaluated (*sañña*) in light of past reactions (*sankhara*): thus ignorance multiplies reaction, and reaction in turn keeps feeding and perpetuating ignorance. (See *Satip. Discourses*, p. 98. The multifaceted role of our reactions is explained particularly well at *Art of Living*, pp. 106-107. Note that in the chain of dependent origination, reaction appears several times, as we have seen: at the second link *(sankhara)*, at the eight *(tanha)*, and arguably at the ninth as well, if clinging *(upadana)* were to be counted separately.)

98. MN 24.9-10 (p. 242).

99. *Udana* 8.3 (Ireland, p. 103; BW 366).

100. Bhikkhu Bodhi, "Nibbana," 1981 Lectures. See SN 34.241 (p. 1242), SN 45.97-102 (p. 1549).

101. AN 8:54 (pp. 1194-1197 [BW 124-26]); AN 4:55 (pp. 445-46 [BW 121-22]), AN 4:61-62 (pp. 449-453); SN 55.7 (pp. 1796-99). See also DN 31.30 (p. 467 [BW 117]) on how husbands and wives should treat each other.

102. *Sutta Nipata* 2.4 (Goenka, *Gem Set in Gold*, pp. 56-57).

103. SN 12:15 (p. 544 [BW 357]).

104. The Buddha's discourse on "The Root of All Things" (MN 1) is his definitive treatment of the dangers of delight, especially MN 1.3-26 (pp. 83-87) and MN 1.171 (p. 89), where the quoted line appears. So severe are many of the Buddha's pronouncements about fostering detachment, disillusion, and even disgust that he can sound like the worst of spiritual killjoys. Right after my first Ten-Day course, I read the *Dhammapada* and was haunted for years by a verse in the chapter on Flowers: "Death carries off a man who is gathering flowers and whose mind is distracted, as a flood carries off a sleeping village." (*Dhp.* IV.4/47) But the Path is meant to be walked joyfully: there is nothing wrong with enjoying the beauty of flowers. As the *Dhammapada* points out right after (IV.6/49), the bee collects its nectar without doing harm —but *picking* flowers (likely with the same sexual connotations in the Buddha's world as in other literatures) hints at our hunger to appropriate and the disregard for what might become of the flowers after their stalks have been cut or broken. The danger lies in how vainly and inattentively we seek happiness where it cannot be found, led around the nose by our thirsty senses and maddened by our blind passion for pleasure.

105. AN 1.328 (p. 121). Thus also MN 49.27 (p. 428, italics added): "Having seen the fear in being ... *I [do] not welcome any kind of being,* nor [do] I cling to *delight.*" And *Udana* 3.10 (Ireland, pp. 48-49):

"The world is afflicted by being, yet delights in being. But what it delights in brings fear, and what it fears is suffering. This holy life is lived in order to abandon being."

No matter how uncomfortable it is for us, we need to recognize that the Path is ultimately about letting go even of the subtle ties that bind us to existence: "The entire course of practice from start to finish can be seen as an evolving process of renunciation culminating in Nibbana as the ultimate stage of relinquishment, 'the relinquishment of all foundations of existence.'" (Bodhi, NEP, III.36)

106. But it should never be taken as a call directed at everyone. The monastic life, especially in its more withdrawn forms, can easily "dull and depress" those who are not cut out for it and become an impediment rather than a inspiration for further spiritual and intellectual development (Rahula, p. 76).

107. Ledi Sayadaw called it "the mainstay of the other perfections" (*Manual of the Excellent Man*, p. 11).

108. See his discourses and *Art of Living*, pp. 58, 63, 67. Also Rahula, p. 47: "No spiritual development is possible without [the indispensable foundation of moral conduct]." "The very starting point of wholesome states," the Buddha says at SN 47.3 (p. 1629), is "virtue that is well-purified and view that is straight... [B]ased upon virtue, established upon virtue, you should develop the four establishments of mindfulness." In the *Dhammapada* it is said that "the fragrance of the good travels even against the wind" and that they "shine from afar, like the peaks of the Himalayas" (*Dhp.* IV.11/54, XXI.15/304).

109. *Truthfulness* as a perfection is a mode of being that begins with avoiding all lies, but goes much further. See MN 110 and 113 on the contrast between true and untrue living in this comprehensive sense.

110. In serving this function, the Paramis are usually intertwined with the Jakata tales, so it is perhaps fitting that I have never warmed to either.

111. In fairness to Goenka, he does emphasize in his courses that there is "every chance" that any practitioner of Vipassana might reach the "final goal." Thus also *Art of Living*, pp. 14, 16, and 124 (my italics): "Whatever [the Buddha] achieved is within the grasp of *any* human being that works as he did... *[A]nyone* who walks on the path is bound to become a noble-hearted, saintly person... [Liberation] must come to *all* who practice Dhamma correctly." See

also Rahula, p. 1: "Everyone has within himself the potentiality of becoming a Buddha, if he so wills it and endeavors." The logic of the paramis doesn't quite deny this universal human potential, but it points in a different direction, namely towards distinguishing the prospects of those who bring more developed qualities from those who do not. I don't deny that there may (or perhaps even must) be such distinctions; I'm just not interested in dwelling on them in my practice. We do enough of that kind of thing in other departments of life.

112. Only a Buddha can make reliable judgments of a person's spiritual development, see AN 6.44 (pp. 911-914).

113. Day 8 Discourse.

114. The contrary view ("There is no kamma, no deed, no energy") was rejected by the Buddha as "the worst among the doctrines of the various ascetics" — "a hair blanket [that] is cold in the winter, hot in the summer, ugly, foul-smelling, and uncomfortable." (AN 3.137 [p. 364])

115. AN 6:63 (p. 963). See also SN 12.38 (p. 576): "What one intends, and what one plans, and whatever one has a tendency towards: that becomes a basis for the maintenance of consciousness." Action that is completely free of ignorance and reactiveness no longer generates kamma. Hence SN 46.26 (p. 1586): "With the destruction of craving comes the destruction of kamma; with the destruction of kamma comes the destruction of suffering."

116. MN 135.4 (p. 1053 [BW 162]) and elsewhere.

117. See Nyanaponika's essay on "Kamma and Its Fruit" in *Vision*, pp. 310-317.

118. Before he became a killer, Angulimala was a model student and his teacher's favorite at the famous university of Takkasila. Out of envy and resentment, the other pupils plotted against him and were able to sow such suspicion and fear in their teacher's mind that he told Angulimala to go away and not to come back until he had collected a little finger from a thousand human beings. Angulimala never paused to consider the possibility of gathering the fingers from the land's open charnel grounds, but proceeded to the slaughter, which ended only on the eve of his thousandth murder, when the Buddha engaged him in a famous show-down. Angulimala kept chasing him, but was unable to catch up. "Stop, recluse!" he finally shouted in frustration. "I have stopped, Angulimala, you stop too," the Buddha answered and managed to awaken the killer from his

murderous nightmare (see MN 86.5 [p. 711] with Note 820 on p. 1292; also *Greatest Disciples*, pp. 319-330).

119. Kisagotami is the mother who cannot accept the death of her infant son and is told to ask for a few mustard seeds (sesame in Goenka's version) from a house where nobody has died (*Greatest Disciples*, pp. 273-276). Patacara is the woman who runs naked in the streets of Savatthi after losing her husband to a snake-bite, her two small sons to accidents during a river-crossing, and her parents and brother to the collapse of their house (*Greatest Disciples*, pp. 294-95).

120. A point also made by Goenka, *For the Benefit of Many*, p. 122.

CHAPTER EIGHT
TICKLISH QUESTIONS DURING A COURSE

What's Goenka's story, and why do many of his students call him *Goenkaji*?

S.N. Goenka was an Indo-Burmese businessman who grew up in Rangoon at a time when half the city's population was still ethnically Indian.[1] His "staunchly conservative Hindu family" was wealthy (textiles),[2] but he was also very successful in his own right by his mid-twenties. When he began to suffer from severe migraine headaches, doctors around the world could only treat his affliction with morphine injections and he was afraid of getting addicted. In 1955, at the suggestion of a friend, he agreed to take a ten-day Vipassana course with Sayagyi U Ba Khin, a high-ranking official in the democratic government of newly-independent Burma. Although Goenka was persuaded to take the course as a "high spiritual path" only, not as a cure for his headaches, they did go away.

After fourteen years of volunteering and training at his teacher's International Meditation Centre in Rangoon, Goenka went to India in 1969 with U Ba Khin's blessings in order to reintroduce Vipassana in the land of its origins, starting with a course for his parents, who had moved there at a time of drastic socialist experimentation in Burma. In 1976 he opened his first meditation center, Dhamma Giri at Igatpuri, a hill station in the Western Ghats, 120 km north-east of Mumbai. Today there are over a hundred permanent Vipassana centers all around the world, and many more sites where occasional courses are held. Goenka died in September 2013.

Goenkaji (like the more generic *Guruji*) is an Indian way to express affection and respect, meaning roughly "our dear and esteemed teacher Goenka." If it sounds unduly ingratiating to you, as it easily can to Western earns, you are under no obligation to use it. The best way to pay one's respects to a teacher is to walk the Path he has marked out.

Goenka pokes fun at the idea that he might be a Great Guru from India who might enjoy his students putting on a Hare-Goenka dance for him.[3] Yet he does seem to inspire a devotion that borders on the cultish. Have you ever wondered whether you might have inadvertently joined a sect?
The thought has occurred to me more than once. Whenever it starts bothering me again, I remind myself of a few basic but reassuring tests. Does anyone in the organization stand to gain materially, especially financially or carnally? No. Is the organization secretive about anything? No. Are students encouraged to distance themselves from friends or family members? No. Is exit more difficult than entry? No. Is any kind of pressure exerted on students outside of the courses? No. That's all pretty good, I would say, and not very compatible with a sect in the alarming sense of the word.

Having spent practically my entire life as either a student or a teacher, I have my own strong ideas about how the relationship should ideally look, and I've never thought, whatever side I was on, that undue deference of students to their teachers was a good idea. In fairness to Goenka, he never did encourage the more cultish kind of devotion; at the outset of the Twenty-Day courses, for instance, the first discourse is a reminder that serious students are expected to become their own teachers.[4] On the other hand, there is no denying the strong tendency among many of Goenka's students to put him on a pedestal, just as there has always been a tendency to move from showing one's respect for the Buddha by walking the Path towards worshiping him in more devotional ways. Goenka stresses that the proper, the purest way to reverence a teacher is to practice his teaching, thus: "*Imaya dhammanudhammapatipattiya, buddham pujemi.*" (I pay respect to the Buddha by walking on the Path of Dhamma from the first step to the final goal [*Gem Set in Gold*, 79].[5]) Beware Goenka and the Buddha, one might adapt a line from Nietzsche's *Zarathustra*, lest a statue slay you.[6] Or as a Zen master would say, "When you meet the Buddha on the road, kill him."[7]

Why should I take refuge in anything other than the Dhamma? Why take refuge in a mere human being, even the Buddha, or in a fallible human institution like the Sangha, to say nothing of "total surrender" to Goenka and his teachers?
Valid concerns, no doubt, but also the kinds of questions that can give you sleepless nights at Vipassana camp if you get too entangled in them.

Taking refuge is not meant to put you in a quandary of conscience, but to give you confidence, to make you feel protected, inspired, and encouraged. If the traditional formula feels like an imposition to you, or even like a burden, then better to subscribe only to the parts that you are comfortable with. (Paying lip-service to the opening formalities because it is expected does not commit you to anything: only the sincere assent of your heart can do that.)

To take refuge in the Dhamma is to take refuge in the natural law and order of things, of which you too are an expression. So you are not only taking refuge in the technique you are about to learn, but more fundamentally in your own true nature. "*Atta-sarana, ananna-sarana*": make yourself your refuge, there is no other.[8] Whenever devout Christians expressed unease about taking refuge in the Buddha, U Ba Khin would let them take refuge in Jesus Christ instead, with the understanding that the refuge taken was not in any person, but in the qualities of enlightenment that he represents.[9] For someone who subscribes without reservation to the Dhamma, it will soon become difficult to see any distinction between the Buddha and his Teaching,[10] but so long as the Buddha seems a stranger to you, there is no need to force anything. (Remember that the Sangha in which one takes refuge is not the established monkhood today, but the *Ariya-Sangha,* the timeless community of the saints, and thus an expression of your own potential to walk in their footsteps and join them eventually.)

The terms in which the Ten-Day course presents the need for "complete surrender" to your teachers seem a little stark to me, and the North American application procedure tones it down, as I have mentioned above. To surrender your critical faculties in an act of blind submission would be against the Dhamma, so just take from Goenka and his teachers what help and support you can get. As soon as you are established in the technique, the process of becoming your own teacher will commence. Let's bring in a bit of Suzuki's Zen, "The moment you meet a teacher, you should leave the teacher, and you should be independent. You have a teacher for yourself, not for the teacher."[11] The worst that can be said of Goenka's crew is that they can be a little narrow in their outlook; but they are there to help you, nothing else. You don't need to marry them.

If you quit a course over this kind of concern, legitimate and even principled as it may seem, you are losing out on the practical benefits you may get from the technique. You should always feel free to raise issues that are troubling you, but don't let them get in the way of giving the technique a fair trial. That is all Goenka and his teachers ask, for your own benefit. After the ten days, you've got the rest of your life to figure out how you feel about Goenka Airlines. The Buddha doesn't need you to sign your name on the dotted line. Pencil it in if you feel like it, or leave it blank if you don't.

My religious beliefs are more than "rites and rituals" to me and I am put off by how Goenka speaks of them. If the Dhamma is as universal as he claims it is, how can he be so disrespectful?

Goenka devotes much of his discourse on Day 7 to questions of faith and what he says can grate on religiously sensitive ears. But if you listen carefully, you will notice that it is all said in the context of what essential *friends* faith and devotion are on the Path, provided they are not blind. Remember that Goenka used to be a staunch Hindu himself ("I've passed through that game") and that much of what he is saying is meant to help students come to appreciate the Dhamma as he did through his own teacher's guidance. The troubles of Indian sectarianism are also never far from Goenka's mind.

Serious followers of all major religions practice Vipassana and insist that it has greatly strengthened their faith and devotion,[12] but it would be disingenuous to pretend that there are no tensions at all between the two. Other commentators, like Walpola Rahula for example, also stress that traditional customs and religious ceremonies "have little to do with the real Path," however beautiful they may be; but Rahula makes explicit, as Goenka does not, that the satisfaction they give to religious emotions gives them their own kind of value.[13] From the high peaks of Vipassana practice, any reliance on rites and rituals can look like a spiritual fetter that becomes irrelevant upon stream-entry. Nor was the Buddha especially friendly towards the religions of his day, though he can't be called their enemy either. Thus he taught that the gods do exist, but that all their powers are inferior to the might of fully developed human wisdom (his own). The idea that there is a single creator-god he flatly rejected. And the priests who rely on tradition for spiritual authority he compared to a file of blind men leading each other and everyone else astray.[14] About the all-encompassing reality that surpasses all understanding, Nibbana, nothing positive can be said in the Buddhist understanding.[15] Thus when Goenka speaks of "entanglement" in organized religion, he is issuing a serious challenge — not perhaps to religion at its most essential, but certainly to how it is usually lived in the world.[16]

I've heard Buddhism called a religion and a philosophy, but many serious students of the Buddha's Teaching, Goenka included, don't seem comfortable with those terms. Why not?
When Goenka insists that he is not teaching Buddhism, nor any kind of religion, nor a philosophy, he is trying to avoid creating contention over mere labels. The Dhamma is meant to identify universal features of life that are accessible to our personal experience, not to feed our instinct for drawing lines and dividing into rival camps. The Buddha's position on devotion and the gods is subtle and complex enough that his Teaching should not be called a religion without careful qualifications. Although it values human sagacity very highly, it is equally insistent in its warnings against the tangle that results from relying too much on intellectual categories and distinctions. I like Goenka's strategy for sidestepping the morass of sectarianism by thinking of the Dhamma as an art of living (or perhaps a *therapy* in the original sense[17]), so long as we are honest and forthright about the philosophical and religious implications of what the Buddha taught — recognizing and frankly acknowledging contentious points without allowing ourselves to be drawn into disputatiousness over them.[18]

In one of his discourses, Goenka tells the story of how U Ba Khin, who is supposed to have been such an admirable person, made the walls of his center tremble with his shouting. What's saintly about screaming at a student? No thanks!
It's not my favorite story either,[19] but it touches on one of the most fundamental and intractable ethical issues of all: what means we may use in the service of what ends. Even Machiavelli, whose name has become synonymous with a cavalier approach to means supposedly justified by ends, in fact never used so crude

a phrase and was intent on making rulers more discriminating in the use of violence and cruelty.[20] How much more so the Buddha who warns us so insistently about the dangers of ill-will, for whom to be "victorious" in conflict is mainly to make new and fiercer enemies, and who would have us refrain from doing avoidable harm even to seeds and plants![21]

Yet the Buddha was quite aware that being compassionate might sometimes mean having to take very drastic action. Thus the *Majjhima Nikaya* recounts an exchange between the Buddha and Prince Abhaya when there was an infant crawling around on the latter's lap. "What would you do," the Buddha asked, "if while you or your nurse were not attending to him, this child were to put a stick or a pebble in his mouth?" The prince answered that he would take the stick or pebble out, *even if it meant drawing blood*, "because I have compassion for the child."[22] The Buddha was only making an analogy with unwholesome speech that people were putting in their mouths and that it was his task to remove, but he let the prince's answer stand. Surely we can all imagine situations, public and private, when we may need to take severe action, for compassion's sake, even if it meets with fierce resistance.[23] There may even times when we might become guilty of "implicit violence" by failing to intervene in the name of non-violence.[24]

How much can be done to prevent violence, even war, by the use of skillful means,[25] the Buddha demonstrated when a king brought him news of his plans to attack a neighbor. Instead of remonstrating with the king or even addressing his ministers directly, the Buddha reviewed the strengths of the intended victims in the ambassador's presence.[26] When word got back to the king, his plans were quietly shelved. But we also need to be realistic about what can be accomplished once conflicts have been brought to the brink of bloodshed, and there were many bitter and bloody clashes that the Buddha was not able to prevent, including the destruction of his own people, the Sakyans, by a neighboring king they had enraged.[27] Rather than having us focus only on the extreme of open violence, as so much law enforcement and diplomacy does, the Buddhist practice would draw our attention to the seeds and roots of aggression we all carry within us.[28] A line from the New Testament's Book of James (4:1) could have come straight from the Buddha's mouth: "What is the source of the wars and fights among you? Don't they come from the cravings that are at war within you?"

Severe teachers may not be the most endearing, but perhaps we need to make allowances in a world that owes the very word *jeremiad* to a prophet. Another, the eater of locusts who baptized the supposed Savior, did so between tirades against a generation of vipers that he gleefully consigned to the fire like so much barren lumber.[29] Meanwhile the alleged Redeemer made a name for himself by denouncing his contemporaries (when he was not physically assaulting them at the temple) as a bunch of hypocrites and thieves, mere "whitened sepulchers" to hold the bones of the righteous they had murdered.[30] If the son of God may be excused for proclaiming in a heated moment that he was bringing fire and the sword, not peace on earth,[31] perhaps we should be able to see the loving side to a martinet[32] of U Ba Khin's temper and temperament — someone orphaned at an early age whose educational ideas would have been shaped by the rod of an early twentieth-century colonial education.[33] If we are not inclined to make any such concessions, let us rejoice that Goenka never shouted at his students — because it reminded him, I've heard it said, of his days as a choleric young businessman and father.[34]

Once the Buddha was asked why sometimes he could be so strict while other times he would let things pass. Some students, the Buddha answered, progress by a limited measure of faith and love, as if they had only one eye to see with. I don't want to risk diminishing their vision, said the Buddha, by taking action and admonishing them in a way they might resent.[35] Others may benefit more from being swiftly corrected or even chastised. Let us hope that U Ba Khin could tell as well when his disciplinarian streak was doing more harm than good.

ॐ

I don't think anything is happening. I'm wasting my time, and I'd rather go home. I'll come back some other time.
If there weren't anything happening, you wouldn't be so eager to go home. It's up to you, but if you manage to stay, you will not regret it, and if you decide to leave, it's not likely to be any easier next time around.

I find the daily schedule too rigid, so I take small liberties with it. But then I feel guilty. What should I do?
A nice case of meditator's guilt, a common affliction in Vipassana circles even though Goenka says that it "has no place on the path of Dhamma."[36]

If your guilt stems from a real conviction that you should be working harder to make best use of the opportunity presenting itself, then forget about the time already lost and make more of an effort to get with the program. If your efforts fall short again, keep trying until you are ready to reclassify your problem.

If you are using the guilt as an alibi — it's OK to slack off, but only so long as I feel lousy about it — then you should work on dropping the nonsense and giving yourself permission to do what you are anyway set on doing. One guy I know does only the group sittings and mandatory instruction segments and spends the rest of his time doing yoga in his room or walking around. The rule against yoga may have been devised with his type in mind, but I admire the way he refuses to tie himself up in knots over it. He may not be making the best use of the opportunity, but he's at peace with himself, which may be even more important. Working hard on a course is only a means: the real end is to become happier, in whatever way may suit you best. In the timeless words of the *Dhammapada*, "You are your own master, who else?"[37]

If your guilt is as deep-seated as your resistance to the rigors of the schedule, then you've got an excellent opportunity to watch both up close. Can you see any change in either from moment to moment? Are there times when you incline in one or the other direction? Are you ever able to let go of the whole business, even to laugh or smile at it? When is the dilemma at its strongest and most troubling? Notice these things but don't get too preoccupied with them: whatever else may be going on, try to stay with the breath or the sensations, whether you are sticking to the schedule or not.

I just don't operate well at 4:30 in the morning. What's the harm in sleeping in? I've also seen others walk or rest during meditation periods. Is that so bad?

The official line is that meditation times are for meditation and nothing else, and for good reasons. The more continuous your practice, the greater the benefits you will take away. A few teachers will send around the course manager to check whether students are really meditating in their rooms in the early morning period, but this is blessedly rare at most centers (in part because servers do not tend to enjoy playing Vipassana Gestapo, however loving the part is meant to be). The three daily hours of group-meditation and certain periods when instructions are given must not be missed and the servers will come looking for you if you fail to show up. Other meditation periods are not policed, though you might invite a gentle reminder if your lassitude gets too conspicuous.

The wider question of how much effort to make and how much slack to permit yourself is one that will stay with you for the length of your journey on the Path. Only you can answer when you really need more sleep or rest, or when a breath of fresh air and a walk would do you more good than a few more minutes of sitting. When you are not sitting, try to stay with the breath and the sensations as you have been taught and you will still be meditating. Goenka asks that students not do their sitting meditation outside because of how easy it is to get distracted and to distract others, as you should be able to confirm by trying it for a few minutes. Remember, too, that all open violations of the rules, even if they are harmless by themselves, do tend to attract a lot of attention and can become a hindrance to others.

What's so bad about daydreaming? Aren't one's wandering thoughts also part of "how things are, not how we would like them to be (*yatha-bhuta*)"?

Yes, one's wandering thoughts are also part of how things are, which is why we should not get frustrated by them. But the premise of the need for *right effort* is that our minds require discipline and direction. The weeds in a garden are also part of how things are, but unless we pull them up, we may not be able to grow much else there. If we practice with them in a good-natured way, on the other hand, we will discover that they make excellent fertilizer.[38] If you have trouble feeling friendly towards your old habits, it's an appropriate Buddhist remedy to recall your own commendable deeds of the past (not to build up your ego, but to remind yourself of your own potential for goodness), or to reassure yourself that you are doing the wholesome work of meditation because some of your acquired merits are coming to fruition! A Ten-Day course may not always feel like a much of a boon, granted, but from a Buddhist point of view that is precisely what it is.

Why the rule against eating in the afternoons? I'm not convinced it's even healthy, let alone that it has anything to do with morality.

The rule against eating after mid-day is part of the Eight Precepts, which are not obligatory for householders and which only apply to returning students on courses. In Buddhist lands, it is customary for the laity to keep the Eight Precepts on certain days of the month and during meditation retreats. With the addition of a rule against handling money, they are also what novice monks and nuns observe before full ordination.

Remember that the precepts aren't only about morality, but

also about creating conditions conducive to mindfulness and meditation. How helpful (let alone nutritionally optimal) it really is to be fasting for three quarters of the day may be up for debate, but not at a Goenka center. (Fasting outright is prohibited.) Most students end up finding the precept quite manageable, at least after a day or two of feeling a bit hungry in the afternoons and day-dreaming about junk food more than usual. My own experience would also suggest, cautiously at least, that there is something to the benefits claimed for meditating on a more or less empty stomach. But see for yourself.

The Buddha ate only once a day, in the late morning, and he claimed that by doing so he kept himself "free from illness and affliction and enjoying lightness, strength, and comfortable abiding."[39] But skipping breakfast was never made obligatory, even in the Sangha, and the Buddha was prepared to make some concessions to followers who complained about so strict a regimen,[40] as the Goenkanauts will also do for newcomers and for anyone who has a serious health-related reason for needing to eat in the afternoons.

Since monks and nuns beg their food from the laity, the Buddhist rules are also meant to limit the burdens put on householders, especially at night-time. The Scriptures mention a woman who was once so startled by a mendicant begging his dinner at night that she screamed out in terror: "Mercy me, a devil has come for me!" "Sister, I am no devil, I am a bhikkhu," the begging monk tried to reassure her, but she would not hear of it. "It would be better to cut off your belly than to go prowling about like an orphan in the thick darkness of the night!"[41]

I smuggled cigarettes (or drugs) into my room. Is it really so bad to go indulge in the woods where nobody will be bothered? Cigarettes are unhelpful, but not against the moral precepts, and I have seen meditators at U Ba Khin's old center in Rangoon smoke more or less openly. But at Goenka's centers, smoking is strictly prohibited, alcohol and drugs are entirely out of the question, and you will be asked to leave without debate if you are caught.

Religious artifacts and even prayers are not allowed during a course. But how can a small Buddha or a meditation bracelet do any harm in a context where the Awakened One is constantly evoked?

Goenka's centers take an unusually strict line on anything that smacks of "rites and rituals." One reason is that Goenka, under the impression of Indian sectarianism and of his own teacher's desire to spread the Dhamma in a universal form, was highly sensitive to anything that might present a religious obstacle to anyone. Another reason is that his interpretation of the Dhamma emphasizes an experimental approach and that the effects of the Ten-Day course should be isolated as much as possible, for better visibility, from all private rituals or observances, even prayers, to which benefits might afterwards be attributed. That said, Goenka's extremely hard line is debatable and the experimental approach cuts both ways. If you wear any visible religious objects or anyone observes you praying or chanting, you will be asked to take off the first and desist from the second. The line between an innocent bracelet or a little prayer and the potentially harmful mixing of approaches and techniques can be a fine one. In the end, what is not visible cannot be policed, but erring on the side of caution would not be a bad idea.

According to the course instructions, yoga is not allowed during Ten-Day Vipassana courses. Does that mean it would be wrong to stretch even in the privacy of my room?

Goenka may not be poster-boy for the fitness revolution, but he knows how beneficial exercise is for spiritual practice and he is fully aware that yoga and meditation are close cousins.[42] The ban at his meditation centers is designed to avoid distraction.[43] With the spread of yoga in the West (and the considerable overlap between the two populations), some centers now clarify that the rule is directed against formal, elaborate exercise routines, not against "simple" or "light" stretching.

Where exactly the line runs is anyone's guess, but you will see for yourself how much the eye can get attracted and distracted by unusual movements during a course, so the least you should do is to keep your stretching out of sight. The second concern is that your exercising may draw too much of your own attention. If you are feeling sore, for example, your instinct will be to make the pain or discomfort go away by stretching, whereas the logic of Vipassana would be to observe and accept it with equanimity, just as it is. (Of course yoga can also be practiced equanimously and thus combined most fruitfully with Vipassana.[44])

Tai chi and kung fu sequences are not allowed. Captain Goenka's "kindergarten of Vipassana" is not a pre-school for karate kids or aspiring Shaolin monks.

Why is there no walking meditation on Goenka's courses?

Walking meditation was widely practiced in India long before the Buddha's day. In the West, too, mental absorption has a distinguished history of association with walking. The followers of Aristotle were called *peripatetics*, those who walk about. Thomas Hobbes did so much of his thinking while walking that he had a cane made with a pen and ink in its knob for ready note-taking on the road.[45] Thoreau was a great walker and his essay on the subject is perhaps the definitive Western treatment.

Many meditation courses offered in traditions akin to Goenka's stress the importance of walking meditation, some even suggesting that beginners should walk before all sittings for as much as forty-five minutes to an hour![46] But such is not the way of Goenka's centers, where the most memorable thing said about walking is the stark warning against moving with artificial slowness in the Old students' morning instructions on Day 1 ("totally prohibited," says Captain Goenka). Let's remember, though, that the ideal way to practice Vipassana is to keep one's attention on the breath or the sensations continuously, in all possible postures of the body, no matter what one is doing. Mindful walking in this sense is encouraged by Goenka and most of his centers provide ample, secluded paths that are ideal for practicing.

Trying to chart a middle course between Goenka's reticence and the enthusiasm for walking meditation in many other traditions,[47] we might say that walking during breaks is always permitted and that during meditation periods it is one of the most orthodox remedies for torpor and drowsiness[48] (also acknowledged by Goenka during his discourses). Traditional instructions for walking meditation would recommend identifying a relatively short path of around twenty paces (the Buddha's own at Bodhgaya is said to measure seventeen), because frequent turns can help to prevent the mind from wandering away.[49] During the Anapana period of a Ten-Day course, try to keep your attention focused on the breath; during the Vipassana period, on any accessible sensations on the body (Goenka's instructions) or else more specifically on your lower legs and feet (especially the soles of the feet). As always at Goenka's centers, fixing your gaze on the ground is recommended, and if you want to be purist, you can make a point of keeping your hands out of your pockets and at your sides or in front of the body.[50] It is true that some teachers recommend slowing down one's movements, but many others emphasize a natural pace just as Goenka does.[51]

When I'm walking, I sometimes notice that I feel like kicking around the pebbles and small cones on the path at my feet. Is even that a form of violence that I should be restraining?
It's always good to become aware of something that you may not have noticed before. The pebbles and cones don't mind being kicked around a little, but any action you take is a reflection of what is happening in your mind. What is going on with your breath and your sensations when you are feeling kickish? Can you feel any tension or frustration that you may be venting, or are you in a playful mood when it happens? If you observe your

footballer's habit in this way, it becomes part of your meditation. (But please don't extend the experiment to living beings, no matter how much you may feel like kicking your annoying neighbor in the meditation hall.)

Why are there mirrors at Goenka's centers? I don't like them!
If you are lucky enough to get a private bathroom, feel free to take the mirror down if it bothers you. (It should come off easily; if not, please don't tear it down or take a swing at it.) But the real problem is never what we see, but how we react to it. You won't get away from yourself by refusing to look in the mirror, any more than Oedipus could escape his torment by plucking his own eyes out.

Meditative practice operates like a mirror on many levels, and much of what it shows us is unpleasant. Not to look may be better than to feed our patterns of blind reaction, but the best would be to develop acceptance of and equanimity with whatever we are seeing. Narcissism is not the Dhamma, of course, but there tends to be much non-acceptance of self lurking behind our supposed vanities. If we can't learn to love ourselves — not in the false and self-defeating style of the ego but with true kindness, in the mirror or anywhere else — how can we learn to love others? A saying attributed by Seneca to Hecato rings as true as ever: "What progress have I made? I am beginning to be my own friend. That is progress indeed."[52]

Is it not a bit absurd to make such a fuss about stepping on an ant or swatting a mosquito?
I remember how appalled I was when I first heard that not killing mosquitoes was part of the practice. How insane, I thought, that human beings should not be free to protect themselves from such noxious predators.

But a few things should be considered here. First of all, the purpose of the precept against killing is not blind to circumstances.

In particular, anything that is done unintentionally does not incur negative karmic consequences. It is not that inadvertently stepping on an ant, or swatting a mosquito in one's sleep, will land one in some Buddhist hell, but rather that we should become aware of how readily our deep reservoir of ill-will leads us to kill and destroy without further thought. No one is saying that we need to share our kitchens with armies of ants or cockroaches, or our walls with termites. But we do need to recognize how readily we resort to destruction without even considering the alternatives. So often there is another way; or there would be, if we were prepared to pause and give it some thought before lashing out against the supposed foes of our species.

Moreover, especially on Dhamma land, we ourselves stand to benefit by deepening our equanimity and enlarging the scope of our forbearance. The anger we unleash on other beings is ultimately lodged in us, and does us greater harm than our victims — the reason, incidentally, why Jesus recommended turning the other cheek.[53] When we are so sure that ants, cockroaches, or mosquitoes are farfetched objects of compassion, are we considering that without the ants, the mighty rainforest would be a barren wasteland on account of the thinness of its topsoil? Or that cockroaches are most attracted not by the scent of feces or garbage, as we might imagine, but by the cleanly fragrance of vanilla? Or that mosquitoes are among a very few species who are content with drawing a bit of blood rather than killing for their sustenance — and that the males content themselves with flower nectar and sweet juices (or Nescafé with lots of sugar), while the females need our blood to have babies? To say nothing of the fact that where there are no mosquitoes, other species who feed on them will disappear. Not that such reflections should make us feel enthusiastic about breeding pests, but it may cast them in a different light, even before the Buddhists have reminded us that our own life-energies and those of our loved ones may once have passed through such lowly vessels.[54]

If all that doesn't help, remember that waving a mosquito away, putting on repellents and wearing long sleeves, or sleeping under a net is perfectly acceptable even on the strictest reading of the Buddhist discipline, which includes explicit provisions for protecting oneself from flies, mosquitoes, snakes, and other "creeping things."[55] The more noxious the poor creatures appear to our judgment, the more they should appeal to our sense of compassion: imagine the horror of living such a hideous life!

It is a marvelous experience when one notices, during a course, that even skittish creatures like chipmunks or rabbits seem unafraid about approaching meditators. I will not forget the two times when I participated in Vipassana rescue operations, both in the middle of a course, coordinated in silence: one involved a giant toad that we needed to get from a bathroom into a bucket in Indonesia; the other a terrified little French Canadian mouse with a birthmark that we needed to catch so that it could be taken back to the woods by chauffeur. One might imagine that these episodes would have been annoyances, but not at all; I remember them as occasions when I made friends.

Arachnophobes eager to reach out to the enemy could wish for no better training ground than the Texas center, ideally in July or August, when Mother Nature's dance with the air con units is at its most macabre and one can watch the cows across the field fainting in the heat.

What about medicines? Don't antibiotics kill bacteria? Does anyone ever suggest that we should learn to be equanimous with treatable diseases?
The Dhamma is not about blindly applying principles to their utmost extreme, but about staying balanced and using common sense.[56] Human life is precious[57] and should be protected. The failure of his ascetic exercises taught the Buddha that the body should be treated with care and kindness.[58] Health and energy are great boons to all human purposes and the Buddha identified them as two of the five factors of striving crucial to meditation.[59] Hence, even on a strict reading of the Discipline, "All is allowed in the case of medicine."[60]

When the Buddha called himself "the supreme physician,"[61] however, he was going further. The deepest illness that the Dhamma offers to cure is the disease of being constantly agitated and perturbed,[62] crudely or subtly, whether we realize it or not: the chronic fever of our grasping minds.[63] Ultimately, what we most need to learn is acceptance and serenity in the face of sickness and death, which will prevail against all our defensive measures before long. The Dhamma is about letting go of our clinging, not about reinforcing the attachments that bind us so powerfully to our bodies. But none of that should be taken as an argument against giving ourselves the loving care that we should show all sentient beings, which certainly includes the use of medicines when needed.

On the mental side, it would be impossible to disentangle many disorders from the defilements that are so central to our mind's ordinary workings from a Vipassana perspective. In his evening discourse on Day 6, Goenka mentions drug addiction, fear (or anxiety), and depression and claims that "all these mental illnesses go away so easily" through the practice. This is one of the times where Goenka's tendency to oversell his product teeters on the edge of irresponsibility. No doubt meditation can offer relief for all kinds of serious psycho-somatic conditions, and there is no telling what a serious Vipassana practice might mean for one's mental health. But it would be unrealistic and possibly dangerous to treat Vipassana as an easy substitute for other kinds of treatment, and many centers now include specific warning and sometimes require waivers to that effect.[64]

There are Vipassana purists who dismiss psychotherapy as dispensable or even as a waste of time and a distraction from the Path. I can't see it that way. To me a well-matched therapist is a gift from heaven, and I owe a great deal to the ones I've worked with, this book included. The way beyond the self leads through not around it. What we do on our side of the river, healing included, needs to be distinguished from what calls us to cross over; but that call is a call on our strength, not out weakness,[65] and we should make use of all the help we can get to augment our feeble powers.

I am trying to focus on my meditation, but my attention keeps getting drawn to the other side of the meditation hall (where members of the other sex are sitting). I also catch myself staring across the boundary lines to where they are walking. What should I do?

"Nothing so obsesses the mind of a man as the form of a woman, nor the mind of a woman as that of a man."[66] Thus begin the 1500 pages of the Buddha's *Numerical Discourses*. We are creatures of the senses living in the realm of sex, and it is not surprising that as your senses are getting more sensitive with every hour, your mind is rebelling against the sparse sensory diet by jumping on every distraction it can find. Don't worry about the magnetic pull you are feeling, but try to focus on your breath and sensations rather than joining the war-dance that your cravings are performing. If you have to join the fray, keep it internal and direct your effort towards not distracting anyone.

I have discovered The Love of My Life on the other side of the room, and I'm ready to kill the guy next to me who keeps disturbing me with his swallowing.

Such are the joys of Vipassana meditation. If you have really found your Great Love, he or she will be waiting for you on Metta Day. Congratulations and good luck!

Your neighbor is an inconsiderate asshole, and he's indeed lucky that you can't give him a piece of your mind. But count your blessings: at least he's not burping. Or if he is, at least he is not farting.

You've heard enough about equanimity for it to come out of your ears by now, but let me tell you a story the Buddha used to tell about forbearance, just to add to your misery. Even if you had been hijacked and your captors were sawing you in two for firewood, a true disciple would feel nothing but compassion towards his tormentors.[67] Not there yet? The Path is long, my friend, and you'd better learn to enjoy the ride.

During my meditations, I keep getting distracted and overwhelmed by vivid images of genitalia in action, or else by misdirected rage and other perverse and disturbing thoughts. What is wrong with me?

It's possible that you are an incorrigible pervert and psychopath, but it's more likely that you are simply seeing the by-products of purifying your mind. When you go diving into your mind's septic tank, you need to be prepared for encountering some turds.

Protracted pornographic episodes are quite common during intense meditation. Nor do only swinish worldlings suffer from the ravages of fornicator's mind. Apparently even the great Thai meditation master Ajahn Chah, when he was still a young man but already a monk, went through a stage when he kept seeing disembodied vaginas everywhere.[68]

Anger, too, can come up in ways that seem nothing short of deranged, along with all manner of other thoughts that no one would want to call his or her own. The key to dealing with them is to remember that you are not meant to own them; they are not, never have been, and never will be yours in any meaningful sense. The whole Buddhist program may come down to this: "Abandon what is not yours and you will be happy."[69] So try to stay with the breath and the sensations as much as you can and let your mind unspool whatever it needs to. The process is often unpleasant, but you will feel better at the end of it all.

At times I find myself overcome by an irresistible urge to masturbate in my room or in the remoter parts of the walking areas. What should I do?

If you succumb and your genitals mysteriously disappear, don't say you weren't warned. Just kidding.

Goenkanauts can be very quick to detect energetic pollutants that only they can pick up with their supersensitive vibrational antennae, and they would surely say that "self-sex" is an impure activity that leaves a stain on the pristine purity of Dhamma-land. I prefer more verifiable standards of right and wrong, but since you are at one of their centers, they get to make the rules, and the rules say that as part of the opening formalities, you have committed yourself to refrain from *all* sexual activity for the duration of the course, self-help included. It's an important part of the training to discipline yourself and learn to observe rather than act on your impulses. "Serious meditators" who would like to sit Long courses for twenty days and more are even reminded on their application forms that they should be working on "coming out of" self-sex altogether, but that is part of a long list of demanding requirements. ("Coming out," in a Vipassana context, marks the end of the party, not the beginning.)

It should be clear that masturbation is not a violation of Buddhist morality so long as it does not disturb or harm others; but it is considered unhelpful in the long-run because it reinforces habits of craving and reaction. So if you must indulge, be sure to do it discreetly and to clean up scrupulously, then see how you feel about if afterwards. If your meditation magically improves, you may have just discovered the fast-track to enlightenment; if it leaves you feeling dirty and depressed instead, don't do it again. In any case, don't dwell on it and go back to working on your restraint.

As for doing your thing outside, please don't assume that you are safe in what seem to be remote corners of the center. Once upon a time, when I was staying in the Amazon at a site that had no toilets, I was eager to identify the most secluded spot to do another kind of private business in the morning. No sooner was I squatting down with my pants around my ankles than the shaman burst through the underbrush with a buddy in tow, both swinging machetes. They laughed and everything was fine, but you may not get off so lightly making mischief on Dhamma-land.

ॐ

When I think that others may be watching me, I make a point of sitting up and staying in the hall. Should it make me feel bad that my meditation seems to be motivated by the desire to look good in front of others?

No, it shouldn't make you feel bad; it's good that you are noticing. If our motivations were perfectly pure, we wouldn't need to do meditation courses. Given that our vanities and competitive instinct will find a way to express themselves no matter what, we might as well use them for beneficial ends. Don't cultivate this kind of ego-tripping deliberately, but don't get too concerned about it either; it's part of our condition, for now. By becoming more aware of the underlying patterns and admitting them to ourselves honestly, we can transform them into part of our practice. That's a big step!

I feel as if I'm competing for the worst meditator award. How come I'm such a loser while everyone else seems to be able to sit like a stone Buddha?

That we should not judge others is not news to most of us.[70] But why judge even ourselves?[71] Meditation is difficult enough when we don't complicate it by trying to define our performance in relation to others, which is a conceit from the Buddhist perspective whether the conclusion is that we are superior, inferior, *or equal* to others.[72]

Meditation is about changing our habit of bolstering the illusion of identity with comparisons. Try thinking of your seat in more impersonal terms as the ground where the meditation-friendly forces of the Five Spiritual Faculties (faith, energy, mindfulness, concentration, and wisdom) are battling it out in close combat with the Five Hindrances (agitation, torpor, sensory desire, ill-will, and doubt[73]) like the Horatii and Curiatii of Roman lore.[74] Sometimes one side will have the upper hand, sometimes the other. *Anicca. Anatta.*

Who cares about your posture? Sure it helps to sit up as much as you can, but look around — not just at the front row where there are such very Old students that they've turned to stone with age, but at the whole scene unfolding before you. Do you see a beauty pageant? (If you do, you may have forgotten to put on the glasses you are supposed to take off for meditation.)

Everyone's mind is a mess, that's the whole point of the exercise.[75] Don't get discouraged or disgusted, but work as patiently and lovingly as possible on observing and accepting things as they are. Take heart: how many "losers" do you know who are willing to spend nine days getting up at 4 am (more or less) and sitting in silence day-in day-out? Something good brought you to the course; honor it.

Your job is not easy, but it's simple: keep your butt on the cushion and observe what is happening, nothing more. You can't help fidgeting because there is so much pain? Good for you that you're not running away! Your head is full of bizarre cravings and aversions? Welcome to the club! The veterans in the front row have more practice with observing their discomfort and keeping still, that's all.

If there's a budding saint in the room somewhere, she's probably one of the martyrs pinned against the wall in the wilderness behind the last row; or he's the burly fellow in the back who was hoping that his collapsible blue beach-chair (the groove for beer-cans holds only kleenex now) would help him through, but who's known better since 5:30 am on Day 1. Or look in the mirror: you may have to squint a little bit or you'll miss the face of the Buddha, but sometimes a blurry image is more true than what we think we are seeing with such clarity.

I'm fed up with the bullshit that Goenka is feeding us. I hate his chanting, his stupid discourses are making me sick, and the teachers never take the time to convince me of anything. Whatever I ask them, they always give me the same answer:

watch your breath or your sensations. I've had it! Beam me up, Scotty!

I hear you. Remember that Goenka does not claim to be Socrates or St Thomas (St Paul would be closer).[76] Think of him as the Ronald McDonald of the meditation scene. Can you expect the organizational genius behind "billions served" to be a philosopher, a saint, and a Caruso as well? You're not required to laugh at Goenka's jokes or to fall in love with him (though a surprising number of students do). And you've got the rest of your life to take on the discourses, if you want. Be warned, though, that Goenka's Happy Meal is no more and no less than Theravadan Buddhism ingeniously repackaged for a globalized age and subjected to a quality control rigorous enough to impress the Swiss. The on-site teachers can be more or less convincing in personal interviews, but they are very serious meditators working from a script that is a lot more compelling, for all its apparent dryness, than it may seem at first sight. Goenka's Golden Arches are a bit like the Hotel California: you can check out any time you want, but you may not be able to leave.

I don't see why I should follow Goenka's boring instructions. I'd rather celebrate the beauty of my free and spontaneous spirit by doing my own thing.

Way to go! I'm glad that the spirit of adolescent rebellion has not died with Kurt Cobain. I especially recommend doing what you are specifically told never to do, such as keeping your attention stubbornly fixed in one place, preferably around the center of your body, and continuously digging down as long and hard as you can manage. If you thought that your bad LSD-trips were fun, wait until you see what it's like to be dancing the polka for twelve hours with a band of raging demons in a sea of burning sulfur.

If you are an intrepid hunter for exotic experiences, there is plenty of other big game to stalk. Go drink Ayahuasca or Iboga if you must. (I'm *not* saying that you should be doing either.

I'm saying that if you are keen on seeing monsters of the deep, that's where you will find them, and not to go looking for them in your meditation.) Vipassana is about staying on the straight path rather than straying into the thicket. It's not about going to extremes or having dramatic stories to tell; it's about becoming more calm, more mature, more sane, more fully reasonable and responsible. Giving the inner child (or adolescent) room to play is important as well,[77] but Vipassana is for growing up.

I do not wish to give meditation instructions, but certain points seem to present particular difficulties to students, in some cases even after they have returned for several courses, so I am adding a few reflections. When such questions arise on a course, they should definitely be taken up with the teachers, who are very well-qualified to answer them.

I'm trying to clear my mind by emptying it of thoughts during meditation, but I am not succeeding. What can I do?

You need to forget the myth that meditation is about clearing or emptying one's mind. This side of Nibbana, there will always be some noise in the mind, whether deafening or almost imperceptible. There is much talk of "taming the mind," by Goenka too, but calming down your inner bucking bronco is not actually your job, any more than it is a contestant's at a rodeo. Your job is to stay in the saddle (that is, keep your focus on the breath) for as long as you can, always understanding that you *will* fall off before long.[78] When you are thrown off, you simply get back on and start over. Again and again. That's all. The wild beast will calm down eventually, but you don't make it; you let it happen on its own schedule with as much patience as possible.[79] When you do get frustrated, let that happen as well, but try not to dwell on it.

Unless I missed something, the map of the body that Goenka draws in his Vipassana instructions on Day 4 has a blank area in

a region that gives a lot of us plenty of trouble. Aren't we told that it's important to scan the whole body without exception?

Goenka must have thought it impolite to get more explicit about the parts between the lower abdomen in the front and the "seat of the trunk" in the back, but you should give them just the same attention as everything else, no more and no less. Don't expect to discover anything too exciting, though, beyond the occasional upward or downward movement. Nobody's primary sexual organs are located between the legs; they are always found between the ears.

What does Goenka mean by "the game of sensations"? I can see where he is coming from, but his account of human action looks like a caricature to me. Are we not also thinking and reasoning beings, rather than creatures blindly driven this way or that by our feelings only?

When Goenka speaks of the game of sensations, he means indulging our habit of reacting to pleasant sensations with elation and to unpleasant ones with dejection. In the context of a Ten-Day course, he is referring to students who make no effort to develop equanimity at all, who come only to enjoy the pleasant aspects of "good meditation" and who dismiss their experiences of unpleasant sensations as "bad meditation." We all play the game to some extent, inadvertently, whether we like to or not, because the basic habit of reaction is so deeply entrenched, reaching down to the roots of our heritage as sentient beings. The very nature of life as we know it, for as long as there have been creatures struggling for survival on our planet, has been to seek out pleasant sensations and to avoid unpleasant ones; that much we have in common with the amoebas, and it is probably encoded in the very cells and genes that have been passed down to us through the aeons. Unlike other organisms, however, we can become conscious of what is going on: we can break the habit, one moment at a time, and we can even liberate ourselves from the basic pattern altogether, stepping outside the cycle of life in

Samsara. It's hard work that requires a lot of persistence, work that those who merely wish to play the game of sensations are not willing to do; but it's possible for us and that's what makes us special as a species: *homo sapiens sapiens*, beings who are not only capable of understanding, but who can cultivate awareness of their own understanding.

What Goenka means by sensations is not just feelings in the crude sense that might be contrasted with thinking and reasoning. What he insist on, and rightly so (it seems to me), is that we never react to thoughts alone, but always to a current of emotionally textured energy that is often so subtle that we don't recognize its directing power.[80] Picture the mind as a supercomputer running all kinds of extremely sophisticated software (our thinking and reasoning at its most powerful). Goenka is not denying the impressiveness of the software; in many ways he emphasizes it (as did the Buddha). If we were not such exceptionally clever beings,[81] we would hardly have arrived at a Teaching that looks simple from some angles, but that is also incredibly profound and comprehensive. Yet even the most elaborate software is made up, at bottom, of binary code, mere zeros and ones — and just so even our most refined and abstract thoughts have their counterparts in particular constellations (or perhaps topographies) of interwoven sensations, pleasant or unpleasant. A particular thought or emotion can never be traced to any one simple sensation; it is always linked to the entire inner landscape of complex, interconnected, ever-changing sensations throughout the body.[82]

What if I just don't feel anything?

Goenka takes up this problem in his discourses on Days 3 and 4, insisting that so long as you are alive, you are bound to feel *something*, and that no sensation should be dismissed as too ordinary to be a fit object of contemplation. To go looking for "something special" is against the spirit of Vipassana.

What gets less attention, however, is how difficult and frustrating it can be to encounter only gross sensations (pain, heat, irritation, etc.) or areas that remain blank or blind throughout a course. Even for someone who can understand and accept the principle of *yatha-bhuta* ("as it is, not as you would like it to be"), it can be discouraging to be feeling no subtle sensations at all when one is also being told that the Path of Vipassana leads from the gross to the subtle[83] — especially if there is still no subtlety by the time Goenka starts talking about *bangha* states on Day 9.

The only counsel and consolation I can give is to encourage you to be patient and to remember, if you can, that what you are trying to learn is precisely not to judge and play favorites among sensations the way we usually do. Try to accept whatever arises as impermanent and impersonal phenomena — not defining or belonging to you, not grounds for comparison or judgment or preference, but merely ephemeral events that you are observing objectively and dispassionately. Even if most of your sensations are far from subtle, surely you will be able to see changes around gross or blind areas: perhaps the edges or boundaries fluctuate a little or the grossness changes texture, however slightly. You will miss much of what is happening if you insist on labeling your experience "the same." You are not noticing the finer differences because you are so convinced that nothing interesting is taking place. So long as you are not giving your sensations any respect, is it any wonder that they are not softening under your gaze?

Goenka does what he can to preface his discussion of *bhanga*-states with stark warnings about how dangerous it is to get caught up with them. Alas, what tends to stick in the mind much more than these disclaimers is the lengthy instructions he gives on Day 9 about how to deal with the body dissolving into subtle vibrations. Evidently some students have this experience even during their first course! Surely I must be a lousy meditator if this "very important milestone" keeps eluding me. Heaven forbid that I might already have returned for several courses — and still no *bangha*! (Same here, I think:[84] so the cat is out of the bag and you can stop reading now.) Thus the milestone turns into a millstone around our necks.

It's one of the central paradoxes of meditation that if you want to get anywhere with it, you'd better forget about going somewhere. The more we curse our coarse sensations, the more entrenched and intolerable they are bound to become; the more we dwell on attaining certain subtle states or sensations, no matter how important they may be, the further they recede from us. Spiritual progress is not an oxymoron or a dirty word, but for it to occur, we need to forget about making it happen. It is said about Ananda and Patacara, for example, that all their efforts to break through to final liberation did not bear fruit until they gave up and retired for the night. Only when they were turning off the night lamp, ready to hit the pillow without having succeeded, did realization finally come to them when they were least expecting it.[85]

The reasons why you are having trouble feeling more subtle sensations are likely to have deep roots in your mental and emotional habits and make-up. There is a lot going on, but for whatever reason, your mind seems to be blocking much of it. All serious meditation aims at softening and unblocking our minds, but this may require a lot of patience, whether in our day or those of the Buddha or Seneca: "There are terrors to be quieted, incitements to be quelled, illusions to be dispelled, extravagance to the checked, greed to be reprimanded: which of these things can be done in a hurry?"[86]

Even if work with the sensations will become indispensable at some point on the Path (which is the strongest claim that can be made for *vedana*-practice), Vipassana isn't always the best access point for a student.[87] The Buddha taught many meditation techniques,[88] always with an eye to different personal temperaments.[89] While Vipassana is highly effective for many students, it is possible that you are not one of them, at least not right now. So give it a chance to work for you, but if it really is not congenial, don't think that you are missing the one and only way to practice seriously.

What does Goenka mean when he distinguishes "sweeping (*en masse*)" from "going part-by-part"? I take it that sweeping has something to do with "free flow," but I'm not sure I quite understand.

These terms are not traditional to Buddhist meditation, but were introduced by U Ba Khin in an effort to develop a more modern, scientific language in his instructions that would be more accessible to Western students.[90] I think of the two modes of scanning the body as settings on your Vipassana search-light. Going "part-by-part" is what Goenka teaches in his initial Vipassana instructions: you pass the flashlight (or laser) of your attention slowly and carefully over every part of the body, pausing a little wherever you encounter either gross sensations or blind/ blank areas. After moving so cautiously for a while, most students will start feeling a flow of subtle sensations in some areas of the body. (If you don't, just keep going part-by-part and don't worry about missing anything.) That's when you can use the second setting to pass your attention more quickly and lightly over the subtle sensations (as if you were "sweeping" over their surface). The second mode is meant to help you develop more of an overall awareness of the body, but after a few rounds of sweeping, you should always go back to the slower, more careful mode so that you don't start getting too superficial in your observations.

Students sometimes wonder whether they are working too slowly (part-by-part) or too quickly (sweeping too much and too superficially). Don't worry: so long as you are doing your best to observe your sensations with detachment and dispassion (objectively and equanimously, without reaction), you are doing Vipassana. The optimal balance between the two settings, and the best speed at which to scan, are ever-evolving refinements of the technique that you will get to fine-tune with experience. As Goenka says in the discourses, don't move so slowly that your mind gets bored and fed up, and don't go so quickly that you're not paying enough attention to the nuances of your sensations. Keep yourself from getting too mechanical by changing your speed and alternating between the "scan settings." So long as you are able to stay alert and interested, you are probably getting things right.

When I am trying to move my attention around the body, intense sensations in some parts keep distracting me. What should I do?

This is the kind of question that Vipassana teachers are best qualified to answer, and you should give yourself a chance to benefit from their expertise by speaking to them about it. The point of moving around the body is to avoid getting stuck on any of the areas you are visiting. As Goenka points out in his discourses, some part of your mind will always go to wherever intense sensations are occurring, but you should not lose sight of what is happening elsewhere in the body. In fact, all sensations are connected on some level: "Like a gong which, having been struck at one point, begins vibrating throughout its structure, so any contact with the senses generates a vibration that spreads throughout the body."[91] So don't worry if you are not able to bring along your entire attention as you are making your rounds, but keep moving as much as possible. The important thing is not to let yourself get bogged down anywhere or deliberately to linger in any one place.

NOTES

1. The British conquered Burma in 1885 after three Anglo-Burmese wars and incorporated it into their Empire. Burma was not separated from India until 1937, and it became independent in 1948.

2. The ancestor who first came to Burma and started the family business from modest beginnings was Goenka's grandfather, around the 1880s. Goenka's family narrative, the details of which I leave to some future hagiographer, is complicated by the fact that he, the youngest of six sons, was adopted at a young age by his aunt and uncle, who had six daughters. (See *Art of Living*, p. 141, *Art of Dying*, p. 9.)

3. Day 7 Discourse, largely devoted to the dangers of blind faith. See also the next question (on religion).

4. See also *Clock of Vipassana*, p. 232: "After ten days it is not necessary that all the time one should depend on a teacher. There is no 'gurudom' in this technique. Nature is the guru and then you have the path and you can walk upon the path."

5. See also DN 16.5.3 (p. 262) on how the supreme homage paid by practicing the Dhamma properly is greater than even the highest honors paid by the gods.

6. *Thus Spake Zarathustra*, Part I, last section.

7. A famous Zen koan attributed to Linji Yixuan (Jap. Rinzai Gigen, d. 866 CE). See *Zen Mind, Beginner's Mind*, p. 9: "A Zen master would say, 'Kill the Buddha!' Kill the Buddha if the Buddha exists somewhere else; kill the Buddha because you should resume your own Buddha nature." See also pp. 42 and 63, said about Zen, but applicable to all Buddhist teachings: "Zen is not something to get excited about... Do not be too interested in Zen... If you are attached to the teaching, or to the teacher, that is a big mistake... You need a teacher so that you can become independent."

8. DN 16.2.26 (p. 245 [following *Gem Set in Gold*, p. 82]). See also DN 26.1,27 (pp. 395, 404) and SN 47.9 (p. 1637), etc.

9. *Clock of Vipassana*, p. 42.

10. Thus SN 22.87 (p. 939): "One who sees the Dhamma sees me; one who sees me sees the Dhamma." See also AN 10.172 (p. 1513) and *Itivuttaka* 92 (Ireland, p. 217).

11. *Zen Mind, Beginner's Mind*, p. 63.

12. Thus Goenka: "A number of times very senior priests and nuns have told me that we are teaching Christianity in the name of the Buddha." (*Clock of Vipassana*, p. 230) The same must have happened with practitioners of other religions as well.

13. Rahula, p. 50.

14. "Who has actually seen face-to-face?", the Buddha asks at DN 13.12 (p. 188). Those who rely on the reports of others when it comes to ultimate things are like "a file of blind men clinging to each other," each believing that the man before him has actually seen something (DN 13.15 [p. 189], see also MN 95 and 99).

15. A thought at home in mystical tradition as well. Thus Meister Eckhart: "Wouldst thou be perfect, do not yelp about God."

16. The authorities in Malaysia, for instance, have threatened the centers there with closure if any Muslims were found taking courses, and their Dhamma literature must carry warning labels on the cover. There is a vibrant Vipassana community in Iran, but it operates at the edges of legality.

17. From the ancient Greek θεραπεία (therapeía): a cure or a course of treatment (physical, mental, or spiritual), but also a service rendered either to another person or to the gods. The Buddha called himself the world's "unsurpassed physician and surgeon," using the terms in their broadest possible sense (*Itivuttaka* 100 [Ireland, p. 226], MN 92.12 [p. 760]). See also the question on medicine in chapter 12.

18. On the avoidance of disputatiousness, see SN 56.9 (p. 1842). Also the Buddha's declaration at SN 22.94 (p. 949): "I do not dispute with the world; rather, it is the world that disputes with me." (If only that were not how every sincere but disputatious person feels!)

19. Day 8 Discourse. Nor was it an isolated incident, but a well-established part of U Ba Khin's reputation. (See for example *U Ba Khin Journal*, pp. 24-25, *Clock of Vipassana*, p. 37.)

20. Thus *The Prince*, chapter x, on how only cruelties well-used, as limited as possible, prompted by necessity, and converted to the greatest benefit for the people allow those who employ them to "*remedy* their condition with God and men" and the *Discourses on Livy*, chapter I.ix, where Machiavelli argues that harsh actions *accuse* the perpetrator and can be *excused* only if they succeed in mending things.

21. On enmity, see SN 3.404 (p. 177). On plants and seeds, see MN 27:13 (p. 272-73) and MN 51.14 (p. 449). The protection of plants is surely meant to safeguard the farmers' harvests, first and foremost. According to the Buddhist cosmology, plants are not liable to suffering and vexation, but they may be home to spirits who are. See the question on the gods in chapter 12.

22. MN 58.7 (p. 499). The same story is told from a nurse's perspective at AN 8.7 (p. 633), where it is made more explicit that such interventions are appropriate only when dealing with the immature.

23. Even Machiavelli rested much of his case on the argument that harsh means, judiciously employed, will prove *more merciful* in the long-run than the alternatives (*The Prince*, chapter xvii). For a few more thoughts on the public and political dimension of the Dhamma, see the question on the precepts in chapter 10.

24. A point raised by Fleischman in his *The Buddha Taught Nonviolence, Not Pacifism*, p. 17. See below.

25. The Buddha could even be a little mischievous in his means, depending on the situation. One of the Buddha's half-brothers, Nanda, seems to have left his bride on the morning of their wedding-day and could not shake the memory of her good-bye. To keep him practicing, the Buddha promised him the favors of "five hundred pink-footed nymphs" — a promise from which he was released when Nanda attained arahanthood (*Udana* 3.2 [Ireland, pp. 35-39]).

26. DN 16.1.1-5 (pp. 232-233).

27. The Sakyans were vassals of the powerful kingdom of Kosala with its capital at Savatthi. (The Buddha was a nobleman by birth, but not a prince, as is often said, because his father was not a king, but one of several leading men in a small republic.) Being politically subordinate, the Sakyans prided themselves all the more on the supposed superiority of their blood. King Pasendi of Kosala, being aware of their pretensions and wishing to strengthen his dynastic position, demanded a suitable bride from them. Because the Sakyans were as unwilling to comply as they were powerless to defy the king openly, they decided to give him one of their slave-girls, suitably disguised with all the trappings of privilege.

Their ploy succeeded until the grown son of the slave-queen, Prince Vitatubha, wanted to pay his maternal relatives an official visit. He was received with all the customary respects, but when he turned back for a sword he had forgotten, he caught his hosts performing a ritual purification over the very seat of honor he had been offered before. When his father Pasendi heard what had happened, he was as offended as his son until the Buddha, whose follower he had become, convinced him that a queen was a queen and not to attach importance to caste-distinctions. But Vitatubha had already contracted so mortal a hatred that he usurped his fathers throne and expiated the Sakyans' insults in their precious blood.

The other major kingdom in northern India at the time was Magadha with its capital at Rajagaha, under King Bimbisara, who was also a follower of the Buddha. Like Pasendi, he had a discontented son, Prince Ajatasattu, who plotted against his life out of hunger for power (instigated, it is said, by the arch-fiend Devadatta). The prince was caught in the act of treason and the king confronted him: "Why do you want to kill me?" "Because I wish to rule," answered the son. "If you desire a kingdom so much, take mine," said the father and handed over his throne (*Cullavagga* 7.3.5). Consumed by fear, his son had him locked away in a prison-cell at Rajagaha (the grounds of which can still be visited today), where Bimbisara is said to have starved to death. Ajatasattu repented only when it was too late, after his wife bore him a child and he realized how great his own father's love must have been.

(Goenka explores the melancholy Sakyan episode and its implications in light of Indian caste-thinking in an article available online, "Why Was the Sakyan Republic Destroyed?" For the kings and clans at the time, see also *Buddhist India* by T.W. Rhys Davids, especially chapters 1 and 2.)

28. The *Mahanidana Sutta* insists especially on the causal chain that runs from our *cravings* to our *pursuits*, from the *gains* we make to *attachment* and *possessiveness*, until our *safeguarding* measures spill over into aggression, "the taking up of clubs and weapons, conflicts, quarrels, and disputes, insulting speech, slander, and falsehoods." (DN 15:9 [pp. 224-225], tr. Bodhi. See also MN 13:7-17 [pp. 180-183] and *Sutta Nipata* 4.11.)

29. Matthew 3:4,7,10 etc.

30. Matthew 21:12-13, 23:27-35. It's one of Osho's better ideas that Jesus, who grew up working on construction sites with Joseph, would naturally have acquired a different tone from a nobleman whose father, fearing that his son might turn out a great saint, made a point of bringing him up with every comfort possible (AN 3.39 [pp. 239-40]).

31. Matthew 10:34, Luke 12:51.

32. Goenka calls him "a very strict disciplinarian" at least twice in his Discourses.

33. Since he was a model student throughout, he may not have been beaten as much as others. U Ba Khin often downplayed his own formal education, but he was a scholarship-student at St Paul's Institution in Rangoon, which was a very highly regarded school at the time. When he passed his final examination in 1917, he won a gold medal and a scholarship to go on to university, but he declined because he felt that he should start earning money rather than burdening his relatives. (See *Clock of Vipassana*, pp. 23-24.)

34. In an interview with the *Indian Express* (3 July 2010), Goenka recalled that before he took up Vipassana, he was very prone to anger and would "beat his children mercilessly." I also remember him mentioning somewhere that he used to be "a devil" towards his employees. When he first began to explore the depths of his mind under U Ba Khin's guidance, he was shocked to find its dark chambers to be "full of snakes and scorpions and centipedes" (*Art of Living*, p. 143).

35. MN 65.27 (p. 547-48). Thus also MN 103.10-14 (pp. 850-51) on not being in a hurry to reproach anyone.

36. *Art of Living*, p. 81.

37. *Dhp.* XII.4/160: *Atta hi attano natho.* The passage is about spiritual self-reliance in a very practical sense; it should not be taken to affirm the self in any way that would cast doubt on *Anatta*, and it is specifically not about one kind of self overmastering another (see Rahula, pp. 59-60).

38. See *Zen Mind, Beginner's Mind*, p. 20: "We pull the weeds and bury them near the plant to give it nourishment... You should not be bothered by your mind. You should rather be grateful for the weeds because eventually they will enrich your practice."

39. MN 65.2 (p. 542). But he never starved himself again after abandoning the severe ascetic exercises of his youth (see the question on the Middle Way in chapter 12). At MN 77.9 (p. 633) it is mentioned that he sometimes ate a full alms-bowl or more and that many of the meals he accepted as a guest were sumptuous ones, to be enjoyed without greed but also without reluctance.

40. MN 65.3 (p. 542).

41. MN 66.6 (p. 552), slightly revised.

42. Goenka, *For the Benefit of Many*, p. 77-78, 103.

43. See also *Art of Living*, p. 139.

44. Goenka says as much: *Art of Living*, p. 139.

45. John Aubrey, *A Brief Life of Thomas Hobbes*, sect. 16 (Memorandum).

46. Thus Dharma Dorje, *Walking Meditation*, pp. 42-43 (see recommended books). Walking is especially suited to the early mornings, to shake off torpor and bring up some energy, and it is said to have been the Buddha's predominant practice at that time of

the day (*Walking Meditation*, p. 19).

47. In the Thai Forest Tradition, for instance, many monks walk for at least five or six hours a day, and as much as ten or fifteen, making walking meditation their main practice! (See *Walking Meditation*, pp. 2-3, 19.) It is said that plenty of meditators have attained the stages of Buddhist enlightenment while doing walking meditation (*Ibid.*, pp. 1, 19; *Vism.* VIII.244 [p. 285]). The case to which I can give the most credit, because of a personal connection and the way it's been related to me, also occurred while walking, not while sitting. "Don't consider walking meditation as a 'second-class' meditation," Ajahn Brahmavamso insists: "Walking meditation is wonderful... If you want to spend most of your meditation time this way, please do so. But do it well and do it carefully." (*Walking Meditation*, pp. 19-20; also Dharma Dorje at p. 25)

48. AN 7.61 (p. 1060).

49. See *Walking Meditation*, pp. 6, 49-50.

50. The traditional instructions frown upon walking with one's hands behind the back as betraying too lax an attitude (*Walking Meditation*, p. 7). On the other hand, if you place your hands before you in too conspicuous a manner, you may alert the Dhamma police to the fact that you are "doing walking meditation."

51. See *Walking Meditation* (pp. 9, 20, 28). Safer to keep it natural while Papa Goenka may be watching from above the clouds: you don't want to be caught doing anything "totally prohibited," do you?

52. Seneca, *Letters from a Stoic*, tr. Robin Campbell, no. VI.

53. For a Buddhist version of the call to do unto others as one would have them do to oneself, see SN 55.7 (p. 1797) and the Buddha's words to some boys tormenting a snake and some fishes in the *Udana* (2.3, 5.4 [Ireland, pp. 25, 69; *Life*, p. 179]).

54. Thus SN 15:14-19 (p. 659): "It is not easy to find any living being that upon this long round of rebirths has not yet, some time or other, been your mother, or father, or brother, or sister, or son, or daughter."

55. DN 29.22 (p. 433), MN 2.13 (p. 94), AN 6.58 (p. 643), etc. See also *Vism.* I.85,87 (pp. 31-32).

56. Thus Goenka stresses that even *sila* (morality), crucial as it is for making progress on the Path, should not be taken to extremes that are not practical of beneficial (*Art of Living*, p. 64).

57. Goenka repeats many times, especially at the outset of a Ten-Day course and at its conclusion, that "human life is so precious" (I remember hearing it multiple times on Days 1, 9, and 11). There may be an ultimate level of reality, beyond all distinctions, where human life cannot be called any more precious than anything else. But on the way towards understanding that reality, as an opportunity for shedding ignorance and suffering, human birth is invaluable and even the gods envy it (see the question on the gods in chapter 12). All beings stand to benefit when a human's extraordinary potential is fulfilled.

58. See the question on the Middle Way in chapter 12.

59. MN 85.58 (p. 707).

60. *Vism.* I.115 (p. 41), speaking of the procurement of medicines by monks; but the phrase can be applied more generally.

61. MN 92.12 (p. 760), *Itivuttaka* 100 (Ireland, p. 226). On the Buddha as a self-described prescriber of "noble purgatives and emetics," see AN 10.108-109 (pp. 1489-90).

62. Thus "being stirred is a disease" (SN 35.90-91 [pp. 1170-71]).

63. When the Buddha said that "all is burning," he was not only using an image that would resonate with former fire-worshippers, he was also referring to our inner fires (SN 35:28 [p. 1143 (BW 346)]). See also *Dhp.* XI.1/146. In the seven pages of the *Aranavibhanga Sutta* (MN 139), the word "fever" appears 37 times (of which Bodhi/Nanamoli only reproduce twenty [pp. 1080-86]).

64. As part of the application process in North America, students are advised as follows: "People with serious mental disorders have occasionally come to Vipassana courses with the unrealistic expectation that the technique will cure or alleviate their mental problems... Although Vipassana meditation is beneficial for most people, it is not a substitute for medical or psychiatric treatment and we do not recommend it for people with serious psychiatric disorders."

65. See MN 64.8 (p. 539) on this very point.

66. AN 1.1,6 (pp. 89-90), slightly contracted.

67. MN 21.20 (p. 223 [BW 278-79]).

68. Ajahn Chah, *Everything Arises, Everything Falls Away*, tr. Paul Breiter (Shambala 2005). The wild parade of temptations that

passed before St Anthony's inner eye during his ascetic exercises in the Egyptian desert (3rd century CE) is the stuff of Christian legend and the topic of many impressive depictions in art (by Hieronymus Bosch, Salvador Dalí, Gustave Flaubert, etc.).

69. MN 22.40-41 (pp. 234-35), SN 35.101 (pp. 1181-82). See also SN 35.71 (p. 1156): "'This is not mine, this I am not, this is not my self.' This itself is the end of suffering." And MN 37.3 (p. 344): "A bhikkhu has heard [and understands] that nothing is worth adhering to... [W]hatever feeling he feels, whether pleasant or painful or neither, he abides contemplating impermanence in those feelings, contemplating fading away, cessation, relinquishment. Contemplating thus, he does not cling to anything in the world. When he does not cling, he is not agitated. When he is not agitated, he attains Nibbana."

70. For the Buddha's equivalent to Jesus's "Judge not" (Matt. 7:1-5), see AN 6.44 (p. 912).

71. Epictetus, *Enchiridion*, chapter 5 (tr. Thomas Wentworth Higginson): "It is the action of an uninstructed person to reproach others for his own misfortunes; of one entering upon instruction, to reproach himself; and of one perfectly instructed, to reproach neither others nor himself." (See also Marcus Aurelius, *Meditations*, x.4.)

72. SN 22:49 (pp. 887-888), SN 35.108 (pp. 1185-1186).

73. Some especially memorable metaphors for the hindrances can be found MN 39.14 (pp. 366-67). "The fifth hindrance, doubt, signifies a chronic indecisiveness and lack of resolution: not the probing of critical intelligence, an attitude encouraged by the Buddha, but a persistent inability to commit oneself." (Bodhi, NEP, V.65)

74. The Horatii and Curiatii were two bands of triplets (not quite quintuplets as the metaphor would require, but close enough) who battled each other on behalf of their respective communities, the Romans and the Albans. The good guys won (at least from the Roman perspective), but only very barely (Livy, *History of Rome*, I.24-25, [Penguin 57-60]).

75. Hence also Goenka's recollection, mentioned above, that when he first began exploring the depths of his mind, he found them to be "full of snakes and scorpions and centipedes" (*Art of Living*, p. 143).

76. Socrates or not, Goenka's intellectual and rhetorical powers are not in doubt. He was already giving lectures on the sacred texts

of Hinduism before he became involved with Vipassana, and his discourses in Hindi are said to be marvels of eloquence. His English Ten-Day discourses may not rise to quite such oratorical heights, but considering that he is operating in his third language and needs to be all things to all people, they are surely impressive enough. Anyone not satisfied with the basic discourses on intellectual grounds might enjoy the Satipatthana discourses, which are also a little more genuinely spontaneous. (The Satipatthana course at which the English recordings were made, held in November 1990 at Dhamma Bhumi in Blackheath near Sydney, was only Goenka's thirteenth, not the 358th like the recorded Ten-Day course. He also answers questions from the students at the end of the course.)

77. See my footnote about the inner child in the context of Vipassana breakfast.

78. See also Fleischman's beach-ball (above).

79. See *Zen Mind, Beginner's Mind*, p. 17: "Do not try to stop your thinking. Let it stop by itself." Or not.

80. See for example *Clock of Vipassana*, p. 101.

81. The literal meaning of *manussa*, used to identify human beings in the Abhidhamma literature, is "those who have sharp or developed minds" (*Abh.*, p. 191).

82. The attempt to connect sensations to their underlying causes is "meaningless waste of energy" according to Goenka: "Observe any sensation that occurs. You cannot find which sensation is related to a particular emotion, so never try to do that; it is indulging in a futile effort. Whenever there is emotion in the mind, whatever sensation you experience physically has a relation to that emotion." (*Art of Living*, p. 128; see also pp. 108, 112.) At times the thoughts going through your mind as you are scanning may happen to give you some indication of what a particular sensation-pattern might represent at a deeper level, but you should never go looking for such connections. Try to keep your attention focused as exclusively as possible on the sensations themselves, without analyzing, judging, or pondering them.

83. Thus Goenka: "The Buddha's teaching is to move from the gross, apparent truth to the subtlest, ultimate truth, from *olariko* to *sukhama*." (*Clock of Vipassana*, p. 59, *Satip. Discourses*, p. 78) The progression from gross to subtle is made clear enough in the Ten-Day discourses, but it is more fully elaborated in the Satipatthana course.

84. One cannot be sure: milestone may remain hidden from view even when they have already been attained, or they may be overlooked as we pass them (*Art of Living*, pp. 77-78).

85. The story is told about Ananda in Goenka's *Satipatthana Discourses* (pp. 16-17). (See also *Cullavaga* 11.1.6 [*Life*, p. 337], *Greatest Disciples*, p. 180.) For Patacara, see *Great Disciples*, p. 297. Thus also Suzuki: "When you give up, when you no longer want something, or when you do not try to do anything special, then you are doing something." (*Zen Mind, Beginner's Mind*, p. 32)

86. Seneca, *Letters from a Stoic*, tr. Robin Campbell, no. XI.

87. Goenka concedes that the starting point can be different at *Clock of Vipassana*, p. 106, and in his *Satipatthana Discourses*, p. 38, where he writes that one might enter the pagoda of meditation from different directions: "but as you enter the gallery they all intermingle in *vedana*."

88. No less than forty by traditional accounts (*Vism.* III.28 [p. 90]).

89. U Ba Khin, in his "Essentials of Buddha Dhamma," also makes it clear that while the technique he taught is the quickest and most effective way of accessing *Anicca* for most students, especially beginners, it is certainly not the only serious way to practice (*U Ba Khin Journal*, p. 33, *Clock of Vipassana*, p. 116). Goenka, too, allow that observing sensations is "the most accessible and vivid" but not the only way to experience *Anicca* (*Art of Living*, p. 100).

90. See *Clock of Vipassana* (pp. 36, 90, 106) on U Ba Khin's reasons for using a less traditional language. Goenka explains the distinction between sweeping and going part-by-part on pp. 104-105.

91. *Clock of Vipassana*, p. 60 (also p. 103).

CHAPTER NINE
LOVE BITES ON METTA DAY

DAY 10, OR METTA DAY, IS TO MOST VIPASSANA MEDITATORS WHAT Christmas morning is to children who believe in Santa Claus. But like every aspect of Vipassana, and of life, it can trip you up when you are least expecting it, and it might be worth watching your steps as you bolt down the stairs to the Christmas tree lest any legs or necks get broken and dampen the festive spirit.

There is nothing special about the morning schedule, which follows the familiar pattern until the end of the group sitting from 8 to 9 am. After the usual short recess, students return to the hall and Goenka gives his instructions for a new kind of meditation on loving-kindness that is advertised as "balm on the wounds" inflicted by the strains of the previous nine days. A wise soul would be put on guard by the very advertisement, since one man's balm is another man's bane, and a woman's too. Generally speaking, however, the Metta session seems to live up to its billing.

Unless it doesn't. When I had waded through the gore of my first nine days at Vipassana camp (interspersed, of course, with moments of elation), I arrived at what I expected to be the balmy beaches of Metta with the most hopeful expectations, only to be bitterly disappointed. To this day, I find Goenka's instructions long-winded, trite, patronizing, and all-round annoying, though my aversion has softened somewhat with time and repetition. I would do better, I think, giving Metta in silence, and it would be nice to see what the session might feel like if one's spirits were raised to the heavens with beautiful chanting or music rather than dragged down by Goenka's croaking. But even an unsatisfactory Metta session will peter out eventually, and at its end beckons the long-awaited liberation from nine days' sensory deprivation. The noble silence is over, in other words, although students are supposed to hold their tongues for a few paces yet, while they are stepping away from the meditation hall. I remember well with what sincere enthusiasm I paid homage, at the top of my lungs, to Martin Luther King: "Free at last, free at last, thank God Almighty, we are free at last!"

The blandest chit-chat suddenly seems enticing, the most unremarkable food irresistible, and faces are blooming with joy and vitality on all sides, especially around the zones reserved to the opposite sex. (The segregation will be relaxed for most of the day, especially in and around the dining areas, but it is tightened again during mealtimes and after 6 pm. Strictly speaking, students are supposed to avoid all physical contact on Dhamma-land for energetic reasons, but hugs abound on Metta Day.) It is astounding to see how the weirdos one has eyed with suspicion or distaste for nine days have suddenly turned into intimate friends and confidants even before a single word has been spoken. No one is pretending either: for once you will be able to engage in serious conversations with nearly everyone, not mere small-talk, and the stories you will hear run no risk of boring you, because they will echo and amplify your own. All earned by one's own hard work. What could be better?

Only there are deeper and darker forces at work that may show themselves on Metta Day as well. After nine full days in the mind's deepest sewers, you cannot count on smelling only flowers when you emerge into the light again. For some, the sudden noble chatter grates. "I liked you all much better when you were silent," I've heard some grouches grumble on Metta Day. Alternatively, you might begin noticing before long how compulsively, almost desperately, you are talking or gobbling down your food at lunch, plate after plate, without any room for the dispassionate observation you thought you had been cultivating. The degree and intensity of attraction you are feeling for students of the opposite sex might strike you as a little disquieting, or perhaps you will encounter a puzzling streak of combativeness in yourself that you cannot quite explain. When the time comes for the afternoon's group sitting (which is still on), you may have to drag yourself to the hall and you may hold out until the last minute before you go in. But since you're an old hand at meditation now, you'll manage another hour without difficulty, or so you imagine. Except that when you close your eyes, the stable frame you have been scanning with your Vipassana apparatus has turned into a writhing tangle of fire of such unclear dimensions that you keep losing your way trying to move around the body. When you retreat to Anapana, you notice that you seem to have lost your ability to stay with the breath altogether and that you are getting sucked into the vortex of your swirling thoughts whether you like it or not. Then parts of your body start hurting that have given you no trouble before, and this for the longest damn hour you can remember having to suffer through at camp. At the end of it all, you are supposed to be in the mood for fifteen minutes of universal loving kindness? Nothing doing!

You run out of the hall and into the arms of renewed chatter, which feels delicious for a while. Before long, alas, you notice a headache creeping up on you. It would be good to rest for a bit, you think, but you can't tear yourself loose. It begins to dawn on you that you're far from the great meditator you thought you had seen in the mirror that morning. How could you have kidded yourself when you're actually a fraud, a loser, an asshole. Why are the people around you so insufferably joyful, when you are feeling like a piece of shit all of a sudden? Maybe you do manage to go to your room for a bit. You stare at the ceiling, maybe you cry a little. But it's too boring being cooped up, so out you go again.

At 5 pm you celebrate the first dinner in nine days by stuffing your face. Afterwards you feel nauseous. The headache has been coming and going in waves, and the last thing you want to do is meditate again. Dragging yourself into the hall is even harder than it was in the afternoon, but you are pleasantly surprised to discover that sitting is a bit easier and that your headache seems to melt away as you put it under the spotlight of your attention. When the sitting is over and it's time for the discourse, you're glad and grateful for the familiarity and the relative quiet of Papa Goenka's story-hour. Afterwards you get involved in some mind-bending discussions, but your brain feels ready to short-circuit if you don't give it some rest. You slink off to your room, where you lie awake for an hour before you can sleep. Your dreams are as crazy as any you've had during the course.

CHAPTER TEN
BACK TO DOING THE DISHES:
QUESTIONS AFTER A COURSE

What if meditation ends up making me passive and apathetic?
This is an old fear, and not just in Buddhist circles. The very
word "apathetic" made its way into English from the term the
Greek Stoics used to express their highest aspirations: *apatheia.*
What they taught, like the Buddha, was a method for coming
out of suffering (*pathos*), not a way to stop feeling and become
indifferent to things[1] — "like a vegetable: let anyone come and
cut me" as Goenka puts it in the discourses.[2]

As a former businessman with a big family, Goenka could
understand such concerns well, but they are still based on a
misunderstanding: meditation does not impede or inhibit the
active life, but clears the way for genuine *action* (sometimes very
strong, but always positive and loving) by diminishing mere
reaction.[3] As Marcus Aurelius puts it: "He who follows reason in
all things is both tranquil and active at the same time, and also
cheerful and collected."[4] Meditation is not for hiding from the
world; to the extent that it involves retreating temporarily, it is
so that by taking a few steps backwards one might jump forward
more effectively afterwards.[5]

The Art of Living offers a nice analogy with music: "There are
those who imagine that always remaining balanced means that

one can no longer enjoy life in all its variety, ... as if one had a piano and chose to play nothing but middle C. But this is a wrong understanding of equanimity. The fact is that the piano is out of tune and we do not know how to play it properly. Pounding the keys in the name of self-expression will only create discord. But if we learn how to tune the instrument and to play it well, then we can make music. From the lowest to the highest note we use the full range of the keyboard, and every note that we play creates nothing but harmony and beauty."[6]

Even so, whether in the Buddha's day or ours, the meditative life has never been immune from suspicions that it may be a mere excuse for the work-shy to shirk their worldly responsibilities. Thus a wealthy ploughman once challenged the Buddha: "I plough, monk, and I sow, and having ploughed and sown, I eat. If you want to eat, you should do the same." "I do plough and sow," the Buddha answered: "Faith is my seed, self-control my rain, understanding my plough and yoke. Mindfulness is my ploughshare, truth the reaping I do, forbearance my unharnessing, and energy my ox. Such is the ploughing I do, and the Deathless is my harvest."[7]

Goenka says several times that awareness and equanimity are like the two wings of a bird or the wheels of a cart: if they don't develop equally, the bird cannot fly and the cart will turn in circles.[8] But is there any guarantee that their development will always be so perfectly synchronized?
There's not much point in getting preoccupied with mere theoretical possibilities on the Path; but this concern can become quite practical. Even during a course, but especially afterwards, you may find that your sensitivity to your sensations has become very keen, while your increased equanimity is not always apparent. If so, you might wonder whether you might be shooting yourself in the foot with your meditation — by making yourself miserable with more sharply felt unpleasant sensations, and by merely reinforcing your addiction to pleasant sensations

that you can feel so much more vividly now! Doesn't seem quite right, does it?

But hold on. Goenka's point is that we need to be careful, in our practice, to keep an eye on both dimensions of our meditation. We need to work on our concentration and on moving around the body so that the mind gets sharper and more able to feel all kinds of sensations, and we need to cultivate equanimity with what we are feeling. Both stand opposed to "playing the game of sensations," that is, merely looking for pleasant sensations to relish and dwell on, with no effort made to observe the full range of possible sensations with detachment, dispassion, and equanimity. So long as we are clear on what it means to practice properly, the two wings should grow apace.

It is easy to get the impression, when you step back into the everyday world, that you have brought only your heightened sensitivity with you, while the equanimity you developed during your course got left behind at the center. But don't worry: nothing goes to waste on the Path, as Goenka says in the Ten-Day course.[9] The strong sensations and reactions that are bothering you have been occurring all along at the depth of your mind (if the Teaching is to be trusted); you are simply more aware of them now. Such awareness may not strike you as cause for celebration, granted: but how to change a pattern until you start noticing it? If you keep up your sittings, your equanimity will revive, and if you don't, your sensitivity will diminish. Either way, the balance between the two should be restored before long. If you find, in the meantime, that your sensations are too overpowering to be observed with equanimity outside your meditation periods, use more Anapana to calm down your mind. But don't quit working with your sensations, or you will lose a crucial part of your practice.[10]

I have just returned home from a course and the noise of the world is overwhelming me. Rather than feeling as good as I was led to expect, I am feeling raw and volatile. Others aren't

sure what to make of me, and they don't seem too pleased either, even my partner. What's wrong with me?

In the Buddha's day as in our own, Buddhists had a reputation for being a conspicuously cheerful lot that seemed to be delighting in their practice more than other seekers. When people imagine a typical Buddhist today, most of them probably picture the big smile of the Dalai Lama. What would you think of someone who introduced himself as an *unhappy* Buddhist?[11] (I'm tempted.)

But how could things be quite so easy, for Buddhists or anyone else, in a world as beset by dissatisfaction and suffering as the Teaching insists it is? The Path leads beyond all misery, but it won't just put you out of *Dukkha's* reach, especially in the earlier parts of your journey. To walk the Path means, first and foremost, to see the world more clearly: how noisy it is, how agitated, and how fundamentally driven by the defilements of craving, aversion, and ignorance — in a word, how miserable. You are not imagining the turmoil: perhaps for the first time, you are hearing and seeing it for what it really is, whereas before, long habit had so accustomed you to all the craziness that you didn't notice it.

You've also just gone through a very deep operation, part of which involved diving down to the mind's *Cloaka Maxima* — the hidden sewage system where your fears and traumas and insecurities are festering in the mind's darkest corners. Is it realistic to expect only sunshine and joy as soon as you resurface? Would you expect the same from a serious medical procedure? Will your teeth feel great as soon as the dentist is done with her drilling? Will parts that have gone under the surgeon's knife, even if it is for your own good, heal overnight? Probably not, and what may seem even worse, "The early stages of convalescence are often worse than the disease," as was known even in Roman times.[12] We tend to find pus repulsive, but what we are seeing is the body cleaning itself; we may resist crying and treat tears as if they were a shameful part of the problem, but they are washing out our wounds so that they may heal better. Courses that take you especially deeply into the practice may even produce results that can seem the opposite of meditative.[13] So best not to expect your mind to finish processing what you've gone through the instant you walk through the Dhamma gates with your honorable discharge papers in your back pocket. The real work begins now, as it always does when you get up from your cushion.

Beyond the element of sheer mental rawness, which may take a week or two to subside, there is the substance of what you may have discovered about yourself and your relationships with others. Much of that is not fun to see, either for you or for anyone else. The Buddha's Path is a path of liberation, not suffering; but as part of the process, the full range and scope of *Dukkha* may need to be faced as you have never faced it before, which can be a profound, unsettling process that will keep germinating within you. Eventually, the light will prevail, because that is the nature of the Dhamma, but you cannot force the pace or set a time-limit. How long does it take the seeds to sprout after you have sown them? How long must a hen sit patiently on her eggs before the chicks are ready to break through their shells?[14] Such things develop on their own schedule, and we only impede them if we try to rush the process. "Do not seek to hasten the ripening of that which is not yet ripe, but rather await its ripening wisely."[15]

You need to consider as well that a Ten-Day course involves not only equanimity, but also a measure of repression. Whether by the Buddhist or the evolutionary analysis, the markers of our long history as pleasure-seeking creatures (billions of years by both accounts) are imprinted upon our minds, embedded in our cells, and engraved on our genes. Our cravings and aversions will not go gentle into that good night; they will rage, rage against the coming of the light. Thus the desperate quality you may have noticed as you are shoveling in your food or mixing it up with your partner; thus the short fuse and the sudden flare-up as your aversions kick up a fuss because you have been neglecting them for perhaps longer than ever before in your entire history as a karmic or a biological being. It's an immense accomplishment to have thrown the switch, even temporarily, but the old circuits have not been erased; they have been tidied up here and there, to be sure, but that is all the more reason for your old habits to fight back now that your attention is being diverted by the usual distractions again. After all, their survival is at stake, and they sense it.

A partner who is not familiar with the dynamics of Vipassana courses, or who may experience them differently, may not know what to make of your difficulties, especially in cases when your relationship, or any aspect of it, is part of what has been coming up for you. In sum, this is when you will need all the equanimity and loving-kindness you can muster. Be as gentle as you can, with yourself no less than with others. Give yourself as much quiet time as possible, at least for a couple of days. *And do try to make time for those sittings, even if they are not very enjoyable*; they will help you maneuver through the straits. Your old habits are bound to reassert themselves; instead of fighting their return to power on a broad front, see whether you can moderate their demands and defenses in those areas, perhaps starting with the precepts, where you see the greatest need for change.

Coming out of my Vipassana courses, especially the first one, I have been eager to share what I have learned with the people closest to me, especially parents and other family members; but I have been discovering that they are among the most unresponsive and resistant to what I am trying to tell them. Is there anything I can do?

Best to do nothing. Remember what Jesus said about no one being a prophet in his own house (or that of one's parents).[16] If the Dhamma is working in you the way you believe, it will show and others will become interested. But if you push, they will quickly pull away. Your job is to work on your own stuff, not to change others.

Committing to ten days of meditation is a daunting hurdle for almost everyone, and you will find that many of your friends, even if they are sincerely interested, will hedge and make excuses and keep talking for years without doing anything about it. The Buddhists would explain this by saying that there are invisible dynamics at work: some have the seed of Dhamma and will respond to the call quickly; others may take a little longer; still others may not be ready for a long time yet. Let the universe do its work; you do yours.

I have practiced for a while now, and sometimes I feel as if I am going in circles or even falling back. Is that possible?
If the Dhamma is real and you are not just a wanderer in the desert, mislead by mirages while dying of thirst, then no, you are not going in circles, nor falling back. But I've often felt the same way.

Phases that feel like unexciting plateaus, where not much progress seems to be made, are as vital to a serious practice as are the sudden leaps that we enjoy so much more.[17] Before you can soar, you sometimes need to gather your forces, or even take what may look like a step back, even if it is ultimately not. In the Dhamma as in all demanding arts, gradual training, gradual activity, and gradual progress are the watchwords.[18] If acquiring any complex skill is said to require several hours of daily practice for perhaps a decade — around 10,000 hours in total — then we can perhaps begin to imagine how patient we need to be with our meditative practices.[19]

Instead of thinking of the Path in two dimensions, as something flat on the ground, perhaps it would help to add a third and think of it as a spiral staircase leading up to the heavens (or to the mouth of Plato's Cave, if you prefer). If you were to look at the staircase from straight above, any upward movement would look circular; but if you looked at it from the side instead, you would see a steady ascent. When you are ready to step out of the Cave and into the sunlight, you will no longer be plagued by such uncertainties. Thus the first three fetters that are said to be eradicated forever at the moment of stream-entry are *doubt*, the mistaken *belief in self*, and the *wrong understanding of rules, rites, and rituals*. "The Teaching is simple. Do what is right. Purify the mind. At the end of the Way is freedom. *Till then, patience.*"[20]

By the Buddhist analysis, life as it is ordinarily lived, in all times and all cultures, cannot give us the lasting satisfaction and peace that we are all ultimately seeking. But long-established patterns of life, however limited from a spiritual point of view, also define human communities and provide a measure of comfort, convenience, and reassurance. When one sets out on the journey towards the other shore, abandoning the benefits of beach-life can feel like a bitter loss. That is why it is said, in the Mahayana literature, that it would be better never to start on the Path than to give up once one has started.[21] I do not see how the warning could be strictly true: any step on the Path surely brings its benefits; pulling weeds from the overgrown garden of the mind can never be mistaken, even if we remove only a few and new ones quickly grow back. But the Mahayana saying still reminds us of something crucial, namely that the waters between the old shore and the new can be choppy, even menacing, and that they must be crossed with resolve, not lingered over, because they are no fit place to settle down. There are storms, too, from which one would be safe on the beach, dark nights of the soul that afflict precisely those who are nearing the other side. That is one of the reasons why a mature and clear-sighted faith is so crucial a friend on the Path.

How strict do I need to be about the precepts in daily life? Must I become a vegetarian if I am serious about being on the Path?
The Five Precepts are enjoined upon Buddhists at all times, but they need to be interpreted. For starters, what gets translated as "precept" is really a *training rule*,[22] that is to say, not an unconditional demand by the Buddha, nor a paternal mandate imposed on sinful mankind by a wrathful God[23] or a categorical imperative issued by our rational faculties, but a generalization

that is helpful (and perhaps necessary) for living peacefully and happily.[24] Rather than dwelling too much on what is "bad," it may help to think of it as simply "what not to do."[25]

The rule against intoxicants is a general safeguard against anything that might lead to heedless or uncaring behavior. It identifies alcohol specifically, but it also applies to any other substance with a tendency to foster irresponsibility. By the same rationale, neither drinking coffee nor smoking tobacco, however addictive, is against the precepts. In the conventional list of ten unprofitable or unskillful courses of action, the use of intoxicants is not included, suggesting that it is not the state of inebriation itself that is so problematic, but its consequences in other immoral directions.[26] There is no denying that alcohol is considered a major obstacle to the spiritual life in Buddhism, but the Dhamma is subtle and even so serious an impediment does not rule out progress on the Path. Thus the Suttas mention that the Buddha scandalized his contemporaries by identifying at least two stream-enterers who were regular drinkers (rare exceptions, it has to be said, among a great many others).[27]

Lying cuts the root of trust and creates a habit of untruthfulness that is the very opposite of seeing things as they are.[28] One of the Buddha's most memorable lessons was given on the subject of lying to his eleven-year-old son Rahula. The Buddha poured a bit of water into a bowl and held it out to the boy: in anyone who is not ashamed to tell a lie, there is as little good as there is water in this bowl. Then he threw the water out: like this a liar throws away the good inside himself. Then he turned the bowl upside down: so a liar turns himself upside down. He held out the empty bowl: so devoid of good are they who do not stick to the truth. There is no telling what might be done by someone willing to tell a lie. You must never speak a falsehood, even in jest.[29] Is it possible to imagine scenarios in which a lie might nonetheless be prompted by nothing but the purest intentions? Perhaps, but if so you need to look at your real motivations very closely and honestly before concluding that a "white" lie is indeed innocent and loving.

Sexual misconduct covers all forms of cheating and deception, breaking faith or vows, taking advantage, or being unkind. Consent is indispensable, age and appropriateness are considerations. Sexual orientation and technique are unimportant in themselves, but one's underlying intentions need to be examined with special care in this craving-prone area.[30]

Stealing extends beyond outright theft to all dishonest business practices, all undue profiteering, anything dodgy or exploitative, any transaction that is not done in good faith. Once more, it is a conscientious look inside that will reveal more than any outward calculation.

Killing applies in the first place to killing human beings, and it is a matter for debate whether there are any circumstances when it may be permissible. Abortion and euthanasia, for example, will not easily avoid looking immoral from a Buddhist point of view, but the scales of karma are not for human judges to calibrate and the forces of karmic gravity always depend on circumstances and motive. Suicide may not be inherently immoral, but it is likely to bring great grief to others and it looks futile and sure to disappoint on Buddhist premises: suffering escaped in this life will have to be faced anew, likely on worse terms, in another life. Even at its most difficult, a human existence offers karmic opportunities that should not be given up without the gravest circumspection.[31]

Buddhist states have not found a way to do without police forces and soldiers, punishments and penitentiaries, and the Buddha never suggested to the rulers among his followers that they dissolve their armies, dismiss their executioners, or open the gates of their prisons.[32] Yet the cruelties of government that may be unavoidable in the world as we know it may still mean a karmic burden for those who shoulder them on our behalf.[33] The ideal of nonviolence that the Buddha teaches, "with stick and sword laid aside," is so demanding that it would have us abstain from injuring even seeds and plants gratuitously,[34] but it is also sensitive to the realities of the world we live in.[35]

Whether the wrongness of killing animals necessarily translates into a compulsory vegetarianism has divided the Buddhist world for ages. Whatever the right answer may be, it is not the eating of meat itself that is objectionable: if I finish the meat left over on the plate of a friend who would otherwise throw it out, say, I commit no wrong.[36] In the Buddha's day, the assumption was that animals for sale in the market had already been killed and could therefore be eaten without scruple. It would look different if an animal had been killed on demand, or anticipating approval; in such cases, it was to be rejected.[37] A complicating factor is that monks beg their food and should not be encouraged to reject anything put in their bowls; with the foreseeable consequence that householders might give them meat if they believed it to be more pleasing, even if the monks did not say so. Environment, too, is a factor: few Tibetan Buddhists are vegetarians because of the relative ease of grazing animals and the difficulty of growing vegetables on so barren a plateau. The Buddha's most aggressive rival, Devadatta, sought to split the Sangha by forbidding all meat-eating to his monks, a proposal that was roundly rejected by the Buddha.[38]

As with all the precepts, the most important consideration is intention. The Sutta most directly concerned with the question of meat-eating stresses that what matters most is not what we eat, but whether our minds are in a loving, equanimous, detached state.[39] Granted that I should avoid buying meat or ordering it at a restaurant, is there anything wrong with eating it when I am invited by someone who was not aware of my preferences? If a more definite answer were required, I would say that a gentle vegetarianism would surely be the most Dhammic line to take on food, hence the diet served at Goenka's centers; but it is clearly not mandatory, and it can undermine the purpose of the precepts if applied with too much rigor and too little concern for context.

What would you say if, after a course, I decided to go back to drinking alcohol and using drugs — not as a matter of compulsion or addiction, but because these substances make a

contribution to my life that I do not want to miss? And what about substances that are not so much intoxicants as spiritual medicines and mind-openers, such as Ayahuasca, for example? You are your own master. Remember the story Goenka tells about the royal first president of Burma (Sao Shwe Thaik) who gave up alcohol so reluctantly during his ten-day course with U Ba Khin and insisted on being left free to drink afterwards (though he ended up not wanting to anymore). The Dhamma is not about telling you what to do, but about giving you generalizations to live by, because in the absence of such rules, we all tend to lose our moral orientation. The question of how to think about alcohol and drugs has many levels, but on the ground floor we all need to reckon with the fact, whether it is welcome or not, that intoxicants are against the precepts for good reasons.

There is little room for argument about alcohol since it is the one substance that the Pali formulation of the precept identifies explicitly.[40] Addiction is rarely a clear-cut matter and compulsion is an even subtler beast, especially with activities that are as deeply embedded in social custom as alcohol is in many parts (or marijuana these days). But assuming that you are making the considered choice you claim, alcohol still clouds the judgment at very low doses. The heavens will not fall over a glass of champagne at New Year's, but it is not easy to stick to so stringent a line, and even one glass may lead one to do thoughtless or inconsiderate things that one might have otherwise been able to avoid. The supposed excuse so often proffered for bad behavior — that one was drunk — is in fact an aggravation and a further accusation.

I cannot imagine a serious Dhammic case being made for entering the basement level of the House of Intoxication, the home of such dangerous residents as Mr Cocaine, Ms Heroin, and Mme Opium. We are not talking about ruling out any and all merits in such substances, let alone in their close cousins the Pain-Killers, whose legitimate medical virtues Buddhists do not dispute even if they aspire to practicing with pain rather than killing it. (Nor are we even touching on the discussion whether such drugs should be illegal or not.) When we approach this problem by way of the Dhamma, we need to recognize that there are spiritual energies that call for a darker vocabulary than the semantics of medical neutrality and that may be more accurately described in terms of possession than of addiction.[41]

On the first upper levels we might encounter substances like marijuana, ecstasy, and the like, to which medical and spiritual benefits may be attributed, but which have a way of shading off into murkier areas. At the intermediate levels we might run into such psychedelics (or hallucinogenics or entheogens, take your pick) as Don Peyote, the Magic Mushrooms Family, or Prof. L.S.D., where the ban against heedlessness loses most of its force and the case for spiritual exploration may be thought strongest. Goenka and his students tend to take a hard line against these as against all drugs,[42] but the classic argument made by Aldous Huxley in the 1950s still needs answering, even if the ensuing decades have not borne out his vision of a responsible and strictly spiritual use of such substances.[43]

The greatest complexities arise at the top of the edifice, where Mother Ayahuasca ("La Madre") has her penthouse and where the Reverend Iboga and other mysterious strangers are said to be regular visitors.[44] In this area, we may still be dealing with intoxicants in the technical sense, but heedlessness and dependency are moot points. If anything, Ayahuasca has a way of breaking addictions and inculcating a keener appreciation for virtuous and loving behavior. Although the Dhamma goes beyond healing, health is not to be slighted on the Path, and the hope that Ayahuasca ("La Medicina") offers in various medical directions cannot just be dismissed as fanciful because it doesn't meet many criteria of conventional scientific evaluation (as yet, at least).[45] When it comes to purification ("La Purga"), where Ayahuasca may reasonably be thought to operate as an extension and an intensifier of meditation, the Dhammic case is even stronger. Anything that helps to open the heart, to build equanimity, and to reduce self-grasping shares in the Dhamma.[46] Whether

Ayahuasca ceremonies really are conducive to equanimity, or whether the often extreme experiences they induce multiply blind reaction instead, is much harder to tell.[47]

On a more cautionary note, those of us who take refuge in the Buddha may pause over the fact that Ayahuasca-journeys almost always expose voyagers to information whose origins and significance we cannot even begin to understand. The Buddha deliberately withheld much that it is possible to know, because he considered it a useless or even harmful distraction from the Path, and we do need to ask ourselves how much of what we might see under the influence of the plants falls into this troubling category. In a Sutta devoted to convincing a prince of the existence of other worlds than our human one, the Buddha also warns against the dangers of seeking those worlds unwisely and prematurely.[48] The lesson needs to be adapted and interpreted because it was not directed at the kind of exploration made possible by Ayahuasca; but the fact remains that mere curiosity about other realms for which one is not prepared (and who is ever fully prepared for what Mother Ayahuasca holds in store?) does not look like a sufficiently Dhammic motive, and may even be a foolish one, though one would have to add that many shamans say the same thing in their different spiritual languages.

Nor is it solely a matter of information, but of energies and possibly entities that most of us do not comprehend at all, for better or for worse, as we step through the portals that Ayahuasca opens up. (The conundrum of whether these are external or internal realities pales, for me at least, beside the question whether and how we should be engaging these dimensions of being.) If we enter such realms in good faith, trusting our spiritual guides and companions, we may be protected to a point by the purity of our intentions, but what do we really know about the energies we are seeking out and inviting in? I am in no position to judge, let alone preach, but devotees of the Dhamma need to be aware that the places we are going may not be nearly as clean, secure, and noble as those safeguarded by meditation under a responsible teacher. Air Goenka will keep you as safe as it is possible to be while flying, and it will take you only to destinations whose wholesomeness it can guarantee. But it is otherwise with flights to the antipodes of the mind,[49] especially with many of the shady operators that the worldwide boom in Ayahuasca is attracting. Of course wolves in sheep's clothes seek their prey in every domain of life, but the smell of Ayahuasca (blended with that of money and the other currencies of power) does seem to be attracting an alarming number of them.

At such junctures, we can only decide for ourselves what we take to be true, what is right and beneficial, what wholesome and good, and what dangers we are prepared to court in pursuit of whatever it is we are seeking. In the end, it comes down to the pivot so often stressed by the Buddha: personal experience and an honest look at how we are affected by it, together with faith and enthusiasm (in the best sense of being filled by something sublime), the heart seconded by the head as much as possible. How so daunting a jigsaw-puzzle of competing considerations is to be put together, I cannot tell anyone, even approximately; I have too much trouble trying to piece it together myself.

Is anyone really able to keep up the two hours of meditation in daily life? And is it true that after one year of faithful practice, it will all become "so easy" and there is no more danger of lapsing?

Yes, there are such Dhamma-heroes. Some characters hit the ground running after their first course and never miss another sitting for the rest of their lives. They're about as common as platypuses outside Australia, but they exist.

If you do not have a history of getting up at 4 am to put in an hour of running and an hour at the gym before work, it may make sense to set your sights a little lower and to make an effort to keep up *any* kind of daily practice, because even sitting for only a few minutes, if you are committed to doing it *every* day, is a great achievement. "By not halting and by not straining I crossed the flood."[50] Another approach would be to accept that you will fall down eventually, and to focus instead on getting up again, even if it is after lying on the ground for a while. In other words, to make yourself pick up the pieces of your practice whenever it has crumbled, perhaps by taking another course.

But there is also the gung-ho approach of stubbornly clocking at least two hours a day, come what may. I tried it for several years, and it was very satisfying. I would say that it got somewhat easier with time and practice, but I still found it a struggle all the way through, and I was tired of it by the end. I thought about suing Goenka,[51] but it's always possible that I was still not practicing strictly enough, because sometimes I would do all my hours in the morning, or all of them at night, and sometimes I would split them up rather than always do two complete hours. Goenka is a salesman, after all, and it is up to us to temper his taller claims with a bit of realism. The Mormon boys who come to your door and promise that if you make it through their book, you will come to appreciate its truth and beauty, are not lying. They may not even be wrong; it's just that in the absence of a faith that moves mountains, getting through such feats of endurance is not humanly possible.

Do I have to keep up my daily sittings even when I am sick?
You don't have to do anything. But meditating when you are feeling sick is supposed to be especially beneficial, because it helps to build equanimity with the class of sensations to which we are most averse — because they trigger our organism's deepest alarms and feel like premonitions of incapacity and death. Our bodies are the products of a long history of struggling for survival, and sickness puts every cells of ours on edge, as we can feel. Yet sickness and death are inevitable, and the sooner we come to terms with them the better. Hence the idea of sickness, aging, and death as "divine messengers" who might wake us up from our dreams of pleasure.[52]

During the Ten-Day course, Goenka keeps emphasizing that "continuity of practice is the secret to success." If that is so, surely it applies in everyday life as well. How is it possible to stay with one's sensations continuously when one is dealing with all the preoccupations and distractions of daily life?

It would be ideal if we could remain mindful all the time — which from a Vipassana perspective would mean keeping in touch with one's sensations around the clock, whatever else one may be doing. But this ideal needs to be qualified in important ways.

Goenka emphasizes that while you are working or taking care of important responsibilities, your attention should always be on what you are doing: that is your primary meditation.[53] You should not aim to focus on your sensations, let alone to do rounds around the body, if this would mean getting distracted from an activity that requires your full attention (driving, for example). That said, you may find that your sensations are easily available for observation without dividing your attention. While you are busy doing other things, making rounds is neither necessary nor practical; simple awareness of sensations anywhere in your body is good enough. If different sensations are accessible to you, try staying with the subtlest and moving around the body in relaxed ways so that you don't get stuck anywhere.

If you find that you are fixating on unpleasant sensations and that you are losing your mental balance as a result, best to go to the breath instead. Goenka's instructions to observe "any" sensations casually during the day can be a little unhelpful when you are not feeling much or you are not sure where to direct your attention. In that case, try observing a few breaths and see whether they help to switch on your awareness (like an "ignition key" as Vipassana teachers say). If you find that working with the sensations requires too much effort off the mat, do not hesitate to practice with the breath instead. Goenka can make it sound as if Anapana were a second-best practice, but it has its own distinctive qualities.

If the entire prospect of continuous practice puts you off at this stage, just leave it aside. As U Ba Khin used to tell his students, anyone still torn between realizing *Anicca* within and the pull of worldly activities outside "would be wise to follow the motto of 'work while you work, play while you play.'" Rather than straining to observe *Anicca* all the time, focus your efforts on your meditation periods until it becomes more natural and intuitive to observe your breath or your sensations throughout the day.[54]

How do you see the relationship between the daily practice and the annual courses that Goenka recommends?

The courses allow for much deeper work than your daily practice. You might think of the latter as brushing your teeth and the former as going to the dentist to get your teeth cleaned and fixed. The equanimity and other benefits you may see in your daily life owe much to your everyday practice, but your daily efforts owe even more to the purification you have done at camp. Regular courses should also help to boost or revive your zest when it has slackened.

When is the right time to go back for another course, or to volunteer as a server?

The time is right when you feel ready. Goenka recommends serving at least one course (not once a year, just one) and coming back to sit a Ten-Day course every year, but those are merely rules of thumb. One course a year can be too much, six a year can be too few, whether sitting or serving. It depends on you.

Is it a good idea for pregnant women to take a Vipassana course?

It is said that doing a course during pregnancy is the best thing you can do for your baby, but that claim has not been validated by the FDA.[55] Since I have no recollection of having ever been a pregnant woman or a fetus during a Vipassana course, I cannot personally vouch for anything, but I can confirm that centers make dietary allowances for pregnant women.

ૐ

Goenka says that Anapana meditation is for concentration, Vipassana meditation for purification. But is the relationship between the two really so clear-cut? I've heard that the Buddha was practicing Anapana under the Bodhi tree, not Vipassana. What if I would like to do more Anapana at home?

The breath and the sensations on the body are two places where the connection between the mind and the body can be observed with particular clarity. Just as the mind and body are interdependent, so the breath and the sensations are linked and the distinction between observing one or the other is not black-and-white. But there is still a difference of emphasis: because the area and range of phenomena observed during Anapana meditation is relatively narrow, it is said to be more geared towards deepening concentration, while the observation of much more differentiated sensations throughout body is thought to be more purifying.

Goenka's more simplistic treatment of Anapana as "just a tool to help you practice Vipassana properly"[56] would be hard to square not only with what other teachers and schools have to say,[57] but also with what we are told in the Canon:[58] "Concentration by mindfulness of breathing is *the one thing* which, when developed and cultivated, fulfills the four establishments of mindfulness."[59] (There is no similarly direct, unequivocal statement to favor the Goenkanauts' insistence on the primacy of *vedana*-practice; they rest their scriptural case on a single vague line occurring half-way through a list towards the end of an obscure Sutta.[60])

The Buddha seems to have taught and praised both techniques, and many more.[61] Mindfulness of the body is certainly recommended: "Even as one who encompasses the great ocean with his mind includes thereby all the streams that run into the ocean, just so whoever develops and cultivates mindfulness directed to the body includes all wholesome qualities that pertain to true knowledge."[62] The need to cultivate non-reaction to bodily sensations may also be thought to follow directly from the logic of dependent origination as we have seen.[63] But the Buddha lavished particular praise on the "peaceful and sublime, ambrosial pleasantness"[64] of mindfulness of breath, and he reported that both before, during, and after his enlightenment, he made a point of "dwelling in this noble, divine dwelling."[65] When the Buddha had taught his son Rahula that "all material form should be seen as it is, with proper wisdom, thus: 'This is not mine, this I am not, this is not my self'" and the boy sat down to meditate on the lesson, he was told to practice mindfulness of breathing so that he might perceive impermanence clearly and abandon "the conceit 'I am.'"[66]

Why put our energies into playing off these two potent techniques against each other rather than into exploring them together? The ratio of two to one between Vipassana and Anapana on a Goenka course is not as rigid as it may sound: students are encouraged to go back to Anapana, using it as their "anchor" whenever the need arises.[67] Once you have become familiar enough with both techniques, you will develop your own sense of how they fit together.

What are "jhanas"?

The *jhanas* are four states of increasingly deep and powerful concentration[68] that the Buddha considered "exclusively pleasant" and that he endorsed as "entirely conducive" to progress on the Path.[69] It is said that he came to appreciate their innocence and helpfulness after he had become disillusioned with his ascetic exercises. He remembered experiencing the first *jhana* as a little boy and asked himself whether it might be pointing him to a better way. "Then, following on that memory, came the realization: 'That is indeed the path to enlightenment.'"[70] On the night of his liberation, the Buddha supposedly experienced the four *jhanas* in succession,[71] and on the night of his death, he ascended from the first up to the fourth, then descended back down to the first before he breathed his last.[72] The Buddha also called the *jhanas* "the Tathagata's footprints."[73]

On the other hand, despite the beauties and benefits of the *jhanas*, it is not for their sake that the holy life is lived.[74] Only wisdom — that is, *insight* into and *equanimity* with the Three Characteristics of *Anicca*, *Dukkha*, and *Anatta* — can purify the mind and pave the way to liberation.[75] Purifying equanimity, however, is attributed to none but the fourth *jhana*.[76] Among the Goenkanauts, *jhana*-practice is therefore associated with Anapana, purification with Vipassana and *vedana*-practice.[77] Any preoccupation with meditative states is strongly discouraged because they can so easily turn into cravings and distractions from *Anicca* and the other characteristics.[78] The so-called "dry-insight" method[79] that does not emphasize the *jhanas* is traditionally said to be a viable path to liberation, but it must do without the nourishing benefits that can come from these states, as the name implies.[80]

How can I tell whether a state I have experienced during meditation was a *jhana* state?

Various kinds of higher meditative states are described not only in the Pali Canon, but also in other spiritual literatures, since *jhana*-practice is not exclusive to Buddhism.[81] Serious meditation can lead you to the strangest corners of your mind, but from a Vipassana point of view, the important thing is to keep an inner distance and treat these curiosities as no more than exotic exhibits in the Zoo of *Anicca*.

This is one of the points on which I most appreciate Goenka's tough line: meditational states are a part of the process, and they can guide us if we treat them as way-markers, but they have no ultimate importance except as testing grounds for our equanimity. Anything that is clung to, no matter how fascinating or sublime, becomes an obstacle to purification.

Too many gurus, in the Buddha's day as in our own, set up shop on the strength of this or that spectacular attainment, which they take to be confirmation of their unique spiritual gifts. For the most part, they may be perfectly sincere, and I don't dispute their "higher" experiences. What I doubt, on orthodox grounds, is that such episodes are as significant as they are taken to be. The ego wears many guises; whatever goes to the head is not the Dhamma.

In the traditional Theravadan scheme, understanding what is and what is not the Path presents one of the trickiest challenges because it is itself a late fruit of purification that cannot be taken for granted even among advanced meditators.[82] Thus Buddhaghosa devoted a full chapter in the *Visuddhimagga* to the dangers that await anyone who allows himself to get attached to higher meditative states or to believe that the serenity he has attained makes him a liberated being.[83] When an unusual meditative state arises, "a skillful, wary meditator who is endowed with discretion examines it with understanding thus: 'This state has arisen. But it is impermanent, conditionally arisen, subject to fading away and cessation.' ... He defines what is the path and what is not the path thus: 'These states are not the path. Insight knowledge that keeps to its course is the path.'"[84]

Goenka doesn't seem to like mantras. Why not?

Goenka acknowledges how much mantras can help with strengthening one's concentration, but their use is not compatible with Vipassana as he understands it because all visualization, imagination, or verbalization creates "artificial" vibrations that do not allow one to observe what occurs "naturally."[85]

I follow Goenka's line, but I keep an emergency mantra at hand for when I need a bit of extra encouragement on the mat: "Better fifteen minutes than ten."

That's it?

When things get really rough, I have a last-ditch mantra: "Better five minutes than none."[86]

When I sleep more, I feel much more energetic, joyful, and equanimous. It seems almost like a kind of meditation to me.

So why does sleep get so little respect?

I've often wondered why so great a blessing as good and plentiful sleep should get such a bad rap. Ask any insomniac about what he is missing, or any scientist who has tested how sleep-deprivation affects performance. I am convinced that we have barely scratched the surface of all the ways the whole organism, body and mind, heals and repairs itself when we sleep. (Among the eleven benefits to be expected from liberating the mind by loving-kindness, the first one the Buddha mentioned is that "one sleeps well."[87])

Yet the campaign against sleep has long united the unlikeliest bedfellows. To the harsher kind of Catholic traditionalist, it might point the way towards mortal sin — a valid concern if anyone really slept "like a sloth," fifteen to twenty hours a day, which even sloths in fact don't. To industrious Protestants, it falls afoul of their sacred work ethic; to those following in Franklin's footsteps, it seems a waste of time, hence of money. Generals, CEOs, and other hardened machos use it to deride wimps and women — Napoleon: "Six hours for a man, seven for a woman, eight for a fool!" — rock-stars and other hipsters to distance themselves from squares who go to bed at 10; they expect to get sleep enough when they are dead (the last place where we should look for rest, according to a more Buddhist perspective). The harried foot-soldiers of modern capitalism don't have time for it (they are said to sleep two hours less a night, on average, than their less urbanized and industrialized grandparents did even fifty years ago) and parents probably never got enough of it in any age.

Among philosophers denunciations of sleep abound. Only Voltaire and Kant had the sense to insist that without the gifts of sleep, hope, and laughter the troubles of life would soon become unbearable.[88]

Self-appointed experts stubbornly perpetuate the myth that there is such a thing as unhealthy oversleeping when in fact it is impossible to force the body to sleep more than it needs. (Lolling about in bed when one has woken up is another matter, as is the sluggishness that results from changing sleep-patterns; but that only seems to be caused by too much sleep, when in fact it is usually the result of recovering from not having slept enough before.)

Spiritual teachers and traditions are among the worst offenders against sacred snoozing, perhaps because sleep and awakening seem to be opposites, if only for reasons of semantics. The ancient ascetic exercise of denying oneself rest seems to have lost little of its appeal and we must count ourselves lucky to be granted even the seven hours that Goenka allots for sleeping at night, which is generous when compared to other meditation centers.

If you need or want more rest, take heart from the example of the Buddha. When a visitor came to him, troubled by rumors that the Awakened One might *sleep during the day* like a lesser being ("some recluses and brahmins call that abiding in delusion, Master Gotama"), the Buddha confirmed that during the hot season, he did indeed nap after lunch. "I fall asleep with mindfulness and awareness," he told his visitor, "It is not in such a way that one is deluded or undeluded."[89] If outright sleeping still seems inappropriate to you, try some *Beditation* (patent pending): lie down in what yogis call *savasana*, in your bed or anywhere else, flat on your back with your chin tucked in a little and your palms facing up. Watch either your breath or the sensations in your palms or on the soles of your feet (or make your rounds, if you prefer). Enjoy whatever you may be feeling in a spirit of detached but cheerful observation: that's what it's ultimately about.

In one of his talks, Bhikkhu Bodhi remembers how he first arrived at a monastery in Sri Lanka after a long and arduous journey, tired but eager to make a good first impression on a monk and teacher that he admired especially (Nyanaponika Thera, I think it was). When the elder monk saw him, he realized how exhausted Bodhi was. "If you are tired, why don't you just get some sleep?" he said. It can be that simple: when it's time to rest, rest.[90]

ॐ

I gather that there is a precept against handling money. Did the Buddha believe that money was dirty and should we try to avoid it if we are serious about the Dhamma?

The last of the Ten Precepts is indeed a rule against accepting money, but unlike the Eight Precepts that get applied to householders on retreats, the Ten are only ever meant for monks and nuns.[91] Cash may be pretty unhygienic, granted, but Buddhist monks and nuns renounce a lot of things that are not dirty at all.

Renunciates don't shave their heads or wear ungainly uniforms because more personal hairdos or wardrobes are dirty (at least they need not be). Getting married, having children, earning an honest living, looking after others and acquiring material comforts for them and for oneself are all good things in their proper place, only not very conducive to confronting our attachments head-on. For those who were not ready to leave behind their householders' delights and responsibilities, the Buddha gave very sensible and practical advice not only about family life[92] and the workplace,[93] but also about protecting "righteous wealth righteously gained" from bandits and grasping governors, fires, floods, and unloved heirs,[94] about generous and balanced living within one's means (and the happiness of freedom from debt),[95] and even about distributing funds between consumption, insurance, and investment.[96]

Over the ages, money has been maligned from all directions. But in a world without it, what Adam Smith called "the propensity to truck, barter, and exchange one thing for another"[97] would not magically disappear, nor the parallel tendency to put oneself first and be greedy, stingy, and hard-hearted in one's dealings with others. It is these underlying inclinations to which money gives expression; were it to disappear, barter would take its place and the same patterns would get expressed in a less efficient but no more benign manner. If the freedom to exchange things were suppressed altogether, it would do nothing to usher in a world of loving-kindness; if anything, the same self-interests would be asserted by more coercive and exploitative means. Slave and warrior societies get on quite well without money; it's relatively free ones that don't.

I agree with everything Goenka says about breaking our addiction to pleasant sensations. So should I be trying to come out of sex?

If you feel the call to be a monk or a nun, you will need to do a lot more than try. The rules for joining and leaving the Sangha are generous: a certain Bhikkhu Citta came and went six times before finally staying the seventh time and becoming an *arahant*.[98] The rules on sex are very strict, however. The life of the monks is governed by 227 precepts (that of the nuns by 311), but only four are considered "defeats for life," and one of them is "sex with any living being" (go figure).[99]

Once Ananda (champion of the bhikkhunis) asked the Buddha how the monks should relate to women. "Do not see them," the Awakened One answered.[100] A little harsh, one might think, even if dire warnings against the dangers of sensual pleasures are nothing unusual, especially when they are directed at young men sworn to celibacy.[101] The Buddha emphasized the need to guard the doors of our senses, including that of the mind,[102] but strictly speaking, it is true that looking itself is never the problem; our reactions are. If we could learn to "look with chaste eyes"[103] upon the things that incite our desires, it would be ideal; a Buddha never needs to avert his gaze.

From a biological point of view, it is only fit that we should like to look so much: the desires of the flesh give their commands with the authority of life itself; their voice is the voice of our evolution, over the aeons, in a long, unbroken chain of survivors and procreators whose heirs we all are. Were it not for such desires, none of us would be around either by the Darwinian or the Dhammic reckoning. Nor is the problem a moral one: we need not worry about incurring the wrath of a disappointed judge eager to chastise us; we must simply live with the cravings we stir up. No one will stop us from stoking the fires beneath the cauldron, quite the contrary: the whole world presents us with inducements to keep burning and boiling, as we all know. So long as we remain convinced that we are having a good time living in this manner, there's no point in being told to change. The question is a practical one: how long do we want to keep watching ever the same show, in all its wearisome repetitiveness? When we get tired of our playthings, or they of us, the Buddha will help us dispose of them; he's not there to take anything away against our wills, nor could he do so even if he wanted to.

That said, it is probably not a good idea for most householders to force the issue on sex.[104] In its playful aspect, it is an innocent part of the joyful path the Buddha discovered. As an expression of love and commitment, it is wholesome and beautiful. Even the pleasant sensations it brings are not themselves problematic: the *jhanas* are supposed to be very pleasurable fruit of concentration, and *metta*-meditation uses pleasant sensations to generate vibrations of universal love. The trouble with sex as with all physical pleasures is the craving, clinging dimension, that is, the addictive, compulsive, obsessive dynamics that usually surround our bodily needs and desires. It is not enjoyment itself that is the problem, but how we relate to it, and what we will do to get it. Behind every broken precept and every promiscuous act is an unwholesome intention; only look closely enough, and you will see how tainted it is with ego, greed, insatiable desire, insecurity, the hunger for power, and so on.[105]

For most householders, establishing sex on healthier foundations will be a safer, more effective strategy than trying to overcome something so primal. Don't give it up until you have found something better is not only common sense, but also sound Buddhist advice.[106] Eventually, when you have deepened your capacity for sharing love in more profound and universal ways, sexual passion may fall away like the worn-out skin left behind by a snake (*Sutta Nipata*). By tearing it off while it is still attached, however, you will only run the risk of bloodying yourself and others. (Anyone married or in a committed relationship will need to take his or her partner's needs into account. Even if you are ready to quit, it is good Dhamma practice to keep going while your partner still needs it. And with gusto, please.)

During the past ten days, I have seen the light. I feel like quitting my job, giving my goods to the poor, and spending the rest of my life meditating in a cave in the Himalayas. What should I do?

You should probably relax and have a beer. The path may prove to be very long: not just a ten-kilometer run or a marathon, but a trek of many, many thousands of miles.[107] Sometimes you will feel like sprinting with shouts of joy; other times you will barely be able to crawl. Forget about rushing; focus on lasting the distance. As I was once reminded by a poster in the Singapore subway (of all places!), "It does not matter how slowly you are going, just so long as you do not stop (Confucius)."

If your work feels uncongenial or unwholesome to you, by all means look for something else. But remember that doing your part by working, especially if others are depending on you, is as important and noble a form of Dhamma service as any other. The Buddha often praised the monastic life, but he also stressed how helpful and necessary it was for monks and householders to support each other.[108] How could one exist without the other? So do not fret if living in a cave is not a realistic option for you.

On the other hand, you are your own master. So if you want to go to India and you have the means, why not? Only remember that you will be bringing yourself along for the journey and that "nothing is a better proof of a well-ordered mind than a man's ability to stop just where he is and pass some time in his own company." The words of the Buddha? No: Seneca's, but the Stoics were pretty good Buddhists without knowing it.[109]

As for India or Thailand or any other place rumored to be especially rife with spirituality, go with open eyes and you will see that the magic and the squalor are about as evenly balanced as anywhere else. Be sure to get your travel vaccines and adequate insurance: the Dhamma is not a substitute for taking practical precautions that are within our power. And don't assume that someone making for your knickers has a spiritual agenda because he is wearing robes or matted hair.

Say what you may, I hear the Tree of Trees calling me and I am going!
I could quote the Suttas — "What need for you to go to Gaya?"[110] — but that would be mischievous because the Buddha explicitly recommended visiting the sites of his birth, death, and enlightenment for inspiration. Only one thing is said to be even more auspicious than breathing your last at a Vipassana center: dying on a pilgrimage.[111]

If you are serious about batting for Team Buddha, the Mahabodhi Temple at Bodhgaya will look to you like the old Yankee Stadium, Wrigley Field, and Fenway Park[112] folded into one and risen from the navel of the universe — besides being equipped not only with gates and gangways for ordinary visitors, but also with portals and pathways for all manner of inter-dimensional travelers. If there are places where the walls between the worlds are thin, this is surely one of them, and at night especially, the Temple seems to be hovering above the landscape like a spaceship ready to depart for some far corner of the universe.

One sometimes wishes the Temple would indeed lift off and move somewhere else, because to call its present location in Bihar the armpit of India would be charitable. Ledi Sayadaw offers a good test of spiritual development: "The truth is that there is no self; there are only phenomena arising and vanishing due to relevant conditions. Thus a leper looking at his sores through a microscope and seeing the carrier germs ever arising and passing away should realize that the sores are not his, but the habitat of the germs only."[113] If you are ready to think along such lines,

Bihar can hold no terrors for you; otherwise, do what you have to do, but mind the state's unofficial motto: "Abandon all hope, ye who enter here."

Gaya Station, where your train will be arriving, if you make it this far, is the kind of place where writhing bodies are strewn all over the floors in the manner of a Boschian painting or an ancient battle-field before the clean-up. The locals will urinate on the sides of the train right as you are boarding or getting off, there will be an ungodly din at all times of the day and night, and if there is any evidence that the New India has arrived here, you will have to go searching for it. Before you even think about going to Bihar, get every vaccination known to man. Not that getting your shots will keep you safe from the attack-helicopters that pass for mosquitoes in these parts, but you have plenty of other stuff to worry about. Buy as much travel insurance as any company is willing to cover, definitely with repatriation benefits, dead or alive, if possible including emergency evacuation to the nearest US aircraft carrier.

So you are ready to hit the road from the train station to Bodhgaya and the vaunted Vipassana center in the shadow of the Great Tree. (Or so you imagine; in reality there is precious little shade at the center, from what I recall.) Trips on Bihar roads should never be undertaken after dark, because they are owned by highwaymen at night, and by the Naxalite insurgents when it's springtime and they are feeling the itch to take hostages or dispose of their mildewed dynamite. Always avoid the rickshaws pedaled by foot, no matter how pitifully you may get accosted by their skeletal owners. And watch your step as if your life depended on it, because it may: there is a good chance that the rusty floor-boards will break right through when you step on them, either cutting your foot off or else giving you blood-poisoning and tetanus. When you get to the center, you will notice that it has walls topped by rusty barbed wire and an armed guard at the gate. The carbine may look as if it has not been fired since the future Edward VII was parking his love-chair in the Hindu Room of his favorite Parisian brothel, but the center has been robbed before, believe it or not.

If you have read *Heart of Darkness*, the scenes awaiting you inside the walls will be familiar from the company station. You will hear objectless blasting and blaring from all directions; you will see a half-finished pathway here, a dripping water tank there, artificial holes and wanton smash-ups everywhere, the pockmarks of a demoralized land alternately rotting in the heat and shivering in the cold. You need not be concerned about any groves of death, at least not inside the center; but then you also can't count on any hairdresser's dummy of a chief accountant keeping up appearances with his starched collars and got-up shirt-fronts. Unless they've hired one to cut down on the few bananas that occasionally turn up to complement the usual fare of potatoes at mealtimes.

The expression "taught with tapes" has become an anachronism in most parts of the world, but when I went to the Bodhgaya center a few years ago (well into the 21st century), *cassettes* were still in use — the rectangular plastic contraptions used for data-storage and for recording your cherished copy of "We Are the World" back in the days of the Commodore 64 and the Ichthyosaurus. The distinctive touch in Bodhgaya is an unsteady supply of electricity that will make the players wobble and break down in mid-sentence, for which, if you are lucky enough to have offered yourself as a server, you will be held responsible although there is absolutely nothing you can do about it. If the gods smile upon your quest, your teacher will be septuagenarian as hard of hearing as he is fond of snapping his fingers at you. He will take himself to be speaking pretty good English, but miss all the nuances; miscommunications will be your fault, needless to say; but never mind, since you will anyway be told to do one thing and expected to do another. He will be obsessed with the monks on the course, yet prepared to send them off for not following the instructions properly; then he will tearfully repent when it is too late. He will also send away two whiney American students on Day 5 — one of whom he has told not to take his thyroid replacement drugs — because he cannot figure out the first thing about them. Your fellow servers, the flower of first-world sensitivity training, will be convinced that Mama India can do no wrong, and they will kiss as many bare feet as possible, though not the soles, whose horrid vibrations they dread as sincerely as any votary of voodoo. A male nurse retired from the Indian army will be sitting course after course at the center in hopes of finally extirpating his secret homosexuality. All servers will mysteriously regress to the age of four-year-olds once the students have gone to bed, and take to communicating with the teachers in baby-talk only — a mysterious phenomenon observable at other centers, too, but with a slightly higher age of regression, six or seven, say. The locals, not content with cooing, will crawl on the floor as they address the saintly apparitions before them.

How good to know that all the problems you may encounter — including your nervous breakdown during the first group-sit at 8 am on Day 1 and your formal resignation from service at 9 am, which will be noted but not accepted — are mere manifestations of your defilements coming to the surface! What better place to deal with them than the holiest of ground with the strongest, purest vibrations in the world!

What are you waiting for?

NOTES

1. Goenka sometimes uses the term "holy indifference" as a synonym for equanimity, but the disadvantages of such usage should be obvious (*Clock of Vipassana*, p. 53, *Art of Living*, pp. 54, 125).

2. See also *Art of Living*, pp. 41, 137; *Clock of Vipassana*, p. 199, 232.

3. See Day 8 Discourse; *Art of Living*, pp. 30, 39, 67, 126, 137-138; *Clock of Vipassana*, pp. 199, 232.

4. *Meditations* X.12.

5. *Clock of Vipassana*, pp. 44. And p. 233: "I keep saying to my students: 'Go to the hospital to gain health, but not to live in the hospital for your whole life.'" See also *Art of Living*, p. 125: "Real equanimity is not merely negative or passive aloofness. It is not the blind acquiescence or apathy of one who seeks escape from the problems of life, who tries to hide his head in the sand. Rather, true mental balance is based on full awareness of problems, awareness of all levels of reality."

6. *Art of Living*, p. 126.

7. SN 7:11 (pp. 266-68), in a free and somewhat condensed combination of the translations by Bodhi and Nanamoli (*Life*, pp. 120-121).

8. A central theme both in his instructions and his discourses; see also *Art of Living*, p. 105.

9. He puts the promise in writing in the printed version of his *Satipatthana Discourses* (p. 64).

10. I will discuss the relationship of Anapana and Vipassana at more length in one of the next questions, and I will argue that the line between the two should not be drawn quite as rigidly as Goenka sometimes presents it. But I am still convinced that *vedana*-practice has special purifying properties that one should not miss — what bothers me is merely the exclusive tone in which the claim is presented.

11. See MN 89.12 (p. 730) for just one example.

12. Livy, *History of Rome*, XXI.39.

13. Bursting into tears for no apparent reason on Metta Day, or during the first few days after a course, is quite common, even while one may also be feeling happy and grateful. I've heard of very serious students going into periods of depression after Long courses, and of others getting strange outbreaks and rashes on theirs skins as a result of especially deep and intense practice. I've often come out of courses feeling the opposite of equanimous, as if my skin — thin at the best of time — had been pulled off altogether. Thus also U Ba Khin: "When one develops [one's awareness of anicca, dukkha, and anatta] ... the impact of this *nibbana datu* upon the impurities within one's own system will create a sort of upheaval, which must be endured. This upheaval tends to increase one's sensitivity to the radiation, friction, and vibration within oneself, which can grow in intensity until one feels as though one's body were just electricity and a mass of suffering." (*Clock of Vipassana*, p. 190)

14. See SN 22.101 (pp. 959-60), MN 16.27 (p. 197), MN 53.19 (pp. 463-64). Breaking through the eggshell of ignorance (AN 4.130 [p. 512]) is an image that the Buddha also used for his own enlightenment, see AN 8:11 (p. 1127-28).

15. DN 23.13 (p. 357).

16. See Matthew 13:57, Mark 6:4, Luke 4:24. History has not recorded how Joseph reacted when he and Mary found twelve-year-old Jesus, after seeking him for three days, discussing theology with the doctors at the temple in Jerusalem and announcing that his parents ought not to have worried because he was "about his Father's business" (Luke 2:41-49). I suspect that Joseph was not inclined to bow to his son (as the Buddha's father supposedly did when he first came upon the boy in serious meditation [MN, Note 389, p. 1230]). "I will teach you about your father's business," would be more likely from the veteran of many a construction site, and in Egypt, too. Jesus may have learned the lesson a little too well: "He that loveth father or mother more than me is not worthy of me" (Matthew 10:37) is not an isolated statement (see especially Luke 14:26 and John 2:4).

17. On "loving the plateau," see George Leonard, *Mastery* (Plume 1992), esp. 39 ff.

18. See AN 8:19,20 (p. 1143, 1147). On the affinities between gradual training in the Dhamma and training in other arts, see for example MN 107.2 (p. 874).

19. No one would have guessed that the ten-thousand-hour idea was destined to become a crowd-pleaser from its beginnings in a plodding academic article (K.A. Ericsson et al., "The Role of Deliberate Practice, etc.," *Psychological Review*, vol. 100, no. 3 [1993], esp. pp. 393-93). Nerds take heart! Yet, however deplorable clichés may be, Goenka would have practiced about that much Vipassana before he started teaching, as have most junior teachers in his organization. Needless to say, few meditators dare be so crude as to count lifetime hours on the mat, or at least to admit it. (I do.)

20. I like Byrom's riff on verses 183-184 of the *Dhammapada* (ch. XIV.5), but he is exceeding his writ as a translator. (The italics are mine, as is the substitution of "purify the mind" for "be pure.") Goenka's version is much closer to the text: "Abstain from all unwholesome actions, perform wholesome ones, and keep purifying your mind. This is the teaching of the Buddhas." (*Gem Set in Gold*, p. 77)

21. Santideva, *Bodhicaryavatara*, VII.47.

22. Or a "step to implement the training" (*Art of Living*, p. 61).

23. There is no sin in Buddhism, only unskillful and ignorant action — though this can of course translate into terrible unwholesomeness and result in the most frightful consequences for all parties concerned. To anticipate dire consequences is not the same as to threaten punishment, however, any more than to point out the dangers of not wearing a seat-belt is to threaten someone with death in a car-accident.

24. See the question on the 227 Precepts for monks in chapter 12. Alas, Buddhists have carried rule-worship to the same extremes as the votaries of other faiths. Thus the wretched story of Maha-Tissa "the mango eater" (or "mango starver": see above), which Goenka applauds with enthusiasm and which seems to be condoned, perhaps even commended, at AN 8.19 (p. 1143).

25. See *Zen Mind, Beginner's Mind*, p. 13. Also p. 120: "Good or bad is not the point. Whether or not you make yourself peaceful is the point, and whether or not you stick to it." This should not be read as a repudiation of morality, however, since without regard for the precepts, there can be no true inner peace from a Buddhist perspective.

26. See MN 41.8-10 (pp. 380-81). The Book of the Tens (AN 10) repeats the list many times from slightly different angles. Also *Vism.* XXII.62 (p. 709). See above for the idea of a compass of the precepts.

27. Ugga of Hatthigama (AN 8.22.1 [p. 1150]) and Sarakani the Sakyan (SN 55.24 [p. 1811-13]). See also Analoya, pp. 254-55.

28. Thus Bodhi: "[D]evotion to truthful speech is a matter of taking our stand on reality rather than illusion, on the truth grasped by wisdom rather than the fantasies woven by desire." (NEP, IV.50) See MN 110 and 113 for "untrue" living in a much more comprehensive sense than mere lying. Also MN 129.2,27 (pp. 1016, 1022) on the fool as "an untrue man" and the wise man as "a true man."

29. MN 61.3-7 (pp. 523-24) (see *Life* 84-85). For the idea that those who are prepared to lie will shrink from nothing, see also *Itivuttaka* 25 (Ireland, pp. 167-68).

30. See also the final question in chapter 12.

31. That is why suicide is considered *blameless* only when it is

committed by an *arahant* under special circumstances (Nanamoli, *Life* p. 199). See the story of the Bhikkhu Vikkali, who cut his throat to escape a deadly illness but is said to have become liberated at the last moment (SN 22:87 [pp. 938-41]) and that of the Bhikkhu Godhika who did the same out of frustration with not being able to make his liberation permanent before (SN 4:23 [pp. 212-214]).

32. The Buddha once asked himself whether it was "possible to govern without killing and ordering execution, without confiscating and sequestrating, without sorrowing and inflicting sorrow, in other words, righteously." Mara, the personification of temptation, sought to encourage him: "Let the Blessed One govern!" but the Buddha was not deceived (SN 4:20 [p. 209-10], tr. Nanamoli).

33. Not that the Buddha condoned harsh or punitive methods: see DN 5.11 (pp. 135-36) and DN 26.61 (p. 397) on the ultimate futility of threats and punishments and the political benefits of kindness and generosity. (Anyone who imagines that human cruelty was less pervasive in the Buddha's times than in our own may want to review the list of common tortures at MN 13.14 [p. 182] and MN 129.4 [pp. 1016-17].) DN 26.9-21 (pp. 398-402) traces the descent of an ill-governed state into poverty, crime, and fierce enmity until even families are divided into hunters and prey and men "mistake one another for wild beasts." The parallels with Hobbes are merely superficial: what cures the situation is a moral awakening ("we became addicted to evil ways ... so let us now do good!"), not the reconstitution of external authority.

34. MN 27:13 (p. 272-73) and MN 51.14 (p. 449), see above.

35. Fleischman touches on many of these complexities, and resolves few, in *The Buddha Taught Nonviolence, Not Pacifism* (Pariyatti Press 2002). See also *An Ancient Path*, p. 21. Asked whether serious meditators would ever be right to join a country's armed forces and to fight if necessary, Goenka answered that they would need to decide for themselves (Goenka, *For the Benefit of Many*, pp. 116, 118). On the great karmic risks of living by the sword, see the Buddha's comments to soldiers in his day at SN 42:3-5 (pp. 1334-36).

36. Goenka does acknowledge that eating meat amounts to indirect encouragement of killing. He also claims that "at a subtler level you harm yourself by eating meat" because "every fiber of [an animal's] body becomes permeated by craving and aversion." (*Art of Living*, p. 66)

37. MN 55.3-5,12 (pp. 474, 476).

188 THE BOOK OF VIPASSANA SECRETS

38. *Cullavagga* 7.3.14-15. The Buddha and his followers clashed with the Jains on similar grounds (see AN 8.12 [pp. 1135-36]). According to the *Cullavagga*, the Buddha's cousin Devadatta sought to usurp the leadership over the Sangha, and even to kill the Buddha. First he dispatched a number of assassins, none of whom were able to carry out the task (*Cv.* 7.3.6-8). Then he hurled down a boulder from the Vulture's Peak, which narrowly missed the Buddha but injured his foot with a splinter (*Cv.* 7.3.9). Finally he arranged for the fierce elephant Nalagiri, trained to kill convicted criminals by trampling them to death, to be made drunk and set upon the Buddha, who often compared himself to a tusker and managed to tame the crazed beast: "Touch not, o elephant, the elephant of men!" (*Cv.* 7.3.11-12, tr. Rhys Davids. On the Buddha's affinity with bull elephants, see also *Udana* 4.5 [Ireland, p. 59]) and AN 9.40 [pp. 1307-1308].) Nanamoli's *Life* devotes a full chapter to Devadetta (pp. 257-272).

39. MN 55.6-11 (pp. 475-76).

40. What I said above about the rare exceptions was for the sake of telling the complete story; it had nothing to do with encouraging drinking.

41. I have heard heroin described as an outright magnet for demonic energies, for example, but that is about as much as I know of the matter.

42. See *Art of Living*, p. 65.

43. Aldous Huxley, *The Doors of Perception / Heaven and Hell* (Grafton 1977 [first published in 1954 and 1956, respectively]).

44. I will limit myself to Ayahuasca, about which I am a bit more informed, but what I have to say may apply equally to some of the other intoxicants in this class.

45. Fleischman engages in another line-drawing exercise (see his comment about New Age, above) when he makes a distinction between the Dhamma and healing: "I hope you won't wander off the path into the roadside weeds where meditation gets tangled with healing." (*An Ancient Path*, p. 30) It's true enough that the Dhamma points *beyond* the struggle for health, towards learning to accept the inevitability of defeat, of disease and of death. But that is no argument against getting what healing we can (see also the question about medicine above). To be human is to be entangled, to live among weeds, to be juggling immediate and ultimate ends all the time. As a psychiatrist, Fleischman knows perfectly well how limited

our arsenals are when it comes to depression and drug addiction, for example, two areas (among others) where any fair-minded appraisal would have to admit that Ayahuasca shows special promise.

46. I know of at least one very serious meditator who called on the Buddha during an Ayahuasca ceremony because he was concerned about the precepts. The Awakened One appeared and told him not to worry: nothing that opens the heart is against the precepts.

47. One of the ironies of issuing a blanket prohibition against Ayahuasca on Dhammic grounds is that it is likely to put off those who are most scrupulous about the precepts, including many serious meditators who might otherwise bring much equanimity to the ceremonies. Another irony is that if the most Dhamma-minded are deterred, the nascent Ayahuasca culture, with all its healing possibilities, is that much likelier to drift off in more unwholesome directions.

48. DN 23.13 (p. 357).

49. The title of the most scholarly Ayahuasca book, by Benny Shanon, who got the idea from Huxley, p. 70: "A man consists of what I may call an Old World of personal consciousness and, beyond a dividing sea, a series of New Worlds — the not too distant Virginias and Carolinas of the personal subconscious and the vegetative soul; the Far West of the collective unconscious, with its flora of symbols, its tribes of aboriginal archetypes; and, across another, vaster ocean, at the antipodes of everyday consciousness, the world of Visionary Experience."

50. SN 1.1 (p. 89).

51. His exact words in the Day 11 Discourse are: "After a year, it becomes so easy in life. All who quit do so in the first year."

52. AN 3:35 [BW 29-30]. See also MN 130.4-8 (pp. 1030-1032) for a slightly more elaborate account. The irony in calling these messengers "divine" is that the gods are less capable than we of waking up. (See my discussion of the gods in chapter 12.)

53. *Clock of Vipassana*, p. 202.

54. *U Ba Khin Journal*, p. 34; *Clock of Vipassana*, p. 118. U Ba Khin points out that for overcoming this inner tug-of-war, the experience of *bhanga* is quite essential (*Ibid.*), but that will come in its due course and cannot be rushed. Craving for it will only make it more remote.

55. Thus Goenka: "The best time to [pass along Dhamma to your children] is before birth. During pregnancy the mother should practice Vipassana so that the child also receives it and is born a Dhamma child." (*Art of Living*, p. 139)

56. *For the Benefit of Many*, p. 121. Fleischman, too, says that Anapana "is not meditation per se, but an exercise in developing the proper type of concentration that is most useful for meditation" (*An Ancient Path*, p. 37). On the other hand, *The Art of Living* acknowledges, supposedly with Goenka's approval, that Anapana is "the technique the Buddha himself practiced," that it is for "exploring inner reality," and that it entails "very powerful moments of purity that challenge all one's past conditioning" (pp. 72, 75-76).

57. The *Visuddhimagga* calls mindfulness of breathing "foremost" among the meditation subjects taught by the Buddha (*Vism.* VIII.155 [p. 263]). Bodhi writes: "By itself mindfulness of breathing can lead to all the stages of the path culminating in full awakening." (NEP, VI.80) Many schools of Buddhism, even ones close to U Ba Khin and Goenka, focus *exclusively* on Anapana. One of U Ba Khin's most revered contemporaries in Burma, Webu Sayadaw (a regular honored guest at the IMC) only taught Anapana, for example. "If you keep your entire attention focused on the spot below the nose above the upper lip, on the in-breath and the out-breath, the whole of the Scriptures is there." (*The Way to Ultimate Calm: Selected Discourses of Webu Sayadaw*, BPS 2001, pp. 55, 71)

58. In saying so, I am not speaking from any personal doubt about the effectiveness of *vedana*-practice, nor from any great fondness for Anapana. In my practice, I follow Goenka's line, but that does not make the scriptural support for his position any more convincing.

59. SN 54.13 (pp. 1780-81), italics added. See the catalogue of benefits enumerated right after: SN 54.13-20 (pp. 1781-87).

60. AN 10.58 (p. 1410). See the box on *Satipatthana* in chapter 6, where I also review different translations of the line.

61. The *Visuddhimagga* speaks of forty meditation subjects taught by the Buddhas (*Vism.* III.28 [p. 90]).

62. AN 1.575 (p. 129), with the benefits enumerated in AN 1.576-615 (pp. 129-132) and the connection with knowledge of the deathless added in AN 1.616-627 (pp. 132-134). The practice of mindfulness directed to the body is made to sound rather daunting at SN 47:20 (p. 1648). One should train oneself as if one were carrying a bowl

of oil filled to the brim on one's head, followed by an armed guard who will decapitate you with his sword if you spill a single drop, all the while making your way through a crowd thronging the most beautiful girl in the land while she is singing and dancing exquisitely.

63. A point developed by Goenka in his evening discourse on Day 5, which I find to be the most powerful of the lot. See also VRI, Vedana, p. xi, and *Art of Living*, pp. 47-50. (Goenka uses the term "conditioned arising" rather than "dependent origination.")

64. SN 54:9 (p. 1774). See also MN 118 (pp. 941-48).

65. SN 51.1 (p. 1765), SN 54.8 (p. 1770), SN 54.11 (p. 1778).

66. MN 62, esp. 3-23 (pp. 527-531).

67. "As and when necessary," Goenka says in his final discourse on Day 11. The image of the anchor is used in *The Art of Living*, p. 114. From my passing familiarity with seamanship in literature, I don't believe that ships actually put down their anchors in "big storms," but never mind.

68. They are described in terms of their basic properties at MN 64.9-12 (pp. 539-540 [BW 397-98]) (also SN 36.19 [pp. 1276-78] and elsewhere), and with some memorable similes at MN 39.15-18 (pp. 367-369 [BW 251-253]), repeated at MN 77.25-28 (pp. 641-642) and MN 119.18-21 (pp. 953-54). Goenka discusses them in his *Satipatthana Discourses* on pp. 93-94.

69. DN 29.24 (p. 434). At MN 79.24-25 (p. 659), he calls them "the practical way to realize an exclusively pleasant world."

70. MN 36.31 (p. 340 [BW 64]). The point is worth lingering over: wholesome pleasure had thereby been radically reclassified from a supposed enemy of enlightenment to one of its crucial supports. Thus AN 10.1 (pp. 1339-40), which spells out the following sequence: virtue leads to non-regret, non-regret to joy, joy to rapture, rapture to tranquility, tranquility to pleasure, *pleasure to concentration*, concentration to knowledge, knowledge to dispassion, dispassion to wisdom and liberation.

71. MN 36.34-37 (pp. 340-41 [BW 65]).

72. DN 16.6.9 (p. 271).

73. MN 27.19-22 (pp. 275-76).

74. MN 79.28 (p. 660). A student of the Buddha "does not give up

the pleasure that accords with Dhamma, yet he is not infatuated with that pleasure" (MN 101.23 [p. 833]).

75. Thus *Visudhimagga* IV.194 (p. 163): "[P]urification is effected by equanimity, not by anything else."

76. MN 36.37 (Bodhi's translation: BW 65), MN 27.22 (p. 276). For a list of the different kinds of equanimity see *Vism*. IV.156-166 (p. 157), especially section 166 on purifying equanimity.

77. See VRI, Vedana, Note 2, p. 82: "The practice of Vipassana [leads] not to the *jhanas* but to purification of mind."

78. The *Visuddhimagga* mentions the danger of "agitation about higher states" (*Vism*. XX.106 [p. 656]).

79. See Note 210 to SN 12.70 (p. 785), *Vism*. XXI.112 (p. 690).

80. One often hears that concentration and wisdom will naturally converge at the end, as they did in the Buddha's case. The argument commonly made for focusing on Anapana is not that insight can be dispensed with, but that the highest concentration is a natural bridge to the highest wisdom.

81. It is said that the word *Zen*, via the Chinese *Chan*, is derived from *jhana,* and the Soto school, at least, may remind a Theravadan of his own *jhana*-practice. Rinzai Zen with its famous koans and partly-open eyes during meditation, not so much.

82. See MN 105.18-21 (p. 864-66).

83. *Vism*. XX.107, 110-113 (pp. 657-58). In structuring his work and assigning such a high place to "knowledge and vision of what is and is not the path," Buddhaghosa followed the progression outlined at MN 24.15 (p. 244).

84. *Vism*. XX.126,128 (pp. 660-661).

85. This follows from Goenka's interpretation of *yatha-bhuta* (see above) and it is spelled out in the discourses (see also *Clock of Vipassana*, p. 228). Once again, one might quibble, but it seems fair to say that mantra-practice, though it may have its own benefits, is quite different from Vipassana.

86. Many meditation teachers set ambitious targets for their students to meet, and Goenka's are certainly among the more demanding. But there's also something to be said for the reminder that any regular practice at all, even if it is just for five or ten minutes a day,

is quite an accomplishment in a world so very prone to distractions (see for example Rahula, p. 70).

87. AN 15.15 (p. 1573). When a prince asked the Buddha whether he had slept well, the Awakened One answered that he was among those (few, presumably) who always sleep well (AN 3.35 [p. 232]). The peaceful sleep of those who practice loving-kindness also appears in the opening stanza of the *Karaniyametta Sutta* that Goenka chants on the morning of Day 3 (*Gem Set in Gold*, p. 35).

88. Thus Kant: "Voltaire said that heaven has given us two things as a counterweight to the many troubles of life: *hope* and *sleep* [*Henriade*, canto vii]. He might have added *laughter* if the means of exciting it in reasonable men were only as readily at hand." (*Critique of Judgment* I.54, my translation) Kant's motto from his famous essay on "What Is Enlightenment?" — *sapere aude*: dare to think for yourself — is just as relevant to the meditator's journey as the capacity for faith and trust in teachers.

89. MN 36.45-46 (p. 342). Sleeping for pleasure is treated less generously, alas (see for example MN 16.11 [p. 195], AN 6.14 [p. 869], AN 7.61 [pp. 1060-61]).

90. Sloth-torpor (*thina-middha*) is one of the Five Hindrances and an enemy of meditation, granted. But sluggishness or laziness is not the same as tiredness, even if the lines can be blurred. I am in no way denying that great exertion is an important aspect of the Path (SN 12:22 [p. 553]). There are times when forgoing sleep makes sense: if you can maintain wakefulness without straining, who would object (SN 35.239 [pp. 1239-40])? What bothers me is the absurdity of telling others that sleep is a waste of time (see Webu, *Way to Ultimate Calm*, p. 5). "All night no sleep — wonderful!" is the stuff of bad jokes (Discourse Day 7).

91. When they are still novices. Once fully ordained, *bhikkhus* follow 227 precepts, *bhikkhunis* 311. (See also the question doubting the need for so many precepts in chapter 12.)

92. AN 4:55 (pp. 445-46 [BW 121-22]), DN 31.30 (p. 467 [BW 117]).

93. See the section on right livelihood in chapter 7.

94. AN 8:54 (pp. 1194 [BW 124]), AN 4:61 (p. 451 [BW 127]).

95. AN 8:54 (pp. 1195-96 [BW 125-26]), AN 4:61 (pp. 450-451 [BW 126-27]), AN 4:62 (p. 452).

96. DN 31.26 (p. 466).

97. *The Wealth of Nations*, bk. 1, chapter 2, par. 1.

98. *Great Disciples*, pp. 172-75.

99. The harshness of the line against sex may be connected to the ease of exit and reentry into the Sangha. Buddhist monks or nuns are not Vestal Virgins sworn to eternal chastity and liable to being buried alive for their transgressions. They may always revert to the householding life if they fall incurably in love; hence there is little excuse for having sex while in robes.

100. DN 16.5.9 (p. 264).

101. Socrates likened infatuation with physical beauty to enslavement and to being bitten by a spider that drives one crazy with pain (Xenophon, *Memorabilia*, I.3). Buddhists use the bloody but evocative image of trying to lick honey off a razor-blade (*Vism.* XVII.63 [p. 541]). For other vivid illustrations of the unavailing nature of sensual pleasure, see MN 54.15-21 (pp. 469-472). The *Udana* (3.3, Ireland, p. 42) calls sensual desire a "thorn."

102. The central theme of SN 35, see especially sections 1-22 (pp. 1133-1140).

103. Marcus Aurelius, *Meditations*, III.2.

104. Thus Goenka: "Sex has a proper place in the life of a householder. It should not be forcibly suppressed... Dhamma offers a middle path, a healthy expression of sexuality that still permits spiritual development." (*Art of Living*, p. 64)

105. Who does what to whom and how is largely irrelevant — except as an expression of attitudes and intentions. If you consider something demeaning and you would not like it done to you, don't do it. If it expresses love, trust, and commitment without bringing hurt or harm to anyone, it does not matter how "dirty" others may find it. Look honestly into your heart and you will know. (Needless to say that I am offering a modernized, Western perspective and that in the lands of the East one can hear some fairly outlandish views on what is and is not permitted in the bedroom. I don't need the bhikkhus to teach me about sex any more than I need a celibate priesthood to do the same, but judge for yourself.)

106. MN 14.4 (p. 186).

107. More on this in chapter 12.

108. *Itivutakka* 107 (Ireland, p. 232, BW 171).

109. Seneca, *Letters from a Stoic*, tr. Robin Campbell, no. II.

110. MN 7.20 (p. 121).

111. DN 16.5.8 (p. 264).

112. I despise sports analogies, but I'm making an exception on account of the fact that baseball is played on a diamond and that it offers an apt metaphor for the stages of Buddhist sainthood. See the question about rapid progress towards liberation in the Buddha's day in Chapter 12.

113. *Manual of the Excellent Man*, pp. 43-44, condensed and edited.

CHAPTER ELEVEN
TO PAY OR NOT TO PAY

AT A WELL-ESTABLISHED NORTH AMERICAN VIPASSANA CENTER, I once heard the story of how the resident teachers had asked an Old student who was a business consultant to review their procedures from a professional point of view and make some suggestions about optimizing them. When the time came to make his presentation, the consultant told them that by the usual standards of his trade, he was not only unable to explain why the organization worked so efficiently, he could not account for how it was able to work *at all*.

One sympathizes with the consultant: how is it possible that several hundred Vipassana centers around the world are able to function without charging anyone for anything, getting by on nothing but volunteer work and donations that may not be solicited and that may not be accepted from anyone but course-graduates? Centers are allowed to make their needs known, and they put out donation desks at the end of courses; beyond that, they depend entirely on the unprompted generosity of students. Although there are emergency mechanisms for centers to help each other out financially, each is expected to be self-sufficient and money collected locally will be used locally. Students may also identify specific uses they wish to support with their donations, and there are a few separate programs to which they can give, including the Vipassana Prison Trust for courses in correctional institutions and the Global Pagoda project. (Opinions differ whether this megaproject outside Mumbai marks Goenka's finest hour or his Albert Speer moment.)

From what I understand, teachers get help with transportation costs, but they are never paid, and neither are the servers. Certain specialized jobs, especially around construction and maintenance, are contracted out and paid for out of donations. In India and Thailand, kitchen staff, groundskeepers, and other support staff are often hired locally and paid, but in the West kitchens are run by volunteers only. So far as I know, there are no secrets around money at Vipassana centers; meetings of the relevant committees are public, budgets are published, and students should have no compunctions about asking anything they wish to know about center finances. But money is often tight, centers do take out loans and mortgages against expected future donations, and so the question of how much to give is one that students coming out of a course often ponder with a measure of perplexity and unease.

The first and simplest answer is to look into your heart and give whatever feels right, however little or however much that may turn out to be. Straightforward as it is, however, that answer rarely satisfies the asker, who would rather know what she owes, more or less. It's important, though, to stress that students at courses don't owe anything; their course expenses have already been covered by other meditators, and they truly need not give a cent if they do not wish to.[1] The approximate cost per student of offering the courses is surely relevant (around $300-500 in North America, depending on the center and how one runs the calculation), but it is not decisive: the case for covering one future student is a good one, but so is the case for covering several, or only a fraction. The sums don't matter; the intentions do. If an income-dependent rule of thumb were needed, I've sometimes thought that giving ten percent of a month's earnings might be right, a variation on the tradition of tithing. Perhaps one should want to give at least as much as one would be spending over the course of ten days on the outside, or as much as one would be willing to pay for a stay at a simple hotel. Or maybe the best method of all would be to set up a monthly donation, however big or small, because this makes for a purer expression of generosity, without reference to what one imagines one owes, and also because such predictable donations help the centers in their dealings with the banks.

An even better way to give (not *back* but forward) is to offer oneself as a volunteer, especially for service on a Ten-Day course. Thus one shares the gift of Dhamma, said to be the most meritorious of all, and certainly most helpful for one's own development as a meditator. After having gotten through a course, you will appreciate better, in light of your own gratitude, how beautiful Dhamma service can be. It's hard work, too, and can get frustrating, but it's always good for you in the end. See whether you can catch one of the servers for a chat on Metta Day; most of them will be glad to tell you about the delights and the difficulties of the role.

NOTES

1. Thus Goenka: "Often twenty-five or even fifty percent of the people don't give anything and leave. So what? Who cares? Money comes and the Dhamma keeps flowing." (*For the Benefit of Many*, p. 55)

CHAPTER TWELVE
BANGING AND WHIMPERING:
LAST QUESTIONS

What kinds of questions did the Buddha refuse to answer and why?

Intellectual life was very vibrant in the Buddha's day and he encountered many philosophical questioners[1] who wanted to know whether the world is eternal or not, finite or infinite, whether there is a soul and how it is connected to the body, and especially what happens to fully enlightened beings after death.

The Buddha's conversation with Vacchagotta the wanderer is a classic exchange of this sort. One by one, Vaccha asks the usual questions and presents what seem to be the only logical possibilities; the Buddha answers by refusing to take any of the positions he is offered and by denying that he holds any speculative views of this kind at all, dismissing them as "a thicket of views, a wilderness of views, a fetter of views beset by suffering and vexation," a mere intellectual fever that leads only to agitation. Vaccha is left bewildered and confused: "The measure of confidence I had gained through previous conversation with Master Gotama has now disappeared." The Buddha smiles and concedes that "it is enough to cause one bewilderment and confusion: for this Dhamma is profound, hard to see and hard to understand, unattainable by mere reason." When a liberated being dies, the Buddha explains, it is as if a fire had been extinguished. Fire requires fuel; when that is used up, it burns no more; that is all. Vacchagotta seems to have been satisfied, but the same questions were asked again and again, even by the Buddha's own monks.[2]

One of them, the bhikkhu Malunkyaputta, got so upset with these unanswered questions during a meditation that he resolved to go see his teacher and demand a straight answer, telling himself that he would abandon the training if he were not satisfied at last. Since the Buddha was dealing with one of his own students now, not a questioner from outside, he got rather sharp with the bhikkhu, calling him a misguided man[3] and reminding him that he had never been promised the kinds of answers he was demanding. Then the Buddha replied to the bhikkhu with one of his most famous images: you are like a man wounded in battle by a poisoned arrow, he told Malunkyaputta. You've been carried to the field-surgeon for treatment, but as he prepares to pull out the arrow, you fight him off and insist that you will not let him operate on you until he has told you exactly who fired the arrow, what his height and social class was, whether he lived in the country or the city, whether the bow he used was long or short, the bowstring made of sinew or hemp, and so forth. Keep obsessing about the questions I have been refusing to answer, the Buddha said, and you will end up like the stubborn man dying of his wound, without either your answers or your life. "Why have I left some things undeclared? Because they are unbeneficial, because they do not belong to the fundamentals of the spiritual life, because they do not lead to dispassion and peace, to direct knowledge and enlightenment. That is why I have left them undeclared."[4]

What is Samsara and why should I care?
Samsara is the wandering of ignorant beings through round after round of rebirth into the sufferings of existence. "What do you think is greater," the Buddha asked, "the stream of tears that

you have shed as you have roamed and wandered through this long course, weeping and wailing because of being united with the disagreeable and separated from the agreeable — this or the water in the four great oceans?"[5]

In Buddhist lands, our wandering through Samsara is sometimes taken, in a more lighthearted spirit, to imply that whatever we fail to learn or accomplish in this life, we will be able to resolve in some other one. As Ayya Khema puts it, "[L]ife is nothing but an adult education class. If we don't pass the subjects, we just have to sit the examination again. Whatever lesson we have missed, we'll get it again."[6] But Samsara has a more oppressive side: our unresolved business, and the suffering that results from it, follows us like a shadow from life to life, inescapably. What is more, we will have no recollection of what we learned in this round, and we may have to keep starting over in kindergarten. What kinds of opportunities for studying and practicing the Dhamma we will find in another life is never certain, nor whether we will be in a good position to take full advantage of what we might find. All this should make us appreciate the preciousness of our current lives and give us a keen sense of the urgency that is the counterpart of our fortunate condition. Today we may advance on the true path; tomorrow, who knows?

How did Samsara get started? How did the world originate?
The Buddha did claim that he knew "the beginning of things" in the sense of understanding how worlds arise, expand, and contract,[7] but not in the sense of identifying any ultimate first cause. Instead he insisted that "this Samsara is without discoverable beginning"[8] and that searching for first causes is futile; what is important is that suffering can be brought to an end by walking the Path to its end.

In another sense, the world (as reflected in our experience) does have a determinate origin in that it arises, every moment anew, in accordance with the cycle of dependent origination, as we have seen. Just as the world originates in dependence on the senses and consciousness, driven by craving and clinging, so "with the remainderless fading away and cessation of that same craving comes cessation of clinging; with the cessation of clinging, cessation of existence; with the cessation of existence, cessation of birth; with the cessation of birth, aging-and-death, sorrow, lamentation, pain, dejection and despair cease. Such is the cessation of this whole mass of suffering, *the passing away of the world.*"[9]

Ultimately, the duality between existence and non-existence is supposed to be no more than a matter of angle: "For one who sees the origin of the world as it really is, with correct wisdom, there is no idea of non-existence in regard to the world. And for one who sees the cessation of the world as it really is, with correct wisdom, there is no idea of existence in regard to the world... *What arises is only suffering arising, what ceases is only suffering ceasing.*"[10]

You don't really believe that any of us will come back as a caterpillars, do you?
I used to find the notion of rebirth bizarre as well, but it no longer seems so strange to me.[11] I have not experienced anything directly that would compel me to believe in rebirth, but what I've heard from close friends has led me to take the possibility seriously. I also see no way to subtract rebirth from the Dhamma without making nonsense of the whole Teaching, and our scientists tell us that according to the Laws of Thermodynamics, energy cannot be destroyed, only transformed. If the vast mental and emotional energies accumulated for at least one lifetime cannot just disappear, then where do they go when we die?[12] The Buddhists do not tell me that "I" will be reborn; they say that the karmic energy I have inherited and augmented will pass from the last moment of this life to the first of another, as it passes from every moment to the next, like the flicker of a flame that keeps a candle burning.[13] And caterpillars have a chance to turn into butterflies!

But it would be best not to dwell too much on an aspect of the Teaching that Ledi Sayadaw called "a really abstruse subject full of pitfalls."[14] For now we see through a glass, darkly. Until we see face to face, we are quite justified, as students of the Dhamma, in either digging in behind our skepticism, suspending our disbelief, accepting the Teaching on faith, or leaving it aside.

If to become fully liberated is to break free of rebirth, wouldn't it be better for highly developed beings to delay their liberation and return to life so that they can keep helping others? Wouldn't they be abandoning the rest of us by checking out of Samsara for good?

I don't want to say too much about the Mahayana traditions of Buddhism because I don't know them well enough, either theoretically or as a matter of practice. But I gather that the notion of a "Greater Vehicle" has something to do with the bodhisattva ideal, that is to say, with celebrating beings who are secure on the path to liberation, but who keep returning to life out of compassion with all suffering beings. From what I have heard, there are even vows not to take the final steps of liberation until one has helped all other beings to do so.

I would rather stay out of this debate except to say that the status of fully liberated beings after death was one of the questions about which the Buddha was often asked, and that he always refused to answer, because he rejected the categories in which it was invariably put to him. Such beings step beyond life, it is true; but they step beyond death as well. They do not become immortal in any sense we could imagine, but by their complete purification, they are surely not just freeing themselves, but rather making the most momentous contribution to everyone's spiritual prospects. Across cultures, saints are described and depicted (with halos, for instance) as extraordinarily radiant beings, small suns that illuminate, nourish, and give warmth to others by their mere presence. If the Laws of Thermodynamics are relevant to explaining rebirth, they apply here as well: where does the energy go when they die? The sun may set, but it does not cease to sustain us even in the darkness. Would we not all say that our practice is still being powered, 2500 years later, by the liberation of a single human being? Are we not being propelled, even today, by the wisdom in Suttas that were compiled, remembered, and transmitted by the efforts of many enlightened beings? To pry deeper into mysteries that the Buddha had good reasons not to broach is perhaps the closest Buddhist equivalent to demanding to meet God on human terms. If we walk the Path to the end, we will find out for ourselves; until then, we should be content to tap into the energy of the Buddhas even if we do not comprehend how it is possible to do so.

Given the nature of the impurities that stand in the way of our enlightenment, it does not make sense for anyone to hesitate before uprooting them, and I am confident that no one will feel the need to pull back from the brink of full liberation when he or she has arrived at that point. "Do not rest content with partial achievements" is the closest thing to a categorical imperative in Buddhism.[15] No point on the Path is meant to be a resting place; only once "the holy life has been lived and what had to be done has been done,"[16] fully and to its ultimate conclusion, only then may we relax our efforts with the Buddha's blessing. If our human calculations seem to suggest that perfectly liberated beings are jumping ship, then that only shows how puny a tool our spiritual math is when it comes to the highest equations. As a practical matter, I doubt very much that any master in the history of Mahayana has ever counseled a student to hold off on finishing his spiritual work, and from what little I understand of their traditions, the tendency is rather to postulate perfectly pure and compassionate beings who somehow keep returning to life. As a matter of strict doctrinal logic, a Theravadan can't make room for such beings; but the important thing here may be pedagogical emphasis rather than any strict logic. If a Theravadan might say "*I* will work out *my* liberation," which does not make any doctrinal sense either, then an advocate of Mahayana might counter with the more salutary, if equally self-contradictory, ideal of an ever-returning Buddha.

If I were to accept rebirth, I would like to know more about my previous lives. How would I go about recovering some memory of them?

According to the Buddha's Teaching, all life is marred by the element of the unsatisfactory. If you were to discover a link with Alexander or Cleopatra, say, rather than with some nameless peasant dying of dysentery, it would not be good news. The great men and women of history rarely leave behind clean karmic trails. Whatever the specifics you might encounter, do you really want to be put in touch with how it felt to lose so many children to disease, so many wives to childbirth, so many sons and husbands to war, not merely once or twice, but hundred or thousands or even millions of times — not just in the world as we know it, but in all the worlds that have ever existed? Do you really need to know what an animal goes through when it is devoured by a predator, or what life is like in a hell-realm?

Once a prominent female lay-disciple, Mother Visakha, told the Buddha that she would like to have as many children and grandchildren as there were people in the great city of Savatthi. Do you realize what you are asking, the Buddha said to her: you would not live another day in your life when you would not be mourning the loss of a loved one.[17] There is a reason why our minds usually spare us confrontations with such aggregated suffering: we've got enough to deal with as it is. Knowledge of previous lives can arise on the Path spontaneously when it is helpful to us, but why pry into such mysteries before we are ready for them?

Goenka seems to promise that Vipassana meditators can count on rebirth in a realm where they will be able to continue

practicing. Does that mean they are safe from the danger of a lower rebirth than in the human realm?

So he tells us in his evening discourse on Day 4,[18] and we even have it in writing: "You need not worry. If you keep practicing regularly morning and evening, then ... you need not fear death — you will be promoted!"[19]

It is said that when we die, very deep sankharas[20] will arise with particular frequencies of vibration (or magnetic forces) that will tune up (or connect) with one of the many planes of existence, higher or lower.[21] These profound mental patterns are not all unwholesome, however: regular meditation, faith and the practice of morality, or the cultivation of other perfections (*paramis*) are equally powerful mental forces that will work to attune the mind to more hospitable spheres where it will be possible to continue on the path of purification in a new life. So long as our minds remain divided between such complex contending forces, how could we be sure that the balance will come out in our favor?

The seeds sown by wholesome actions can only ripen in happiness, those of unwholesome actions, in suffering. Yet in his "great exposition of action," the Buddha presents the unsettling possibility that someone who has lived a life of immorality and unwisdom might be reborn "in a happy destination, even in the heavenly world," while a moral and wise person might reappear "in a state of deprivation, in an unhappy destination, in perdition, even in hell."[22] Such seemingly perverse outcomes are possible because the kammic seeds that come to fruition at death have been accumulated over many lifetimes, and older ones may well arise at the last moment.[23] It follows that there are no guarantees when it comes to rebirth and that a sense of complacency in the face of death is always misplaced (at least this side of sainthood). Hence the Buddha's urgent insistence that we must not "rest content with partial achievements."[24]

It will also be crucial whether, at the decisive moment, right view will predominate within us or not.[25] In dying as in living, a mind attuned to impermanence, to *Anicca* and *Anatta*, will point the way to liberation, while all clinging to the flicker of life will do the opposite. Thus the "all-important recognition," stressed in the supremely evolved Tibetan art of dying, that whatever may flash through our minds during life's final moments, however dazzling or threatening it may seem, is still *Anicca* and *Anatta* and has "no existence separate from the nature of mind." Whatever happens we must recognize for what it is, a final passing show, a tremendous display perhaps, but nothing to be either feared or delighted in: "However terrifying the appearances may be," says the *Tibetan Book of the Dead*, "they have no more claim on your fear than a stuffed lion."[26] *Anicca, Anicca, Anicca.*[27]

Without strong roots in practice and habit, however, such good counsels are likely to be blown away by the first gales of the final tempest, when some of the deepest and darkest energies lodged in our minds are likely to be unleashed as the dying organism fights its last losing battle. Equanimity is possible, even in the face of such hurricanes: at the eye of the storm there can be calm, but it must not be taken for granted. When Shunryu Suzuki, one of the first Zen masters in the United States and author of the near-iconic *Zen Mind, Beginner's Mind*, was dying of cancer, his last words were not an edifying haiku but "I don't want to die." (The response of another master at his bedside, Katagiri Roshi: "Thank you for making the effort to let me know.")[28] It is not just Zen masters who don't die easily. There are several stories in the Pali Canon of accomplished monks "not bearing up" on their deathbeds and needing to be consoled by the Buddha; some even took their lives to escape their misery.[29] Most of us won't have the benefit of a certified Buddha sitting by our bedside when we die. That's why we need to anticipate, in our practice today, what we would usually prefer not to think about at all.[30]

On the other hand, we should not look ahead to death with dread or anxiety, but only with a wise prudence and a suitable sense of urgency. On one occasion a lay follower came to the Buddha distressed about his lapses into unmindfulness. If I die in such a muddled moment, he asked, what will become of me?

"Do not be afraid, Mahanama, do not be afraid!" the Buddha answered. "When your mind has been fortified by faith, virtue, learning, generosity, and wisdom, your death will not be a bad one."[31] As ghee must rise in water, so a mind unburdened of immorality and lightened by confirmed confidence in the Buddha's teaching will naturally ascend at the time of death.[32] "Now go and practice!"[33]

Has anyone ever died during a Vipassana course?

I've heard that a lot of people die when they think they are having fun on cruises. Others are killed when their lighters explode, when they fall from chairs or buckets they've been using as ladders, or when they get eaten by bears. On the day I visited Machu Picchu, someone who may have been dead was carried downhill, feet-first, on a stretcher. People die everywhere, so naturally they also die during Vipassana courses. But it doesn't happen very often, either in absolute or in relative terms. So if you are the worrying type, but you'd like your anxieties to bear some resemblance to rationality, worry about the drive to the center, not your stay there.

Besides, you should be so lucky: they say that nothing raises the odds of a favorable rebirth like dying on Dhamma-land. One of the teachers appointed by Goenka is said to have died on the first night of a course after bowing three times to pay her respects to Goenka at the beginning of his evening talk.[34] A little much, perhaps, but there sure are worse ways to go.

My friend's mother slipped in the bath, hit her head against part of the shower, and died on the spot. I'm bothered by the idea that such freak accidents should have anything to do with karma.

The basic logic of karmic law may seem straightforward (for every action there is a reaction), but its workings in the world are subtle and complex, and we should never use facile imputations of blame to distance ourselves from suffering or to judge anyone.

Reflecting on karma when we are trying to make sense of seemingly senseless events is not about assuring ourselves that if something bad has happened to you, you must have earned it with bad behavior in the past, but about recognizing that beneath what we can readily ascertain, there are deeper causal undercurrents made up of old, possibly ancient, intentional energies. These dynamics are not ultimately unfathomable, but so long as we have no direct access to them, we need to proceed with great caution. If thinking in terms of karma bothers you more than it helps you, and if living in a world of freak accidents makes more sense to you than living in one where events are causally ordered in invisible ways, just leave karma aside. It's a central, profound aspect of the Teaching, to be sure; but anything that gets in the way of living with more joy, more compassion, more open hearts, and more peace is not the Dhamma.

I've heard that the Buddha and many of his disciples walked out on their wives and children in order to lead "the holy life." What a joke! Why should I listen to any of what such assholes have to say?

Now, now. The future Buddha was married at sixteen, which was probably typical then.[35] People also lived in extended families, so the core family wasn't the object of obsession it has become for us. Fathers were considered much more dispensable than mothers (one reason why there was so much resistance to admitting women to the Sangha), and when the Buddha sired a son before leaving, he may have been more dutiful than irresponsible. There is a story told of an early monk, Sudinna, who had left his wife without a child and whose mother came pleading with him to give them an heir, at least. He obliged and agreed to sleep with his former wife three times, though he repented later and got into a lot of trouble with the Sangha. But his family was grateful.[36] By the standards of his times, the Buddha, at 29, was quite old to have a first child, especially after thirteen years of marriage, so he must have been deliberately holding out. The Pali Canon doesn't tell of any negotiations with his old man, except to acknowledge how much grief the departure caused, but perhaps the two made a deal in which the father agreed to let the son go in return for an alternate heir. The Buddha may have been wavering, too, tearing himself loose on the night of the birth because he knew that he would never be able to do it afterwards. It is said that he was very much in love with his wife.

If we are serious about the Path, we need to recognize that the ends of a family man or woman and those of a determined seeker cannot always be expected to line up. A time may come when you will need to decide where your priorities lie and at what cost, to yourself and others, you are prepared to pursue them. If it's any consolation, things turned out well for the Buddha's family in the end. The Buddha's father, wife, and son Rahula are all said to have died fully liberated *arahants*. His mother, who survived his birth by only a few days, is said to have been reborn in a heavenly realm. His maternal aunt and foster-mother Gotami became the first woman ordained as a bhikkhuni, as we have seen, and a future Buddha according to the Mahayana Lotus Sutra. Things ended less happily for his people as a whole: the Sakyan republic was overrun and annexed to a neighboring kingdom amidst great slaughter towards the end of the Buddha's lifetime[37] — an important reminder of how brittle all worldly securities are, even the most basic.

The Scriptures say that even after the Buddha's enlightenment, a god needed to plead with him to teach, and that his first attempts were clumsy at best. I would have expected an Awakened Being to do a little better!
Teaching is beautiful, but even the best and happiest teachers will tell you how scary and frustrating it can be, especially in the beginning. The most inspired teachers make mistakes, too, and if we could imagine perfect teaching, it would still have to contend with incomprehension and misunderstanding. Who knows how

much nudging the Buddha really required; perhaps what got dramatized as a divine intervention wasn't more than a moment of indecision.[38] There is no room for fear or resentment in the heart of a Buddha, but does that mean that awakened beings must never hesitate, even for an instant?

When he had become enlightened, the Buddha had some very profound things to say; but teaching isn't just about the message, it is also about how to convey it most effectively to others who are not always ready. Why should it be to anyone's discredit if he needs a bit of practice and experience before getting more sure-footed about what works and what doesn't? The Buddha's first encounter with a prospective student, a wandering seeker he met on the way to Benares, may have been a fiasco, but so what? (Asked who his teacher might be, the Buddha rattled off a list of unheard-of distinctions to show why he had outgrown any teacher in the world. The wanderer shrugged: "May it be so," he said and departed, shaking his head.[39]) If you have never swum before and you become enlightened overnight, don't count on being able to do the butterfly in the morning.

The Buddha was not a superman,[40] but a human being who needed to rest his aching back and who took naps after lunch in the hot season when he got older.[41] When his friends Sariputta and Moggallana had just died, he looked over the assembly of monks left before him and said that it seemed empty to him now.[42] When he knew that he was about to die as well, he was sad to see the beautiful city of Vesali for the final time, and one of the last meals he ate (a deadly dish of bad mushrooms or pork, served with the best intentions by a blacksmith who meant to offer something especially delicious) gave him such violent pains (and bloody stool) that even the great being was wearied.[43] The news that his people, the Sakyans, had been massacred by their neighbors in a brutal invasion reached the Buddha not long before his death. So it goes, even for a Buddha.

"Shame on you, sordid age, maker of ugliness!"[44] Do those sound like the words of an enlightened being to you?
If you expect the deterioration of the body to be a pretty process, you haven't spent enough time at hospitals and at the kinds of institutions where the less presentable cases of senility are hidden away. The Buddha wasn't a wide-eyed dreamer imagining that he could evade the realities of life; he was a hard-headed realist in many ways, who taught us to face our difficulties squarely. We all hope to escape the worst, but the suffering and ugliness that come with old age are facts of life, even if there is a higher perspective from which they can be transformed.

How free are we really?
We are not free *from* anything; there are no autonomous selves that could rise above the interdependent, ever-changing matrix of things. Nothing has sharp boundaries when it is looked at under a sufficiently powerful microscope — whether one furnished by our science or the one of seeing things through the lens of the Dhamma.

But there is still the freedom *to* act, in this moment, to change in a wholesome direction, to give expression to a purer intention, to remain equanimous with a situation rather than to react blindly — a freedom that will grow as we shed our ignorance and break the force of our bad habits. That freedom points the way to liberation; it underpins the Buddha's conception of karma, and it is the cornerstone of his Teaching. The Buddha denied any hint of fatalism or nihilism and devoted at least one discourse to spelling out all the ways in which our initiative is real and vital.[45] Philosophical and religious accounts of our place in the world that might lead to passivity and resignation he roundly rejected as false and contrary to the Dhamma, even evil.[46] We are the heirs of our past actions, but the masters of our present karma[47] — not mere playthings of fate, or of the gods, or of an indifferent universe in which nothing matters.

Speaking of freedom: why so many rules? The Dhamma is a raft for crossing over, not something to cling to.

So the Buddha said. "When you know the Dhamma to be similar to a raft, a time will come to abandon even the Teaching."[48] But first you have to cross over to the other shore; the far bank will not come to you just because you are calling out to it from dry land.[49]

There are and always have been spiritual teachers promising a fast-track to enlightenment,[50] but the Buddha's Path is not about this or that moment of awakening to greater awareness. It is about gradually purifying the mind to its depths. "Just as the great ocean slants, slopes, and inclines gradually, not dropping off abruptly, so too, in this Dhamma and discipline penetration to final knowledge occurs by gradual training, gradual activity, and gradual practice, not abruptly."[51] There are instances of very rapid progress mentioned in the Suttas,[52] sometimes in the course of hearing a few words, but these need to be balanced against the fact that even stream-enterers (whose progress is said to be irreversible) may still harbor enough defilements to fuel several more rebirths. And their remaining impurities are to what has been purified as a bit of dirt under the fingernails is to the soil of the great earth![53]

How much karmic baggage any of us are carrying is anyone's guess and not worth speculating about. Chances are that it will be a long path for us, perhaps a very long one.[54] When you have finally arrived, you will leave the raft behind, but to abandon it while you are still struggling in the water would be imprudent, and while you are still on the near bank, mere folly.

But there is only Now!

Yes, yes, I've heard the rumors. "Time is but the stream I go a-fishing in. I drink at it; but while I drink I see the sandy bottom and detect how shallow it is."[55] Hillel, too: "If not now, when?"[56] Not to mention our own day's prophets of Now proclaiming their gospel of instant liberation from every roof-top armed with a satellite dish. "Let be the past, let be the future," in the Buddha's version.[57] "Today the effort must be made; tomorrow death may come, who knows?"[58]

Having dabbled in Kant, I would even suspect that time does not belong to the nature of things at all. That wouldn't leave it any less real, however, than space or causation, or the distinction of things into objects and selves, categories of how our minds make things appear to us, not of how they really are in themselves. By the Teaching, such constraints are left behind when we are ready to go beyond the All,[59] the field of the Five Aggregates, beyond the senses, beyond mind and matter, to witness Nibbana — but not until then.[60] In the meantime, neither spiritual exhortation nor philosophical or scientific speculation will bring us closer to that ultimate reality: it needs to be experienced. So long as we have to go by the assurances of others, we are like moles trying to understand color, and we'd better stick to our tunnel-vision, crude as it may be, until we have found something better — something we truly *know*, not something we have been told[61] — to keep us from bumping our heads into a lot of walls and other unyielding objects.[62]

Even if you were right (and I'm not saying you are!), 227 precepts for the monks and 311 for the nuns would still be ridiculous!

As the Buddha prepared to die, he told Ananda that "the Sangha may, when I am gone, abolish the lesser and minor rules."[63] The monks later gave Ananda a hard time for not asking which rules were the lesser ones,[64] but surely they were missing the point: the Buddha was telling them that the Dhamma would be their teacher now and that they would need to use their own judgments.[65]

If life is so rife with suffering, crude and subtle, then why should I perpetuate it by having children, especially when they take up so much time that I could be devoting to the Dhamma?

Some meditators decide that they want to walk the Path as quickly and resolutely as possible, and they become monks and nuns. The Buddha left his wife and child, and he always endorsed the monastic route as the most direct, because householders are so very prone to getting caught up in the distractions and entanglements of daily life. Families and loved ones make for fierce attachments and grave sorrows:[66] not for nothing did the Buddha named his son "Shackles" (Rahula).[67] So how does it help to get married and have children?

It helps because to commit yourself to someone in good times and in bad, and to raise children in a truly loving manner, is a formidable training in selfless service, and selflessness is exactly what we need to break through our delusions. Granted, the selfless part tends to be more honored in the breach than in the observance in families, but similar things could be said about many of the unglamorous realities of monastic life. The aspiration to pure love is as valid, valuable, and viable in a householder's life as in any monastery, and just as difficult. There's another dimension, too, in that from a Buddhist point of view, having children does not actually create or perpetuate life in the way we imagine; it merely provides a vehicle for karmic energies that would exist anyway.[68] Human birth is considered a great blessing in the Buddha's Teaching, and one could hardly do the world a greater service than to provide a spiritually wholesome environment for a human child to grow up in. From a Dhammic point of view, the progress of each is the ultimately the progress of all, and to raise a potential Buddha is as good, possibly even better, than to be a potential Buddha oneself.

When it is said that we need to help ourselves before we can help others, are we not opening the door to selfishness?
It's possible, of course: the story Goenka tells about the king and queen (Pasendi and Mallika) who realize that they love only themselves applies to all of us.[69] The ego is crafty and loves to hide behind pretenses. But the story also shows how we can begin

to overcome our selfishness once we are able to see it clearly.

The Buddha used the image of being stuck in the mud: how can we hope to pull out anyone else if we are sinking ourselves?[70] As we all know from air-travel, put on your own oxygen mask before trying to help your loved ones. We may even have an obligation to help ourselves, because if we don't, we will never keep our miseries to ourselves but will always infect others with them.[71] Physician, heal thyself.[72]

The question of what is truly effective help raises wider and deeper questions. In the Buddhist view, the world that appears to be so solid around us is ultimately a projection of the mind. As Goenka translates the opening of the *Dhammapada*: "Mind precedes all phenomena, mind matters most, everything is mind-made."[73] The apparent good we do while acting with an impure mind (a mind tainted by cravings, aversions, and ignorance) does not lose all its merit; someone may still be helped. If purity of mind were a strict precondition for helping others, not much good would ever be done. Our motivations, so long as we are not Buddhas, will always be mixed — but so will the ultimate benefits we bring to ourselves or to others.

In a world where "political realism" is taken to mean that we must, to secure ourselves, respond in kind to all provocations and aggressions, and where most "welfare" politics presumes that just as much good can be done with a dollar extracted by force of law as with one freely and lovingly given, in such a world the Buddha's Teaching is radical in the truest sense of the word: it takes us to the root of the problem within ourselves, not merely to the visible fruits borne by our impurities.[74] The implications of the Teaching for our public affairs cannot be identified with this or that side of the Procrustean bed of ideological politics. It doesn't finally matter much on which end of the bed the chopping is done.

From a higher point of view, that of true equanimity and pure love, the very distinction between loving ourselves and loving others loses its meaning.[75] Triumphs merely multiply envy and breed enmity; only love conquers truly, only love dispels hate.[76] Thus the Buddha's pronouncement that "Protecting oneself, one protects others; protecting others, one protects oneself."[77] If only we saw more clearly, our generosity would lose all its forced character: "If people knew, as I know, the result of giving and sharing, they would not eat without having given something... Even if it were their last morsel, their last mouthful, they would not eat without having shared it, if there were someone to share it with."[78]

The Buddhist ideals of renunciation and detachment sound unsociable to me. Make an island of yourself? What about friendship?

There is a time for engagement and a time for withdrawal, but there is no Dhamma without friendship. "Make an island of yourself, make yourself your refuge"[79] is meant to foster self-reliance, not to negate human relationships.[80]

Once Ananda, after hearing the Buddha give a talk, exclaimed: "At last I understand: good friendship is half the spiritual life!"

"Not so, Ananda, not so!" the Buddha corrected him. "Good friendship is the entire spiritual life."[81]

Did the Buddha really urge us to practice "as if our hair were on fire"? Isn't that a bit over the top?

So it says several times in the Scriptures,[82] but you need to figure out what it means and how to live it. Human birth is an extraordinary opportunity,[83] said to be greater than any other in the whole realm of existence, preferable even to that of the gods, who are too contented to seek liberation.[84] Since time is limited, possibly much more so than we realize, we should feel a great sense of urgency in our practice. *Life is as short and fleeting,* said the Buddha, *as a drop of dew on the tip of a grass-blade just before the sunrise; it is like a bubble in the rain, like a line drawn on water with a stick.*[85] "What if I were to die tonight?" is therefore a question, for the Buddha as for Montaigne, that should never be far from our minds.[86]

We must not kid ourselves: the house *is* on fire.[87] (The Buddha spoke of aging and death as "a great mountain high as the clouds coming this way, crushing all living beings."[88]) Like busy and distracted workers in a large building that is on fire, we may not want to hear that there is an emergency, and we may dismiss the reports coming in as mere rumors. But the image also reminds us of something else: if we want to get out safely, and we want to help others do the same, we need to find the exit both quickly and calmly. Panic will only get us trapped: we need a balanced, clear, and tranquil head, whether it is on fire or not. How to reconcile dispatch with detachment and effort with ease is one of the great challenges you will have to face throughout your practice.

One of the Buddha's disciples, Sona, had been a wealthy young man known for his delicate feet, a lute-player. After he became a monk, his eagerness to make progress was such that when he did his walking meditation, he worked at it until his feet were bloodying the ground. Yet, despite his great energy, he did not feel that he was getting anywhere, and he considered returning to lay life. The Buddha reminded him, and all of us, to think of our practice as if we were making music. Unless the strings on your instrument are taut, you will not be able to play on them, and you may need to keep tightening them so as not to sound flat (a problem only too familiar to string-players even today). But keeping in tune is a delicate matter: one turn too many, and you will be sharp, two turns and the strings may break. Under-striving leads nowhere, over-striving to agitation only.[89] It is by a balanced effort, neither halting nor straining, that we may cross over to the other shore.[90]

When you notice yourself getting frustrated with what you take to be your poor performance on a Ten-Day course, it may help to remember that you are not there to please anyone, to prove or accomplish anything, but to do something good for yourself. In the end, you are not even there to work, whatever Goenka may say; you are there to become happier. It may take some effort, so Goenka's exhortations have their place; use them to motivate yourself, but don't allow them to make you feel pushed around. Once again: you are your own master. Take responsibility for your actions, be considerate of others, and do what seems best. *An it harm none, do what ye will.*

You mentioned "the gods": what gods?

The Buddhist cosmology may seem to take us a long way from the reliance on personal experience that is the hallmark of Vipassana, but all its realms are supposed to be observable phenomena, if not in everyday life then at higher levels of meditative discovery. Rather than philosophical or creedal commitments, the various spheres of existence are "outward reflections of the internal cosmos of mind, registering in concrete form the subtle gradations in states of consciousness."[91]

The connection of the different realms with distinct states of consciousness is clearest when it comes to the higher planes, which are described in terms of corresponding meditative states, as we shall see. According to the logic of dependent origination — the fundamental law according to which *all* things are said to arise and pass away — consciousness *precedes* the arising of matter (including the mind-body phenomenon).[92] Yet this must not be understood the way philosophical idealism might take it, as a denial of the reality of matter; instead the Buddha insisted that mentality-materiality, once it has arisen, subsists in a complex interdependent relationship with consciousness in which neither can be said to predominate.[93] Thus the inner and the outer worlds flow together in a stream too complex to disentangle, except practically, by applying the Buddhist program for bringing about cessation and escaping from Samsara altogether.

Intertwined with the human world, but considered the first lower realm, is the world of the animals with which we are all more or less familiar, except that we often misunderstand it. From a Buddhist point of view, there is nothing innocent about an existence dominated by even coarser cravings and aversions than our own, and mired in a far more impenetrable ignorance. Animals may gain higher rebirths — like the frog Manduka who happened to be listening to the Buddha's voice when his head was crushed by a wanderer's staff[94] — but the odds are slim and the suffering in the animal realm is profuse. It is not bucolic scenes of lambs and lions lying side-by-side that characterize *nature, red in tooth and claw* (as we well know but like to forget), but the blind terrors of prey about to be torn limb from limb by predators, without comprehension or hope of respite.[95]

Lower still are the realms of aggravated anguish and misery — some dominated by particularly fierce kinds of insatiable hunger, others by extreme aggression, still others by all the shades of torment that can be unleashed by unwholesome mind-states.[96] Though sites of great suffering, these realms are not places of punishment by an indignant authority; they merely provide the stage upon which the crudest, most violent, and most painful energies play themselves out until they have been dissipated and exhausted. Nothing is permanent in the Buddhist cosmos, not even hell.

All the higher planes of existence correspond to mental states that can be experienced in meditation: the four most accessible and proximate to conceptions of "heaven" in other traditions are equivalent to the four *jhanic* states, from the paradisiacal bliss and rapture of the first up to the serene equanimity of the fourth. Above these are the "pure abodes" of ever more expansive and subtle mind-states rising to the "immaterial spheres" of infinite space, infinite consciousness, nothingness, and a final realm where the very distinction between being and non-being, perception and non-perception breaks down.[97] Even here, however, in divine spheres whose vastness and longevity we cannot even imagine,[98] the fundamental problem of existence has not been solved. However minute the taint of the unsatisfactory, it has not been fully expunged and beings there have not made their escape from the Dominion of Dukkha.

In contrast to how the gods are almost universally conceived (with the rare exception of the august aloofness depicted by Lucretius[99]) the divine beings in the Pali Canon, called devas and brahmas, do not govern or even concern themselves with human affairs as a matter of course.[100] They may take themselves to be the creators of their worlds, but by the Buddhist understanding, they are mistaken.[101] In the Canon, they appear on the human stage mostly for dramatic emphasis and the punctuation of key moments in the Buddha's life.[102] Nor does it bespeak great reverence when the gods are likened to swarms of flies contentedly settling on a pole or pail.[103]

Not immortal, only extremely long-lived by our standards, the devas and brahmas remain engulfed in the cycle of Samsara, however subtle their unease. Because they are so powerful and comfortable, they are in a less advantageous position than we are to understand their place in the world and learn from it.[104] Thus it is said that when the time comes for devas to pass away, they encourage each other with the prospect of a human rebirth.[105] "Even the gods envy those who are awakened,"[106] and divine beings often sought out the Buddha for instruction.[107] "I know of very many gods whose splendor the radiance of the sun does not match," said the Buddha on one occasion, claiming that he knew of much greater splendors still. On another occasion, the Buddha tells a god outright that "I know more than you do" and gets him to agree.[108]

Plants have a highly anomalous status in the Buddhist cosmology. They are said to be born and alive, but they are not considered sufficiently sentient or self-aware to be liable to suffering on the wheel of Samsara.[109] Followers of the Buddha are enjoined not to injure plants or even seeds gratuitously,[110] primarily out of respect for farmers and their harvests, but also because they are said to be the homes of "garden deities, park deities, tree deities, and deities inhabiting grass and medicinal herbs."[111] The power of plants themselves to convey teachings to human beings, which drinkers of certain plant-medicines insist they have experienced, would be hard to reconcile with a Buddhist perspective; the possibility that the beings inhabiting plants would find a way to communicate with us, less so. Either way, the Buddha's Teaching, if it is real, goes beyond anything that even the gods could teach us, and the idea that plant-induced visions, however sublime they may be, could take one beyond the Dhamma is not intelligible from a Buddhist point of view.

Pali accounts mention "the divine eye" that came to the Buddha on the night of his enlightenment, as well as other supernormal powers supposedly attainable through meditation. That sounds awesome! Are such powers real?

Real or not, supernormal powers are mere distractions from the path of insight and purification.[112] Asked about telepathy and other psychic powers and superhuman feats, the Buddha denounced them: "Seeing the danger of such miracles, I dislike, reject, and despise them."[113]

Remember the story about the leaves left on the floor of the forest: much more can be known than is necessary or useful for living well. There are some profound truths in Goethe's poem about the sorcerer's apprentice who discovers how much easier it is to invite powerful spirits than to control and get rid of them again. The Buddha's Path is clear and clean, well-marked and safe.[114] No one can stop you from heading off into the underbrush if you see an enticing opening, but you do so at your own risk and responsibility.[115]

The Pali accounts make it sound as if the attainment of Buddhist sainthood was very common during the Buddha's lifetime. Today it seems to be practically unheard-of and is talked about only in hushed tones. Why?

Theravada Buddhism recognizes four stages of sainthood, from *stream-entry* and the first glimpse of Nibbana via two intermediate stages to full and final liberation, *arahanthood*, with specific fetters eliminated at every stage.[116] One might think of these stages as the stations on a baseball *diamond* (a prime Buddhist symbol for cutting through ignorance and attachment[117]), with the biggest challenge that of making it across the no-man's-land that separates the batter from first base, and the important difference that moving from one base to another is supposed to be a mere matter of time. Thus it is said that having experienced Nibbana, a stream-enterer will be reborn no more than seven times before arriving at full liberation.

The Pali Canon reports many instances of rapid advancement when students were personally instructed by the Buddha. Even a few words seem to have been enough in some cases, as if home-runs were an everyday event then but had quickly ceased after the Awakened One's death. If the Buddha was not a miracle-worker, but merely a pointer of the way,[118] and if the Path remains as it was, why the change? A tough question on which I can only offer a few speculations, no definite answers. One is that whether the Buddha could (or would) work miracles or not, he must have had an extraordinary capacity for inspiring others who were already carrying the seed of enlightenment in them, speeding up the process even if he was not driving it. Another thing to consider is that the earliest adherents of a powerful new faith are bound to be not only especially energetic, but also most eager to attribute the highest accomplishments to their first practitioners. We should not simply dismiss reported breakthroughs to sainthood, but neither do we need to put our trust in all of them, especially when numbers in ancient texts tend to be used symbolically, whether we are reading Homer, the Bible, or the Pali Canon.[119] "Seven" rebirths are not meant to be counted off on one hand and two fingers, nor the many other instances when the Buddha promises that something will occur in the course of seven years, seven months, seven weeks, or seven days.[120] Likewise the calendar of five 500-year periods of decay in the Teaching, followed by an age of revival, may be taken as literally as one wishes — so long as one is willing to ignore everything we know about the literary practices of ancient times. (The completion of the first 2500-year cycle was celebrated in Burma in 1956. Whether the renewal that may indeed have occurred since then owes more to the power of numbers than to that of self-fulfilling prophecies, we must all decide for ourselves.)

Revival or not, one sometimes hears that enlightened beings are supposed to be more scarce today because we live in a particularly degenerate age. I am not convinced: as soon as the Buddha was dead, the Buddhist world erupted in bitter disputes over his very ashes.[121] Folly is not the prerogative of any century, nor wisdom that of any other. There are good reasons why stream-enterers and other advanced walkers on the Path alive today would be discreet; but such cases do exist, in our age as in every other. True teachings are not easy to identify, as the Buddha conceded in his discourse to the Kalamas; but making one's search for meaning depend on first finding a certified saint is not a very promising strategy, as he emphasized in the same discourse. Some traditional criteria for the true Dhamma are that it must be clearly expounded, to be seen and realized for oneself by any reasonably intelligent person; that it must give results here and now, inviting one to come and see; and that it must lead straight to the goal.[122]

What is the Middle Way?
The Middle Way is a path of moderation that avoids two extremes: undue hedonism or sensual self-indulgence, and undue asceticism designed to beat the body into submission.[123] Wisdom calls for simple living, not penance.[124]

The Buddha experimented with the first in his youth, when he is said to have had an entire palace of dancing-girls at his disposal, and he carried the second to extreme lengths during a period of brutal self-mortification in the final months before his breakthrough. He pulled out his hair; he spent his nights among the beasts in dark forests; he slept on spikes and amidst the rotting corpses at funeral grounds where the dead are left exposed to the animals and the elements; he fed on grass and cow-dung, even on his own urine and excrement; he suffocated himself without mercy and otherwise so tormented his body that the deities said to be watching over him thought that he must have ended by killing himself.[125]

At last the Buddha realized that his austerities were getting him nowhere and a memory arose in him: how happy he had been as a small boy when he had sat in the shade of a rose-apple tree, absorbed in spontaneous meditation while his father was presiding over a ploughing ceremony in the surrounding fields. Why fear such innocent and wholesome pleasures?[126] Thus was born "the safe and good path to be traveled joyfully."[127] Knowing oneself and doing things in moderation go together as naturally in the Buddha's teaching as they did on the walls of the Delphic oracle.

Meditations on the loathsomeness of the body, including charnel-ground contemplations, are no doubt authentically Buddhist techniques for loosening sensual attachments.[128] Goenka downgrades them to mere beginners' exercises,[129] but they make up the longest section in the Satipatthana Sutta and they have a troubled history of being taken all-too seriously by the monks. In the early days of the Sangha, a group of them got so carried away by revulsion that twenty or thirty killed themselves in a single day.[130] The Scriptures make it very clear that fear and loathing of our human nature, or disgust with it, is far from liberating, but is rather another form of craving, namely for annihilation.[131] Thus the Buddha, when he heard of the suicides, immediately switched the remaining bhikkhus to the "peaceful and sublime, ambrosial and pleasant" technique of Anapana. The technique of reflecting on the supposed repulsiveness of the human anatomy remains on the books, but it should be used with care and caution.

The failure of his ascetic exercises taught the Buddha that hostility to our bodies is just as "ignoble and unbeneficial" as is the preoccupation with sensual pleasures.[132] So when the Buddha derides the body as a mere lump of digested rice and porridge, as a "tumor" or an "affliction" or a "calamity,"[133] he is attacking not nature, but our propensity to identify unduly with all that is so unstable and insecure about the physical frames of our being.

What are the "Seven Factors of Enlightenment"?

Many factors contribute to the process of enlightenment, but seven (called the *bojjhangas*) are emphasized especially:[134] mindfulness (*sati*), keen investigation of phenomena (*dhamma vicaya*), energy (*viriya*), joy or rapture (*piti*), tranquility of body and mind (*passaddhi*), concentration (*samadhi*), and equanimity (*upekkha*).[135] They are said to have an especially close relationship to the four divine abodes of equanimity, loving-kindness, compassion, and sympathetic (or altruistic) joy.[136] A whole chapter of the *Samyutta Nikaya* is devoted to them,[137] as is Goenka's morning chanting on Day 7. If you prefer a more dramatic illustration of the Seven Factors' alleged powers, it is said that when the Buddha got gravely ill, he had one of his monks recite the Seven Factors and was cured.[138]

I do not share the Buddhist taste for spiritual grocery-lists with overlapping items, but let me add that a super-smoothie of 37 requisites for enlightenment is commonly concocted by blending the following ingredients with the seven above:[139] the Noble Eightfold Path, the four foundations of mindfulness from the *Satipatthana Suttas*,[140] the four right kinds of striving,[141] the four bases for spiritual power,[142] as well as the five faculties and powers.[143]

What are the "worldly vicissitudes" and what is their significance?

The *Lokavipatti Sutta* identifies eight vicissitudes that come and go like winds agitating the whole world: gain and loss, praise and blame, repute and disrepute, pleasure and pain.[144] "To be at peace, rest like a great tree in the midst of them all" (Ajahn Chah).[145] In the *Mangala Sutta*, it is said that the greatest blessing of all is for the mind to remain unshaken by these vicissitudes, ever sorrowless, stainless, and secure.[146] In other words, equanimity.

What makes the lotus such a special symbol for Buddhists?

Lotuses floating peacefully on cool water with their beautiful open petals have an obvious appeal as symbols of liberation, and they are sometimes specifically linked to equanimity in the Pali Canon.[147] Their opening at the surface might be likened to the opening of the heart, and Buddhists take note of the way water does not adhere to the petals, just as sorrow drops off from those who are wise.[148]

What is just as interesting as the beauty of the flowers is how long a journey they must make to rise from the muck and mire at the bottom of a pond, through murky waters, until they finally arrive at the surface.[149] Truly an image worth pondering for the process whereby spiritual progress can be made in the world.

And what about the lowly onion?

Onions have many minute layers of skin that become transparent as they are peeled off: to Buddhists that suggests the shedding of layer after layer of impurities. Under the microscope, onions reveal a very clear cell-structure: like mind-moments seen for what they are when they are magnified in meditation. Once properly cooked, onions are sweet, but raw ones often make one cry.

It seems to me that the Buddha's teaching is everything the world is not. How can it make sense to break so radically with life as we know it?

Because the Buddha realized how contrary his Teaching was to the ordinary ways of life, one of the first things he called it was "this abstruse Dhamma that goes against the worldly stream."[150]

So long as the world as you know it makes sense to you, there is no reason to break with anything. The Path is not something to be imposed on anyone. Like a kindly therapist, the Buddha is ready to help you if you would like to go see him, without charges. But you should never feel pressured into visiting him against your will, let alone forced to swallow suspicious pills prescribed for your supposed good. Such perverse and coercive situations might arise in certain spiritual settings, even among Buddhists, but they have nothing to do with the Dhamma.

It's when we cannot make sense of things any more, when we are looking for a refuge, that the Dhamma really comes to life, and then it won't feel like a provocation or mere source of cognitive dissonance any more. Until then, have fun; just keep an eye on whether you are really enjoying yourself.

Let's say that blind reaction really is at the heart of our difficulties in life. Even if reaction is a habit that can be changed, not an inevitable part of our human condition, it must be an incredibly deep groove in the mind. What realistic hope can there be of making such a drastic turn?

Reaction is the deepest habit of all, so central and so entrenched as to be nearly synonymous with life itself. By the Buddhist account of dependent origination, one might say that we are not the creatures of God, but the creatures of our own reactions and thus the authors of our own suffering! That is why the Buddha could be so scathing about existence, saying that even the least bit of it smelled like feces. Only fully liberated beings step beyond the reach of all reaction; only they break through the bounds of *sankhara* and *Dukkha* within which life normally traps us. (That is one reason why it is so difficult to say what happens to liberated beings when they "die": even before the end, they have already quit the confines of life along with the last traces of reaction and impurity.)

But let's be more practical. If we are dealing with a habit, it must be possible to overcome it the same way it got established: by repetition. As with all deep habits, we should not expect miraculous, instant transformations. Glimpses of freedom will come as conditions ripen, but we need to keep going back to the hard work and discipline of changing the orientation of our minds one thought and one reaction at a time. Suzuki puts it nicely: "After you have practiced for a while, you will realize that it is not possible to make rapid, extraordinary progress. Even though you try very hard, the progress you make is always little by little. It's not like going out in a shower in which you know when you get wet. In a fog, you do not know you are getting wet, but as you keep walking you get wet little by little."[151] I sometimes think of our minds as giant tankers traveling between continents. Such behemoths cannot just be swung around: they must be turned by degrees so tiny that they may escape notice, and yet even the most minute changes in direction make a big difference over time.

If your habit of reaction were truly too deep to change, then your meditation at the end of a course should be as shallow and volatile as it was at the outset. Not likely! When doubt assails you, remember yourself being equanimous, even if it was only for a few moments, during a tough sitting. Could you have done such a thing even a few days earlier? When you return to everyday life, the change may be less visible, granted, and the garden of your mind, which you weeded with such care and effort during your course, may appear altogether overgrown again before long. But to use that as an argument against meditation would be to argue like the kid who doesn't want to brush her teeth because they will get dirty again. Sure they will: but not as dirty as they would get if you had never brushed them at all. Every little bit counts, as the vagabonds say. They can be wiser than we.

If the Teaching is true, our habits of reaction are unimaginably ancient, going back not only for billions of years on our planet, but endlessly, aeon by aeon and world-system by world-system. Think about what a remarkable thing it is, after an eternity of reaction, to change the programming, even if were just for an instant. Who knows: it may never have happened before in your history as a karmic creature![152] (Or if that version is too bizarre and Darwinian terms sound more reasonable to you, think what a remarkable change you are making to a pattern that may be encoded in cells and genes that you have inherited from an unbroken line of survivors and procreators going back to the very origins of life on our planet billions of years ago!) Either way, the remarkable thing is not that change at so fundamental a level is difficult; the remarkable thing is that it is possible at all. And can there be any doubt, in light of your own experience during a course, that some change, however minute, is indeed possible?

If you discover a more efficient way to bring about change at the most profound level, please let me know: I would like to hear about it, because I get tired too of the effort that Vipassana requires. But until we find something better, why fret about progressing slowly? If the journey is worthwhile, we need to keep taking our little steps, puny as they may seem.[153] Snails can be hard to watch because their movements are so pitifully slow; but who has not been astonished to see how far they can travel when we are looking the other way! Or to see how the steady drip of a faucet, which can seem so paltry at any one moment, fills a sink or a bucket, or even a bathtub, in a way that we might not believe possible if we had not seen it happen.

Whatever else you may say, ten days of silence and solitude sound very boring and lonely to me. What's there to like?
When I tell people how many times I've put myself through the Goenka wash-cycle, they sometimes respond by saying "you must really like to be on retreat." Bah! Humbug! Of course the experience is bound to have its enjoyable moments, but I definitely don't do the courses for fun. I do them because they help me to process what lies behind me, to prepare for what lies ahead, and to become a little more at ease with living in the present. Don't get me wrong: I'm very glad that such a tool exists, just as I am grateful for the state of dental or medical technology. But to me Vipassana is a course of treatment, not a vacation — "all included," to be sure, but very far from Club Med. Sure there will be times when you will feel bored and lonely on a course, or miserable for some other reason. But such is life. Suffering there will always be, crude or subtle; during a course it is more likely to be therapeutic, that's the only difference.

It all sounds very interesting, but I still don't understand why anyone would feel the need to do a Ten-Day course!

Why does anyone agree to sit in a dentist's chair or to submit to any other painful or unpleasant operation? Not because it sounds interesting, that's for sure, but only because one realizes that something is wrong, that it won't go away by itself, and that something can be done about it. If the Buddha's diagnosis does not apply to you, congratulations. Be happy!

If you are waiting for things to sort themselves out with no great effort on your part, however, you are probably deluding yourself. Effortlessness and "great inaction" at the right time are also important, granted, but right effort is required even on the way to effortlessness.[154] If you do need help, but you doubt that Vipassana can help you, by all means be skeptical and try whatever else makes most sense to you. But if you find yourself unable to get to the root of the problem, consider wagering ten days. You have nothing to lose but your chains — Marx hardly invented that. Rest assured that nobody will, or can, take your precious burdens away from you against your will.

Once and for all, is sex un-Buddhist? What about specific sexual techniques?

How could something that is so central to who we are as human beings be contrary to a Teaching that is meant, above all else, to be realistic? We do not only owe our natural biological conception to the union of the sexes, but the karmic spark of existence would not have brought us into this life if it had not been for the current of sexual desire flowing this way. *Yatha-butha* applies here as well: like it or not, we are sexual creatures living in a sexually charged world, and as much as the Teaching would encourage us to find a way to transcend the sufferings of existence altogether, so much would it counsel careful attention to the actual state of our current development.

Certainly, the Buddha's Teaching warns us with great vehemence and persistence against the dangers of blind entanglement in our sense-desires. Combined with the very severe pronouncements against sex in a monastic context — directed at so many young men who would have found celibacy difficult — one can easily get the impression that the Buddha was disparaging the world of sensuous enjoyment altogether. Yet one should always be wary, in dealing with so subtle a teaching, of rushing to premature conclusions. To be sure, one must expect to pay a price for one's amorous adventures and sexual excitements, which feed our cravings and agitate the mind (as does much else that is not objectionable in itself: such is the texture of creatureliness). It may even seem obvious, from a higher point of view, that the price is not worth paying. But we need to be careful with anticipating such higher, let alone ultimate, points of view for which we may not be ready. Thus dieting is hardly a Buddhist exercise if it gives one no reprieve from food cravings, but intensifies them further, and sexual abstinence is no better when it merely leaves one boiling in unfulfilled desires or twisted with repressed ones. (St Paul's "better to marry than to burn" and his insistence that we must act in accordance with our very different gifts are both sound Buddhist reminders as well.[155]) There may even be those for whom sexual exercises (one thinks of tantric practices for example) may retain there usefulness even at the highest levels of spiritual development. For the rest, the characteristically Buddhist response to the problem of our overweening desires and our ever-ready addiction to pleasure it is not rejection but *attention*. Even the word *detachment* that is so often used in characterizing the Buddhist approach can be misleading because it seems to suggest a pulling away, when what is really needed is simply an observer's stance, a not attaching rather than an aggressive distancing.

Ultimately (such a slippery and dangerous little word), the Path should lead us to transcend our sexual desires along with all else that attaches and binds us. But eventually leaving our desires behind, in a light and a joyful release, in favor of something better, is a very different proposition from denying and repressing our natures as they currently present themselves. For one who is ready to take renunciation to the next level, a free and easy-going celibacy may indeed be a higher calling than that of an ordinary worldling who revels in his desires and pays the price for them in turmoil. But such things must not be forced, and few are those who are ready to leave the fetters behind without having to tear them off and make a bloody mess.[156] A story is told of two monks who were traveling by a river when an unaccompanied woman appeared who needed help with crossing. So the first monk took her in his arms and carried her over. The second monk kept his peace until he could stand it no longer, then scolded his companion for having broken his monastic commitments. "I have put her down a long time ago," replied his friend. "Why are you still carrying her?"

It would be painfully easy to compile all manner of stark proclamations from Buddhist worthies, past and present, on what must not be done with whom. But such injunctions often acquire a life of their own that has very little do to with the Teaching in whose name they are paraded. The ground rule for all Dhammic activity is not very different from the golden rule of the Christians or the Wiccan Rede, for that matter: be scrupulously careful not to hurt or harm anyone, and when in doubt, treat others just the way you would wish them to treat you. Do not lie or deceive anyone to get what you want, especially when it comes to sex. Be kind and caring and generous, always giving before you think of getting, in the bedroom or anywhere else. Never be cruel or manipulative or let yourself in for the temptations of abusive power. Be discreet and do not talk about your exploits in a way that might reflect badly on someone else, especially a bedmate. Be grateful and never dismissive or disdainful of the favors you have received. We know these things well enough, but we also know that they are hard to practice, so we may imagine that it would save us time and trouble to be done with sex altogether. Yet we should take heed, for so many supposed shortcuts end up taking us on unavailing detours or get us lost altogether.

Whether in the domain of sex or anywhere else in human life, the Teaching is less concerned with *what* we do with *whom* than with *how* we do it. *That which is done mindfully* is shorthand for every action on the Path, bedroom deeds included: because behavior that runs contrary to the Dhamma is such that no mindful person would wish to engage in it, since it tends to one's own harm and that of others. *That which is done with loving-kindness* is another reasonable abbreviation, if only we are capable of real honesty with ourselves, willing and able to look beneath our specious pretended motives at the darker stuff that so often lurks beneath. The Teaching acknowledges our physical realities without blinking or blushing, but there is nothing particularly Dhammic about exercising our basic body functions or exchanging body fluids. Yet, where the spirit of love enters and makes a closer connection between human beings — even if it is just for a moment and not free of impurities — there the Dhamma is at home, however ephemerally. Since the act itself tends to be clouded by the heat of passion and its intense sensations, a good test is to ask what happens afterwards: when the fires die down, is there a warm glow left behind or just the ashen taste of consumed desires? Does the connection persist or does it dwindle away with the receding armies of our lusts?

The Way of Sex should not — at least in ordinary cases — be expected to work wonders for one's concentration, one's equanimity, or one's meditative development in general. But the spiritual path is long, winding, and often full of surprises. Who can say with confidence what twists and turns might not, unexpectedly, reveal particularly splendid and enlightening vistas? There are many lessons to be learned in this life, and the school of sex has its of own profound ways of teaching us, with all its joys and beauties, its limitations and letdowns. When we look at a river meandering through a landscape, we may wonder at its many apparently senseless diversions, not to say aberrations; but to a geologist it will be evident that given the prevailing physical conditions, the water is in fact finding the quickest way to the sea.[157]

NOTES

1. Six teachers were especially famous in the Buddha's day, including the founder of Jainism (see MN pp. 50-51 for an overview). Even the Buddha's very last student, who refused to be content with paying his respects at the Awakened One's deathbed, wanted to know which of these teachers had realized the truth (DN 16.5.26-27 [p. 268]). (Goenka mentions the episode in his discourses, but not the questioner's most urgent preoccupation.)

2. MN 72 (pp. 590-94 [BW 367-69]). Also SN 56.8 (pp. 1841-42) and MN 122.12 (p. 974), the latter on questions that are among unprofitable kinds of speech.

3. Only Devadatta gets called worse, "a wastrel, a clot of spittle" (*Cullavagga* 7.3.1, following Nanamoli's translation [*Life* 258]).

4. MN 63 (pp. 533-36 [BW 230-33]); see also SN 56:31 (pp. 1857-58 [BW 360]) (above).

5. SN 15:3 (p. 652 [BW 18]).

6. *Being Nobody, Going Nowhere* (Wisdom Publications, 1987), p. 148 (also p. 32).

7. DN 24.2.14-15 (p. 381) and DN 27.10 (p. 409). On the dissolution of a world-system and the migration of the beings living there, see AN 10.29 (p. 1379). Whatever else may need to be said about the Buddhist cosmology, it is certainly vast: references to thousand-fold, ten-thousand-fold, even hundred-thousand-fold world-systems abound in the Pali Canon (see for example MN 120.12-18 [pp. 960-61]).

8. SN 15.1 (pp. 651 [BW 37]).

9. SN 12:43-44 (pp. 580-82 [BW 358]), italics added.

10. SN 12:15 (p. 544 [BW 356-57]), italics added. The Sutta continues by making a connection with the Middle Way understood more abstractly than usual: "'All exists': that is one extreme. 'All does not exist': that is the other extreme. Without veering towards either of these extremes, I teach the Dhamma by the middle." (*Ibid.*)

11. As Schopenhauer points out in chapter 41 of *Die Welt als Wille und Vorstellung* (vol. II), the belief in some variant of rebirth is so widespread outside the three Abrahamic religions that it might be called the "consoling original faith of mankind" (*tröstlicher Urglaube*

der Menschheit). It's not only central to Hinduism, Jaininism, and Buddhism, but also to the religion of the Egyptians and to virtually all nature-based aboriginal faiths the world around, including the Druidic. The Greek mystery cults (most famously the Eleusinian) presumed it, the Pythagoreans taught it, and Plato adopted it in his *Republic*. The doctrine survived even at the margins of the Abrahamic faiths: Orthodox Christianity repudiated it, but many Gnostic Christians upheld it, and it remains part of Islamic mysticism and the Jewish Kabbalah tradition.

12. By the same measure, where do they go when we sleep? To me this is an open question and I would not want to issue any challenges over it. For Fleischman it is an opportunity to do just that: "If you think there is something as absolute and final as death is often construed to be, then you are being *non-scientific*, since the essence of this scientific world-view is continuity of causality." (*An Ancient Path*, p. 126)

13. Apart from the karmic imprint, "nothing whatever passes over" (*Vism.* XIX.22-23 [p. 624]), not even consciousness, which arises every moment anew at the six sense-doors, including that of the mind (MN 38.1-8 [p. 350-351]).

14. *Manual of the Excellent Man*, p. 98. To understand rebirth fully, one would need to be able to see the arising and passing away of creatures in accordance with their karma, which is only revealed to the "divine eye" at a very high stage of spiritual development (DN 2.95 [p. 107], MN 27.23-24 [p. 276], *Vism.* XIII.72 [pp. 418-19]).

15. DN 16.1.7 (p. 233).

16. The traditional formula for *arahants*, as pronounced by the Buddha on his own liberation at MN 36.43 (p. 342).

17. *Udana* 8.8 (Ireland, pp. 114-115; *Life*, p. 156). See also *Udana* 2.7 (Ireland, pp. 28-32), especially the conclusion.

18. In his discourse, Goenka declares that "every Vipassana meditator dies consciously and smilingly" because there is a "promotion" (favorable rebirth) awaiting her. This bold promise is based, he says, on the experience of several hundred of his students, with only a single doubtful case (as of 1991, when the standard English discourses were recorded). See also *Satip. Discourses*, p. 59: "If Vipassana has been properly practiced ... the Vipassana vibration is so strong that at the last moment [it will connect a meditator] with a plane where Vipassana can be practiced." The promise is affirmed

in Goenka's text on "What Happens at Death" (pp. 31-32 in *The Art of Dying*).

19. *The Art of Dying*, p. 86.

20. The idea that some sankharas are much deeper and more entrenched than others is illustrated by Goenka with images from AN 3.132 (pp. 361-362), namely lines drawn on stone, on the ground, and on water, respectively (see Day 4 Discourse and *Art of Living*, p. 38). In the Sutta, however, the images get used not with reference to reaction in general, but in order to distinguish three types of angry persons.

21. See also *The Art of Dying*, pp. 14-15, 31. On the basics of Buddhist cosmology, see the question on the gods below. At the outset and conclusion of the course, Goenka makes passing remarks to the effect that this "getting tuned up" with salutary vibrations happens throughout life and might be called grace or mercy.

22. MN 136.6,8 (p. 1060).

23. MN 136.17-21 (p. 1064-65).

24. DN 16.1.7 (p. 233).

25. MN 136.17-21 (p. 1064-65).

26. See Sogyal Rinpoche, *The Tibetan Book of Living and Dying* (Harper 1993), esp. chapter 17, pp. 280-288.

27. Here as everywhere in one's practice, faith in the Buddha and his Teaching, or in a beloved teacher one has known personally, or in a congenial divine representation of the highest spiritual qualities, has its place, and some traditions encourage us to call on them for assistance in these difficult final moments. From a Vipassana perspective, such faith is not emphasized, but neither is it discouraged, provided only that it does not come at the expense of staying mindful of *Anicca*.

28. Natalie Goldberg, *Writing Down the Bones*, p. 167. These words have also been attributed to Ikkyu, a famous 15th century Zen iconoclast.

29. See the stories of Phagguna (AN 6.56 [p. 937]) and Khemaka (SN 22:89 [pp. 942-46 (BW 402-406)]). The bhikkhus Vakkali and Channa cut their own throats before dying of their illnesses and supposedly became *arahants* at the last moment (SN 22:87 [pp. 938-41, 1082]), SN 35:87 [pp. 1164-67]).

238 THE BOOK OF VIPASSANA SECRETS

30. The best way to prepare in a general way for dying, I have no doubt, is to cultivate equanimity with impermanence. So far so Vipassana. But if I've ever felt that I was *rehearsing* dying, it was in the realm of Ayahuasca. If so, what greater boon could one imagine? How dare we imagine that we have the right to prohibit such a thing, whether in the name of morality or of the law? (On drinking Ayahuasca as practicing and preparing for death, see chapter 13 of *The Shaman and Ayahuasca* by Don José Campos [2011].)

31. SN 55.21 (pp. 1808). When someone challenged the Buddha by saying that surely everyone is afraid of death, the Awakened One denied it (AN 4.184 [p. 550]).

32. SN 55.21 (pp. 1809). A variation on the theme of ghee and pebbles in water (the basis of Goenka's story in the discourses) appears at SN 42:6 (pp. 1336-38). The importance of "confirmed confidence" (as opposed to blind faith) in conjunction with morality as the foundation for stream-entry is stressed throughout SN 55 (pp. 1788-1837). "Stream-entry" is used loosely in this chapter (see also AN 10.64 [p. 1419] and Bodhi's Note 2087 on p. 1847) as synonymous with the entire Noble Eightfold Path (SN 55.5 [pp. 1792-93]), not as a marker for its final stages only. Learning and comprehension seem to be emphasized more here than elsewhere: "If these great trees could understand what is well-spoken and what is badly-spoken, I would declare them to be stream-enterers." (SN 55.24 [p. 1813]) At any rate, the threshold for irreversibility does sound more readily attainable here than elsewhere (see for example SN 55.7 [p. 1799]).

33. Not a rude command, but something I am adapting from a story told about the Jewish sage Hillel (d. 10 CE). Once a non-Jew went to another rabbi, Shammai, and said to him, "I will convert to Judaism if you can teach me the whole Torah while I balance on one leg." Shammai chased him away with a tool he was holding. So the questioner went to Hillel and presented him with the same challenge. Hillel answered, "What is hateful to you, do not to your neighbor: that is the whole Torah; the rest is commentary. Now go and learn it!" (Babylonian Talmud, Shabbat 31a)

34. Tara Jadhav, at the age of 82, at Dhamma Giri in 1996 (*The Art of Dying*, p. 43).

35. Brides may have been younger still, though the Buddha's wasn't. MN 13:18, dedicated to the dangers of material form, presents an imaginary girl "at the height of her beauty and loveliness ... in her fifteenth or sixteenth year" (p. 183).

36. *Suttavibhanga* 3.17-21 (Vinaya Pitaka), see *Life*, pp. 157-59. In the *Udana* (1.8, Ireland, p. 18) a former wife tries to a get a monk to take responsibility for a child he fathered before going forth, but gives up when she realizes that he won't even look at it.

37. See my long footnote above.

38. MN 26.19-21 (pp. 260-62).

39. MN 26.25-26 (pp. 263-64).

40. To translate *mahapurisa* as "superman" (as Nyanaponika Thera does in his *Abhidhamma Studies*, p. 60) is misleading. According to the *Mahapurisa Sutta* (SN 47:11 [p. 1640]), a "great man" is anyone who has liberated himself by dwelling in mindfulness, not a super-human.

41. On resting his back, see DN 33.1.5 (p. 480), MN 53.5 (p. 461), AN 9.4 (p. 1251). On napping, see MN 36.45-46 (p. 342).

42. SN 47.14 (p. 1644-45). The Sutta stresses that "there is no sorrow or lamentation in the Tathagata"; but the Buddha still missed his friends, though without attachment or suffering. Ananda, by contrast, was still very much shaken by death, to the point of feeling "as if his body had been drugged," and the Buddha told him to be more mindful of the impermanence of all things (SN 47.9,13 [pp. 1636, 1643]). A few days before dying himself, the Buddha caught Ananda weeping bitterly, because he felt that he had so much left to learn and now his teacher was about to leave him; the Buddha had to console him that he was closer to breaking through than he thought (DN 16.5.13 [p. 265]).

43. SN 16.4.1,21 (pp. 254, 257).

44. SN 48:41 (p. 1687), following Nanamoli's translation (*Life* 274).

45. AN 6.38 (pp. 900-902). The Nigantha Nataputta (Mahavira) described the Buddha as a "proponent of non-doing" (AN 8.12 [p. 1130]), but that charge is mentioned to make the Jains look ill-informed.

46. See for example AN 3.61 (pp. 266-70). DN 23.2 (p. 351) identifies the following *evil opinions*: "There is no other world, there are no spontaneously born beings, there is no fruit or result of good or evil deeds." On nihilism and the denial of moral efficacy, see also MN 60.5-28 (pp. 507-516) and MN 76.7-19 (pp. 619-623).

47. A point stressed by Goenka in his Day 8 Discourse (*Dhp.* XII.4/160), see also *Art of Living*, p. 40.

48. MN 22.13-14 (pp. 228-29).

49. DN 13.24 (p. 190). There is no "dry way across": we must get into the water and swim. Hence Goenka's story about "swimology" in the last discourse on the morning of Day 11 (see also *Art of Living*, pp. 10-11)

50. Not a new phenomenon: see DN 1.3.19 (p. 85).

51. AN 8:20 (p. 1147). Gradual training, gradual practice, and gradual progress are a bridge between the Dhamma and all kinds of arts, including architecture, archery, and even accountancy (MN 107.2 [p. 874]).

52. According to MN 85.59 (p. 708), a bhikkhu instructed by a Tathagata "might arrive at distinction" in the course of a single day or night. See also my discussion of Buddhist sainthood a little further down.

53. SN 13.1 (p. 621); see the rest of the chapter (pp. 621-626) for similes to the same effect.

54. Thus Goenka in his discourses; see also *For the Benefit of Many*, p. 44. It is true that the Buddha, when asked how long it would take a bhikkhu "practicing in accordance with the Dhamma" to become an *arahant,* answered "Not long" (SN 38.16 [p. 1300], SN 39.1 [p. 1301]). Likewise, serious meditators ("intelligent, sincere, honest, and straightforward") are promised at DN 22.22 (p. 350) and DN 25.22 (p. 393) that within as little as seven days of diligent practice (probably not to be taken literally, see below, but still "not long"), they may break through to the ultimate wisdom. (Getting to Antarctica or reading the Book of Mormon from cover to cover is not a big deal — once you have boarded your flight or taken the leap of accepting Joseph Smith as your prophet.)

55. Thoreau, *Walden* ("Where I Lived"), [Vintage p. 93].

56. *Pirkei Avot* I.14.

57. MN 79.7 (p. 655), MN 80.16 (p. 664).

58. MN 131.3 (p. 1039), part of the "summary and exposition of one who has had a single excellent night" that is repeated eight more times (pp. 1041-1052).

59. On the All, see SN 35:23,26 (p. 1140-42 [BW 345]), *Itivuttaka* 7 (Ireland, p. 159), and my discussion in chapter 7.

60. Even hard-headed scientists have some surprising things to say about what we are ultimately leaving behind: "It is important to realize that there probably isn't anything here anyway... Of course we are part of and surrounded by things; but at a deep level there is nothing... The total electrical charge of the universe is zero ... for otherwise the enormous strength of the interaction between unbalanced charges would have blasted it apart as soon as it had formed... The universe does not rotate: its overall 'angular momentum' is zero... No one knows whether the total of all the contributions to the total energy of the universe is in fact exactly zero, but the near-cancellation of the positive contributions by the negative is highly suggestive... The bottom line, prejudiced with a dash of speculation, is that the initial endowment of energy at the creation was exactly zero, and the total energy has remained fixed at that value for all time... *What we see around us is in fact nothing, but Nothing that has been separated into opposites to give the appearance of something.*" (Peter Atkins, *On Being* [OUP 2011], pp. 13-17, italics added) But one needs to be careful: the meditative vantage point from which it appears that "there is nothing" is a very high one, but there *is* Nibbana to be reckoned with (MN 102.4 [p. 840]).

61. Thus once more the discourse to the Kalamas (AN 3:65 [p. 280 (BW 89)]). Even the great plausibility of a claim, the acknowledged competence of a speaker, or the fact that one has accepted someone as a teacher cannot take the place of knowing for oneself. "I teach the Dhamma ... [so that you may] attain to and dwell in the fullness of perfected wisdom by your own insight and realization." (DN 25.23 [p. 394])

62. Thus Goenka: "Both this wall and my head are ultimately vibrations, but apparently solid. The wall will still break my head on impact!" (*Satip. Discourses*, p. 102)

63. DN 16.6.3 (p. 270) (tr. Vajira-Story). At MN 104.5 (p. 854), also speaking to Ananda, the Buddha calls disputes about the *Patimokkha* (the 227 precepts for monks) "trifling."

64. *Cullavagga* 11.1.10 (*Life*, p. 339).

65. DN 16.6.1 (pp. 269-270); see also MN 108.9-10 (p. 882). At the other extreme, an old monk by the name of Subhadda expressed relief at the news of the Buddha's passing: "We are well rid of the Great Ascetic! Now we can do what we like!" (DN 16.6.20 [p.

274], *Cullavagga* 11.1.1 [*Life*, pp. 329-30]) The unguarded comment prompted Mahakassapa to convene the First Council to ensure that the rules would not be loosened (*Cullavagga* 11.1.1 [*Life*, p. 336]).

66. See SN 42.11 (pp. 1348-1350), MN 87 (pp. 718-722), *Udana* 8.8 (Ireland, pp. 114-115, *Life*, p. 156).

67. On the other hand, the Buddha never treated families with derision or contempt. See especially AN 8:54 (pp. 1194-97) and AN 4:61-62 (pp. 449-453) for the kind and pragmatic things he said about the happiness of householders (BW 124-28). In the *Sutra of Forty-Two Chapters* (taken to be the first Indian Buddhist sutra translated into Chinese) the family is likened to a prison (chapter 23), but not in the Pali Canon.

68. Parents must do their part, of course, but their contributions are merely necessary, not sufficient, that is to say, there is a crucial kammic element that must connect parents to their prospective offspring in order for conception to take place (MN 38:26 [p. 358]; see also AN 3:61 [p. 269]).

69. SN 3:8 (pp. 170-171), *Udana* 5.1 (Ireland, p. 65). See also *Art of Living*, p. 81.

70. MN 8.16 (p. 130). See *Art of Living*, p. 137. The *Visuddhimagga*, too, stresses that loving-kindness "should, first of all, be developed towards oneself, repeatedly: 'May I be happy and free from suffering.'" (*Vism.* IX.8 [p. 289])

71. See Nyanaponika Thera, *Vision*, p. 308. Also SN 12.22 (p. 553) on the need for "manly exertion" not just for one's own good, but also for the good of others. And SN 16.5 (p. 667): "You are practicing for the welfare and happiness of the multitude, out of compassion for the world."

72. See Luke 4:23.

73. *Dhp.* I.1 (following *Gem Set in God*, p. 77).

74. See the "dark chain of causation" by which "the taking up of stick and sword" is traced to its roots within (DN 15.9 [p. 224-25 (BW 36)]).

75. Theravada Buddhism identifies four divine abodes — equanimity, loving-kindness, compassion, and sympathetic (or altruistic) joy (see AN 4.125 [pp. 507-508 (BW 216)]) — but they all look like the meeting place of equanimity and love to me.

76. SN 3.14.404 (p. 177), *Dhp.* I.5 (tr. Byrom). See also the *Itivuttaka* 27 (Ireland, p. 169-70): "Just as the radiance of all the stars does not equal a sixteenth part of the moon's radiance, which surpasses them and shines forth, bright and brilliant, even so all worldly and meritorious things do not equal a sixteenth part of love, the liberation of heart." (Combining translations by John D. Ireland, Nyanaponika Thera, and Nyanatiloka Thera.)

77. SN 47:19 (p. 1648-49).

78. *Itivuttaka* 26 (tr. Bodhi: BW 169; Ireland, p. 168). Also AN 3.57 (p. 255): "One acquires merit even if one throws away dishwater in a refuse dump or cesspit with the thought: 'May the living beings here sustain themselves with this!' How much more, then, does one acquire merit when one gives to human beings!"

79. DN 16.2.26 (p. 245 [following *Gem Set in Gold*, p. 82]); also DN 26.1,27 (pp. 395, 404), SN 47.9 (p. 1637), etc. Variations on the exhortation can also be found in the *Dhammapada* II.5/25 and XVIII.2/236.

80. Thus also the *Sutta Nipata* (5:10): "To those who stand midstream, facing the flood, overwhelmed with aging and death, I proclaim the island: *having nothing, clinging to no thing: that is the island, there is no other.*" In the ultimate sense, Nibbana is the island (SN 43.14-43 [p. 1379 (BW 365)]), a refuge that no one can reach as a self. True insight, real liberation cannot be "mine": Nibbana is, but no person can enter it (MN 1.26 [p. 87], *Vism.* XVI.90 [p. 521] and XX.83 [p. 650]). If we saw more clearly, we would understand that we are lost at sea, in an ocean of suffering, and that we should fly straight towards Nibbana, the island, like a land-finding crow kept by sailors (*Vism.* XXI.64-65 [p. 679], XXII.14 [p. 699]).

81. SN 45.2 (pp. 1524-25 [BW 240]). See also SN 46.12,48 (pp. 1579, 1596); AN 1.71 (p. 101) and AN 8.54 (p. 1194); *Itivuttaka* 17 (Ireland, p. 162).

82. SN 56.34 (p. 1859), also AN 6.20 (p. 879), AN 8.74 (pp. 1222-23).

83. SN 56.47-48 (pp. 1871-72).

84. See my discussion below of the gods in the Pali Canon.

85. AN 7:74 (p. 1096 [BW 206]). See also *Vism.* XXI.27 (p. 667).

86. AN 6.20 (p. 879). AN 6.19, 6.20, 8.73, and 8.74 are all devoted to "mindfulness of death." One of Montaigne's central contentions in

the Essays is that we should "have nothing on our minds as often as death," since he agrees with Cicero that to philosophize is nothing else but to prepare for dying. (See *Essays* 1.20, tr. Donald Frame.)

87. For the image of a house on fire, see also *Vism.* XXI.94-95 (p. 687).

88. SN 3:25 (p. 192 [BW 27]).

89. AN 6:55 (pp. 932-33), *Life* 170-71.

90. SN 1.1 (p. 89). Two other images for well-balanced effort are that of a surgeon in training who must learn to use his scalpel with just the right amount of pressure, and that of a clever skipper who knows just when to hoist and when to take in the sails (*Vism.* IV.68,70 [p. 134]).

91. *Abh.*, p. 188.

92. Thus the *Visuddhimagga*: "No world is born if consciousness is not produced; when that is present, then it lives; when consciousness dissolves, the world is dead." (*Vism.* VIII.40 [p. 234])

93. See the section on dependent origination in chapter 7.

94. *Vism.* VII.51 (p. 204).

95. Thus the description of the animal realm at MN 129.18-26 (pp. 1020-21): "There mutual devouring prevails, and the slaughter of the weak."

96. To make the distinctions more graphic, the inhabitants of the first are commonly thought of as hungry ghosts (*Peta Loka*), the denizens of the second as *asuras* or anti-gods, usually called titans in translation (a refinement made by later Buddhist tradition, not in the Suttas: see MN 12.35-36 [pp. 169 and Note 190 on p. 1199]). In the commentaries, the topography of hell was elaborated with enthusiasm, distinguishing eight major hells, each surrounded by a host of minor ones with prison terms ranging from a few days to millions of years (*Abh.*, pp. 189-90, 196).

97. For the full scheme of classifications as worked out in Abhidhamma, see *Abh.*, pp. 186-199.

98. The Canon refers to all manner of gods that are associated with thousand-fold, ten-thousand-fold, even hundred-thousand-fold world-systems (see for example MN 120.12-18 [pp. 960-61]). An aeon, the life-span of one world-system, is so vast that no intelligible number can be put on it: "Suppose there was a great stone mountain

seven miles long, wide, and high, made of solid rock. At the end of every hundred years a man would stroke it once with a piece of fine cloth. That great stone mountain might by this effort be worn away and eliminated, but the aeon would still not have come to an end." (SN 15:5 [p. 654 (BW 38)])

99. In William Ellery Leonard's translation (*The Nature of Things* II.69):

> For all the gods must of themselves enjoy
>
> Immortal aeons and supreme repose,
>
> Withdrawn from our affairs, detached, afar:
>
> Immune from peril and immune from pain,
>
> Themselves abounding in riches of their own,
>
> Needing not us, they are not touched by wrath
>
> They are not taken by service or by gift.

100. There are traditional Buddhist formulas for calling on their protection and for sharing our merits with them. Thus the *Puññanumodanam* that concludes every Vipassana group sitting (*Gem Set in Gold*, pp. 68-69).

101. What built this world and all worlds according to the Buddhist account of dependent origination is not the will of any creator-god, but simply reaction. MN 49 (pp. 424-430) describes the Buddha's encounter with Baka the Brahma, who takes himself to be immortal, the Great Creator, the "Master and Father of those that are and ever can be" (although these are Mara's words, the god does not object to them). In fact he is lord over no more than the lowest of the higher realms and comparatively short-lived by divine standards, but he has no understanding of his real position. AN 3.61 (p. 267) raises the perennial point that if all could be traced to some god's creative activity, then so could the failings of his creatures.

102. At his birth, he is received by four deities, though they are outshone by "an immeasurable, splendid light surpassing the glory of the most powerful devas." (DN 14:1.17-26 [pp. 203-204], MN 123.7-17 [pp. 980-82]) At his passing, the gods throng the site like spectators crowding into a stadium and grumbling because one of the monks is blocking their view (DN 16.5.5 [p. 263]). They mourn alongside the humans and are consulted about the funeral arrangements (DN 16:6.10-15 [271-73]).

In the *Mangala Sutta* (*Sutta Nipata* 2.4, *Gem Set in Gold*, p. 55) the story is told of a twelve-year debate about what brings the greatest happiness and blessings in life. When neither the gods nor the humans can resolve this question, "a certain female deva of surpassing beauty" is sent on an embassy to solicit the Buddha's answer. It strikes me that the gods in Homer or Hesiod, too, would have thought of sending the most attractive *goddess* to see the most sagacious man. (See also Sakka's use of the love-song just below.)

103. MN 127.12 (p. 1004).

104. Not unlike Greek tragedy, the Buddha's Teaching identifies our human vulnerability to suffering, in conjunction with our great mental capacities, as the key to attaining wisdom. The gods are too comfortable and complacent; the animals and other denizens of lower realms are too trapped in misery. Only human beings face enough adversity to make them want to break free, but not so much that it would be impossible to do so. (See Ledi Sayadaw, *The Noble Eightfold Path*, p. 29.)

105. *Itivuttaka* 83 (Ireland, pp. 207-208). Thanissaro translates: "The human state, monks, is the devas' reckoning of going to a good destination."

106. *Dhp.* XIV.3/181.

107. For the pageantry of the gods at its most extravagant, see DN 20 on "the great assembly of the gods" (pp. 315-320). Many devas also come to watch the Buddha's son Rahula being liberated by a teaching (SN 35.121 [pp. 1194-96], MN 147 [pp. 1126-1128]). When Sakka, the ruler of the devas, wants to consult the Buddha at DN 21, he has a divine minstrel attract the Awakened One's attention with a love-song (DN 21.1.5 [pp. 322-23]). Before we get to the actual lesson, we are told the story of Gopika, a girl who would rather be a man and finally succeeds (DN 21.1.11-12 [p. 325-28]). The teaching (DN 21.2.1-9 [pp. 328-333]) is a serious one, but we know that on another equally serious occasion (MN 37.3 [p. 344]), when Sakka is advised that "nothing is worth adhering to," he is depicted as too busy and distracted to heed what he is being told as urgently as it deserves (MN 37.8, 11 [pp. 345-46]).

108. MN 49.10 (p. 427). See also MN 99.22 (p. 816), where the Buddha insists that he understands Brahma and his world better than they understand themselves.

109. MN 98.8 (p. 800). Samuel Butler's *Erewhon* contains a memorable argument, in chapter 27, for why the unconsciousness of plants should not be taken for a sign of unintelligence, but rather for their particular perfection: "Each stage of development brings

back the recollection of the course taken in the preceding stage, and [in the case of plants] the development has been so often repeated that all doubt — and with all doubt, all consciousness of action — is suspended... [Action by the laws of nature] will become unconscious as soon as the skill that directs it has become perfected."

110. MN 27:13 (p. 272-73), MN 51.14 (p. 449). Among the monks' rules requiring confession (*Pacittiya*-rules), the eleventh affirms that living plants must not be damaged deliberately.

111. MN 27:13 (p. 272). The *Udana* mentions a class of originally benevolent nature-spirits (the *yakkhas*) who seem to have turned hostile after the arrival of Buddhism, perhaps because so many early Buddhist monasteries were built on the sites of their shrines (Ireland, pp. 118, 131). At *Udana* 1.7 (Ireland, pp. 17-18), a *yakkha* seeks to frighten the Buddha; at *Udana* 4.4 (Ireland, pp. 56-58) a more aggressive spirit tries to kill Sariputta with a brutal blow to the head.

112. Thus *Vism.* III.56 (p. 97): "Supernormal powers are an impediment that should be severed by one who seeks insight." Nonetheless, several are mentioned in the Canon, including the ability to pass through walls, walk on water, travel in space, and read minds (see SN 51.11 [pp. 1727-28]).

113. DN 11.1-5 (pp. 175-76). Also DN 24.1.4 (p. 372): "What purpose would the performance of miracles serve?" And SN 42.13 (p. 1360) on how the Buddha understood magic but rejected it.

114. MN 19.26 (p. 210 [BW 420]).

115. Working with plant-medicines like Ayahuasca to purify and open the heart has its place, but I would not encourage anyone to make whoopee in the twilight zone. Mother Ayahuasca is a guide who will take you where you need or want to go, but you are responsible for setting a direction and for determining whether you are being led too far afield. Shamans come in all varieties, but the more Dhamma-minded will encourage you to meet all suspect energies with a firm pledge that you are journeying to learn, to love, and to purify, and that you are not welcoming any unwholesome energies.

116. See Bodhi, BW 373-380 and NEP, VIII.117-19, for an overview of these stages and their respective fetters.

117. In the Mahayana tradition with its emphasis on the *Diamond Sutra* (see above), it is one of the most prominent symbols of all, but

even in the Pali Canon, there is mention of "the person whose mind is like a diamond" and who is liberated by cutting through the taints (AN 3.27 [p. 220]).

118. *Dhp.* XX.4/276. Also MN 107.12-14 (p. 877-78) where Goenka gets the outlines of his story about the road to Rajagaha (Day 2 Discourse, *Art of Living*, pp. 21-23). A variation on Goenka's story about the pot of ghee and the pot of pebbles (*Art of Living*, pp. 55-56), illustrating the Buddha's insistence that one's own actions and nothing else will lead to a good or a bad future, can be found at SN 42:6 (pp. 1336-38).

119. If support were needed for a fairly obvious point, Rhys Davids and William Stede, in the entry for "*satta*" (seven) in their *Pali-English Dictionary* ("based on astronomical conception (Babylon!), this science being regarded as mystic, it invests the number with a peculiar magic nimbus") give many relevant examples.

120. Perhaps the most salient such passage occurs in the *Mahasatipatthana Sutta* (DN 22.22 [p. 350]), where serious meditators are promised that within seven years ... seven months ... seven days they might break through to the highest wisdom. See also DN 25.22 (p. 393), where it is said that anyone who is "intelligent, sincere, honest, and straightforward" may, if he or she practices the Dhamma diligently, reach the final goal within seven years/days. To establish seven-day courses on this foundation, as is commonly done, may be a valid expression of faith, but it would be unwise to measure the symbolic power of the number by reference to the calendar.

121. SN 16.6.24-25 (pp. 275-76).

122. Dhamma Vandana (*Gem Set in Gold*, p. 80).

123. SN 56:11 (p. 1844 [BW 75-76]), MN 139.3 (p. 1080).

124. Seneca, *Letters from a Stoic*, tr. Robin Campbell, no. V. Whether Seneca lived by his own counsels is another matter, but the phrase captures the Buddha's meaning well.

125. MN 12.44-52 (pp. 173-75), MN 36.20-30 (pp. 337-340).

126. MN 36.31-32 (p. 340 [BW 64]). Thus the Buddha came to stress that as mental defilements are dissolved, the result will be happiness and delight (DN 9.40 [p. 167]). *Joy or rapture (piti)* is one of the enlightenment factors (see below), and the pleasures of the *jhanas* (see above) are supposed to be "entirely conducive" to progress on the Path and to Nibbana (DN 29.24 [p. 434]). (Different kinds of

rapture, from the carnal to the "more than spiritual" are discussed at SN 36.31 [pp. 1283-84]). But of course any enlightenment factor, if it is clung to, turns into an impediment and one always needs to be careful to observe pleasant sensations with detachment (*Satip. Discourses*, p. 72).

127. MN 19.26 (p. 210 [BW 420]). On the importance of joy for the Buddha's Path, see also DN 34.2.2.1 (p. 519).

128. See DN 22.5, 7-10 (pp. 337-39), MN 10.10, 14-30 (pp. 147-49), and MN 119.7, 9-17 (pp. 951-52). Once, when a famous courtesan had just died (Sirima, who used to charge a thousand gold pieces for the pleasure of a night's company), King Bimbisara arranged for the corpse to be left to putrefy for three days until it was swollen and crawling with worms, "so that it looked like a pot of rice boiling on the fire with bubbles rising to the surface." The king decreed that all adult inhabitants of Rajagaha were to file past the corpse, on pain of a fine of eight gold coins. (See *Great Disciples*, pp. 304, 307.)

129. *Satip. Discourses*, p. 43.

130. SN 54:9 (p. 1774). See also MN 145.5 (p. 1119). It is said that Cleombrotus of Ambracia, a student of Plato's, once gave so devastating a lecture on the miseries of life that several hundred auditors did away with themselves (Robert Burton, *The Anatomy of Melancholy* [New York Review Books, 2001], I.2.3.x [p. 279] and I.4.1 [p. 438]).

131. MN 102.12 (p. 842 and Note 948 at p. 1308).

132. SN 56:11 (p. 1844 [BW 75-76]).

133. MN 74.9 (p. 605).

134. Bodhi: "In the preliminary stages of the path they prepare the way for the great realization; in the end they remain as its components. The experience of enlightenment, perfect and complete understanding, is just these seven components working in unison to break all shackles and bring final release from sorrow." (NEP, V.72)

135. DN 22.16 (p. 343), SN 46.5 (p. 1574).

136. SN 46.54 (pp. 1609-10).

137. SN 46, see especially sections 5-7 (pp. 1574-77).

138. SN 46.16 (p. 1581-82).

139. See MN 77.15-21 (pp. 637-38) for the complete enumeration. See also DN 28.3 (p. 418): "This is the unsurpassed teaching ... and beyond it lies nothing further to be comprehended."

140. DN 22.1 (p. 335) and MN 10.2-3 (p. 145 [BW 281-82]).

141. Striving to foster wholesome states and to avoid unwholesome ones, both arisen and unarisen.

142. Zeal, energy, purity of mind, and keen investigation.

143. Faith, energy, mindfulness, concentration, and wisdom approached from slightly different angles and thus counted twice.

144. AN 8.6 (p. 1116 [BW 32-33]).

145. See AN 10.27 (p. 1375), where "making an end of suffering" is equated with no longer being moved by the eight vicissitudes. Marcus Aurelius uses a similar image of being "like the promontory against which the waves continually break, but [which] stands firm and tames the fury of the waters around it" (*Meditations* IV.49).

146. *Gem Set in Gold*, pp. 57, 81.

147. MN 39.17 (p. 368 [BW 252]).

148. MN 152.6 (p. 1148); *Dhp.* XXIV.3/336, XXVI.19/401; *Vism.* XIV.143 (p. 468), XXI.63 (p. 679).

149. See SN 22.94 (p. 950).

150. MN 26.19 (p. 260).

151. *Zen Mind, Beginner's Mind*, p. 31.

152. Vipassana teachers stress, accordingly, how powerful even the briefest moments of equanimity are, because they reverse the tide of the ages (*Art of Living*, p. 110-111).

153. Thus Marcus Aurelius: "Practice even things which you despair of accomplishing. For even the left hand, which is ineffectual for all other things, holds the bridle more vigorously than the right hand because it has been practiced in this." (*Med.* XII.6)

154. Thus Suzuki: "It is necessary for us to encourage ourselves and to make an effort up to the last moment, when all effort disappears." (*Zen Mind, Beginner's Mind*, p. 21)

155. That is, burn with desire or passion (1 Cor. 7:9). The key passage on our different gifts is Romans 12:6-8.

156. Hence the central image of the *Sutta Nipata*: a snake shedding its skin without pain or effort when the time is ripe.

157. I wish I could take credit for this fabulously evocative image, but I got it from one of Joseph Goldstein's talks at Barre ("The Meandering River," 30 June 1994).

Post-Coital Reflections

ARTHUR SCHOPENHAUER WAS NOT ONLY ONE OF THE FIRST WESTERN philosophers to take Buddhism seriously, he also wrote a remarkable chapter on "The Metaphysics of Sex" in which he dismissed the traditional disdain for so important a subject and disparaged the meager contributions made by the great minds of the past.[1] Plato, Schopenhauer sneered, did not get beyond the sphere of myths, fables, and jests; what little Rousseau had to say was false and inadequate; Kant simply did not know what he was talking about when it came to sex; and Spinoza's ideas on the subject were so exceedingly naive that they deserve mention for their entertainment value only.

"All romantic love," Schopenhauer contended, "no matter how ethereally it may present itself, is rooted in nothing but the sexual impulse that has been focused, narrowed, and individualized."[2] Not only in our shows and novels, but in the real world too, Schopenhauer insisted, "the sexual impulse is, along with the love of life itself, the most powerful and active of all motives, which not only lays constant claim to half the energies and thoughts of the younger portion of mankind, but is the ultimate goal of almost all human endeavor... What we are dealing with here is no trifle, ... but something that really is more important than all other human ends, ... for what is decided by it is nothing less than *the composition of the next generation.*" At bottom, what we feel in the dark undertow of desire and the incessant ebb and flow of sexual passion is nothing other than the eternal tide of life itself.

The inference that the riddle of life might be easily solved if only we learned to play in the surf was drawn long before the Beach Boys enthused about getting around and finding two girls for every boy. Much of what we associate with the Age of Aquarius can already be found, at least in outline, in Goethe's proto-romantic *Sorrows of Young Werther*[3] — the childlike hope and exuberance no less than the Altamont moment when poor Werther spends all night dying from a blundering bullet to the head, his veins half-opened but not leaking enough to grant him the hoped-for rest. All of which would have little to do with the Dhamma if we weren't in the habit of associating the Buddha's Teaching with the adventures and follies of a generation that had trouble growing up but also happened to produce the first wave of Western Buddhists (the repercussions of which can still be seen at every bookstore where Buddhism is made to share a duplex with various mysticisms in the ever-hip but chaotic suburb of Esoterica). In the Buddha's view, even children eventually get tired of playing on the beach and either scatter their castles or gladly abandon them to the waves.[4]

Thinking of the art of living as learning to surf would be all right if it were clearly understood that getting bloodied on the rocks, breaking one's neck, or drowning in brine is as much part of the deal as coasting on the crests and making a timely escape before the towering waters come crashing down over one's head. A lone wave, one might say, imagines that it perishes when it founders on the shore; but if it could learn to see itself more clearly, it would realize that it is no more than the edge of a boundless sea. What we must also recognize, however, is that although the Buddha's Path is meant to be a joyful one, the great ocean of life is not a fit place for us to linger and amuse ourselves, but a sea of suffering that we must cross while we can, lest we run out of time and add our bitter tears to the salty waters, as we have so often done in the past.[5] Our sensual pleasures are baited hooks for unwary fish,[6] our bodies repositories of repulsive substances,[7] our very selves are built upon delusion, and life itself is so fearsome and so foul-smelling to a sufficiently sensitive nose that not even the most trifling amount of existence is deserving of a Buddha's praise.[8]

Yet as Freud pointed out, it is a mark of neurosis to object to the fact that "we are born between urine and feces" into a world of sex.[9] The Buddha would have agreed: unlikely as it may seem in light of his harsh indictment of existence, there is no greater blessing than to be human, because the very tensions and contradictions that are woven into the fabric of our lives can be made fruitful. Our perplexities open the door to insight, our vulnerabilities should keep us alert, and our sufferings point the way towards wisdom and liberation. The Path may prove long and arduous, frustrating and discouraging at times; but when we are losing heart, we need to remember what a stupendous legacy the Buddhas have bequeathed to us. If only we persist, they have promised us, the day will come, in this life or another, when we will step beyond sorrow altogether. From the terraced heights of wisdom, which only human beings can scale unaided, having at last overcome all craving and clinging, we will see life as it is meant to be seen, and the entire suffering universe will reveal itself before our perfect equanimity, before a peace and love that surpasses all understanding.[10]

"But is it true?" you might well ask.

Que sais-je?[11]

Nietzsche wrote that one repays a teacher badly if one always remains nothing but a student.[12] Perhaps something similar could be said about writers and readers. If you have learned anything in these pages, and you would like to repay me, go find out for yourself and bring back word. Beware of putting anyone on a pedestal, lest a statue slay you.[13]

Tomorrow death may come, who knows?[14] So let us go and practice today. If not now, when?

NOTES

1. Schopenhauer, *Die Welt als Wille und Vorstellung*, vol. II, ch. 44 (in my own translation after consulting Haldane-Kemp).

2. At about the time that Socrates was pursuing the truth in the streets of Athens, a group of young philosophers got into a quarrel over which part of a woman was most desirable and pleasing. They referred their controversy to Lais of Corinth, considered the most beautiful woman of the day and the most expert in all matters amorous. She smiled at the young men: "What young fools you are. If you had me where you wished, what would you seek first?" (Robert Burton, *Anatomy of Melancholy*, III.2.2.ii, p. 82)

3. First published in 1774, the book made Goethe an instant celebrity at 24 and triggered a craze, among Europe's sensitive young men, for dressing like the novel's hero (and perhaps for dispatching themselves as well, a disputed point of history).

4. SN 23:2 (p. 985).

5. *Vism.* XXII.14 (p. 699), SN 15:3 (p. 652 [BW 18]), SN 35.228-229 (p. 1226-1227). Thus also Nyanaponika Thera: "[Life is] a vast ocean of suffering of unfathomable depth, on the surface of which beings swim about for a little while, or navigate in their fragile nutshells of which they are very proud. True, there are spells of calm on the waters, but those with open eyes and minds are not deceived by these short moments of respite: they know the overpowering fierceness of a storm-swept sea, its dangerous currents and whirlpools, the demons and monsters of the deep. They know that even under the most favorable conditions, the feeble strength of man will soon be exhausted by the impact of life's elemental forces." (*Vision*, p. 232)

6. SN 35.230 (p. 1228). For other such images, see MN 54.15-21 (pp. 469-472), *Vism.* XVII.63 (p. 541).

7. DN 22.5 (p. 337), MN 10.10 (p. 147), MN 119.7 (p. 951), AN 9.15 (p. 1270). The point, once more, is not to malign the natural functions that a healthy body performs so admirably, even beautifully, but to emphasize that the infatuations that so enthrall our senses invariably rest on illusions. In "The Lady's Dressing Room" by Jonathan Swift (1732), a prying lover pays the price of his indiscretion when he discovers secrets for which he was not prepared. He slinks away having lost his appetite for women altogether:

> Thus finishing his grand survey,
>
> Disgusted Strephon stole away
>
> Repeating in his amorous fits
>
> Oh! Celia, Celia, Celia shits!

Many are the paths that lead to the monastery. But before we run after him, let us consider Swift's conclusion to the poem:

> If Strephon would but stop his nose, (...)
>
> He soon would learn to think like me,
>
> And bless his ravisht sight to see
>
> Such order from confusion sprung,
>
> Such gaudy tulips rais'd from dung.

Hardly a Dhamma-discourse, you may say. I wonder. The image of a lotus-flower growing on a dung-heap beside the roadside (*Dhp.* IV.16/59) could hardly be more Buddhist, and is well-worth pondering.

8. AN 1.328 (p. 121), MN 49.27 (p. 428).

9. *Civilization and Its Discontents*, chapter IV, footnote 7. The Latin complaint, *inter urinas et faeces nascimur*, is usually attributed to St Augustine.

10. *Dhp.* II.8/28 (Philippians 4:7).

11. Montaigne's personal motto: What do I know?

12. Nietzsche, *Thus Spake Zarathustra*, Part I, last section.

13. Nietzsche, *Ibid.*

14. MN 131.3 (p. 1039).

More Books to Read

Of making books, there is no end, and much study brings much weariness, it rightly says in *Ecclesiastes*; but that is no argument against reading, only for being more discerning and selective in our choice of pages.

For anyone wondering how even the most skeptical and ambitious Western worldlings might end up walking the Buddha's Path, step by step, until they are surprised to find themselves in the suburbs of faith, there is perhaps no better starting point than Dan Harris's *10% Happier* (Dey Street 2014).

Within the Tradition:
Both as an introduction and as review, ***The Art of Living*** (HarperOne 1987), written by **William Hart** but authorized by Goenka himself, is the most obvious companion to a Vipassana course. **Goenka's *Satipatthana Sutta Discourses*** have been published in a slightly condensed version edited by Patrick Given-Wilson (Vipassana Research Institute/VRI, 1998). ***For the Benefit of Many*** (VRI 2005 [3rd ed.]) is a collection of talks and answers by Goenka to common questions raised by students. Goenka's ***Gem Set in Gold*** (VRI 2006) contains translation of all the Pali and Hindi terms, phrases, and chants used in the Ten-Day courses.

A collection of miscellaneous materials pertaining to Goenka's teacher **U Ba Khin** were published under the title *Sayagyi U Ba Khin Journal* by the VRI in 1998 to mark the twentieth anniversary of his death. U Ba Khin's best-known discourses on "The Essentials of Buddha-Dhamma in Meditative Practice" and "What Buddhism Is" are also available online and in a collection entitled *The Clock of Vipassana Has Struck* edited by Pierluigi Confalonieri.[1] A version of "The Essentials" read by U Ba Khin himself was recorded in the 1960s and is available from Pariyatti. com as a scratchy audio-file.

I know of no better concise treatment of *The Noble Eightfold Path* than the little book of that name by **Bhikkhu Bodhi** published by Pariyatti (2000) (cited by chapter and page). His **1981 Lectures**, available for download from Bodhi's website, offer a sophisticated introduction to the Buddha's Teaching as a whole. From what I have read and listened to, everything by Bodhi is worth studying. For anyone eager to go directly to the Buddha's Suttas from the Pali Canon, there is no better place to start than **Bodhi's anthology** *In the Buddha's Words* (Wisdom 2005 [cited as BW]).

Over the past few years, Wisdom Publications has put out magnificent editions of the complete **Long, Middle-Length, Connected, and Numerical Discourses**, giving the enthusiast many thousands of pages to work through should Bodhi's anthology not go far enough. (Long: *Digha Nikaya*, cited as DN; Middle-Length: *Majjhima Nika*, cited as MN; Connected: *Samyutta Nikaya*, cited as SN; Numerical: *Anguttara Nikaya*, cited as AN.)

The Questions of King Milinda, published in an abridged English version edited by N.K.G. Mendis (BPS 2007), is one of the most interesting and original texts in the Pali Canon: a Greek king reigning in the Punjab in the aftermath of Alexander's conquests challenges a Buddhist sage with his Hellenic intellect.

I love **Thomas Byrom's translation of the *Dhammapada***, the most popular collection of sayings attributed to the Buddha, because it makes the work sing with inspiration, even if one might have some objections to the poetic licenses taken with the text. The audio-version read by Jacob Needleman is lovely and comes with his astute commentary on the Buddha's significance.

The Visuddhimagga has been called "the epitome of Pali Buddhist literature" by none less than the Dalai Lama and it is a weighty resource in every sense. Compiled by the scholar-monk Buddhaghosa in 5th century Sri Lanka from all the commentaries then still extant, it is second in authority only to the Scriptures themselves. The classic translation by Bhikkhu Nanamoli is available in a handsome recent edition under the title *The Path of Purification* (BPE 1999). Give it a go, but don't be disappointed if you find it somewhat indigestible despite its grandeur (or perhaps because of it).

The Buddha's Path to Deliverance by **Nyanatiloka Thera** (BPS 2000) brilliantly reconstructs the architecture of the Buddha's whole Teaching based on excerpts from the Pali Canon. *The Life of the Buddha* by **Bhikkhu Nanamoli** (BPE 1992) brings the Pali Scriptures to sparkling life by using them to tell the Buddha's story chronologically. For the lives of the Buddha's most prominent followers, see *Great Disciples of the Buddha* **edited by Bodhi** (Wisdom 2003).

What the Buddha Taught by **Walpola Rahula**, first published in 1959 (cited edition by Gordon Fraser, 1978), was written in a spirit akin to U Ba Khin's with a view to satisfying Western curiosity about Buddhism in a manner both rigorous with respect to the Canon and accessible to the modern rationalist mind. Rahula was the first Buddhist monk to become a professor at a Western university and his book provides a bit of geographical balance by giving voice to someone originally from Sri Lanka, which was for so many centuries the refuge and heartland of Theravadan Buddhism.

Nyanaponika Thera is perhaps my favorite Buddhist commentator, and I especially like his essays collected under the title *The Vision of Dhamma* (BPE 2000) and his reflections on *The Heart of Buddhist Meditation* (BPS 1996). The first essay in his *Vision* ("The Way to Freedom from Suffering") is a marvel of concision that lays out the full range of the Teaching in a mere fourteen pages.

Ledi Sayadaw can sound be a bit stern for our age, but his *Manual of the Excellent Man* (BPS 2000) is still a fine resource when one is in the right mood for it.

Paul R. Fleischman (the author of *Karma and Chaos* [Pariyatti 1991] and *An Ancient Path* [VRI 2008], not the writer of children's books who may come up first on Amazon) is a psychiatrist, a senior Vipassana teacher, and Goenka's ambassador to academia. He's probably the organization's most credible and original intellectual, but still a true-blue Goenkanaut.

Joseph Goldstein's Dhamma talks, available from his website, are excellent and take a line recognizable to Goenka students, though more ecumenical with respect to other Buddhist interpretations. His *One Dharma* (HarperOne 2003) — not just a title but a program — may answer some of your questions if you are getting confused about the tangle of seemingly contradictory Buddhist traditions.

The study of **Abhidhamma** offers a highly elaborated but rather arcane angle on the Buddha's Teaching. If you must, try reading *Abhidhamma Studies* (Wisdom 1998) by Nyanaponika Thera and *A Comprehensive Manual of Abhidhamma* (BPS 2007) edited by Bhikkhu Bodhi.

On *Walking Meditation*, see the little booklet of that title by BPS (2007) with contributions by Ajahn Brahmavamso, Ajahn Nyanadhammo, and Dharma Dorje.

Sherwin B. Nuland's reflections on *How We Die* is a brutal but salutary reminder of what is ultimately at stake in our practice. On Vipassana as an art of dying, no less than an art of living, see Goenka's "What Happens at Death," available online,[2] and *The Art of Dying*, collected and edited by Goenka-appointed teacher Virginia Hamilton (VRP 2014). *The Tibetan Book of Living and Dying* by Sogyal Rinpoche (Harper Collins 1994) looks at death through the eyes of a tradition rather different from Vipassana, but one that has evolved unrivaled resources for this life's final chapter.

Beyond the Tradition:

Eckart Tolle's *Power of Now* will not win him the Nobel Prize in Literature, but it does strike some deep chords that resonate profoundly with the Vipassana approach.

At the end of one Ten-Day course, a fellow meditator gave me a copy of *The Buddha Said* by Osho and insisted that I absolutely had to read it. I did as I was told and enjoyed it more than I would have expected. My main objection is that it needs a more accurate title: *What Osho Said...* (I did not imagine that I was being very original when I picked the title of my own book, but I was still unaware that both Osho and Deepak Chopra had used it already, to say nothing of Rhonda Byrne. The sales figures alone — perhaps a million to one — should suffice to dissociate my project from theirs.)

Approaching Zen from a Vipassana direction can be confusing (perhaps Zen is confusing no matter what), but *The Empty Mirror* by Janwillem van de Wetering is still one of my favorite books about stumbling towards wisdom along Buddhist paths. Shunryu Suzuki's *Zen Mind, Beginner's Mind* (Shambhala 2011), first published in 1970, is the great classic of Soto Zen practice adapted to North American circumstances.

Reading the *Sermon on the Mount* (Matthew 5-7) through the lens of a Vipassana course can be a most enlightening experience. For majesty, literary beauty, and poetic resonance, nothing beats the Authorized or King James Version (KJV); for a sensible scholarly update, try the Revised or New Revised Standard Versions (RSV/NRSV).

The *Meditations* of Marcus Aurelius, ancient Rome's most philosophical emperor, present some of the West's most compelling reflections on the practice of equanimity, especially in George Long's translation. Epictetus is the closest thing to a Buddhist sage in Western literature: thus his *Enchiridion* (or

Manual) or his *Discourses*, most accessible in the translation by Robert Dobbin (Penguin 2008). If Epictetus's wisdom got James Stockdale through seven years of captivity and torture at "the Hanoi Hilton" after he was shot down over Vietnam, perhaps it can help you, too. (Alas, it did not save Stockdale from embarrassment as Ross Perot's running mate in the 1992 presidential election. "Who am I? What am I doing here?" were serious questions meant to bring philosophy to debating on TV. Needless to say they were taken as either parody or signs of senility on Stockdale's part. So it goes.)

NOTES

1. Also in *U Ba Khin Journal*, pp. 31-52.

2. Also in *U Ba Khin Journal*, pp. 124-126, and in *The Art of Dying*, pp. 29-34.

Made in the USA
San Bernardino, CA
12 October 2016